critical praise for

The Struggle for Modern Tibet
The Autobiography of Tashi Tsering

"The Dalai Lama instructed Mr. Tsering, 'Be a good Tibetan. Study hard. And use your education to serve your people and your country.' It's what he has tried to do, against sometimes spirit-crushing odds. He has now documented his exceptional life in a readable, at times startling, autobiography."

—*The Wall Street Journal*

"The considerable value of Tashi's briskly told life story is that it complicates our view of modern Tibet. . . . His is a harrowing but remarkably unbitter story with a happy ending for him, if not for Tibet. Recommended for academic and larger public libraries."

—*Library Journal*

"A compelling account of survival and rebirth. . . . [A] fascinating life story."

—*The Seattle Times*

"What sets this carefully crafted account apart from other publications documenting the experiences of Tibetans . . . through the successive upheavals that have affected their homeland in the last fifty years is Tashi Tsering's apparent readiness to work within the Chinese system imposed on Tibet. . . . This fine piece of historical scholarship deals lucidly with a complex subject matter. . . . It is the book's earnest efforts to portray education as a touchstone of Sino-Tibetan relations, while scrutinizing a wealth of complex historical issues, that makes *The Struggle for Modern Tibet* worthy of attention and respect."

—*The China Journal*

"An inspiring and enthralling story. . . .*The Struggle for Modern Tibet* is the struggle . . . of one man to find his destiny: it is a heroic saga of passion, anger, folly, betrayal, injustice, bloody-mindedness and determination. It is the story of man's unconquerable mind. Melvyn Goldstein and William Siebenschuh, who are responsible for the translation, have done a good job in capturing Tashi's style and vitality of expression from his oral tapes. . . . Tashi Tsering *tse ring po sho!*"

— *Tibetan Review*

(over)

"Tashi Tsering's captivating life story is [an] example of how good the literature on Tibet can be. This is far from the first autobiographical account by a Tibetan, but . . . it represents one of the finest examples of the genre. . . . Tashi's narrative is riveting, but told without bitterness or anger. Its matter-of-fact tone is compelling and moving, as is its tale of perseverance and commitment. I suspect the polemicists on both sides will be considerably unhappy with Tashi's story—which is why it is so important that it be widely read."

—*China Review International*

"The book is of interest on two levels, the personal and the political. On the former level, any non-Tibetan reader is bound to be surprised at the mores of traditional Tibet. . . . On the political level, the Western reader is also likely to be surprised, for the book does not adopt the anti-Chinese stance we have come to expect from Western writings on modern Tibet. . . . It makes us privy to Tashi's internal struggles as he weighs up the old and new societies, the former represented by the monk-aristocrats in exile in India, the latter by the ordinary people who have remained in Tibet."

—*Asian Studies Review*

"This book may be read in several ways. At one level, it is the story of the left-wing sympathizer savaged by the very system he tries to support, a tale familiar from the writings of Orwell, Koestlet, Djilas, and many others. . . . At another level, the book portrays the psychology and development of an individual, convinced of the failings of the old society. . . . A very worthwhile read for anyone concerned with Tibetan studies."

—*Pacific Affairs*

"Tashi Tsering speaks honestly of life in Lhasa under the Lamaist theocracy and examines some of the cultural assumptions on which life there was based."

—*Far Eastern Economic Review*

AN EAST GATE BOOK

M.E.Sharpe

Armonk, New York
London, England

The Struggle for Modern Tibet

The Autobiography of Tashi Tsering

Melvyn Goldstein, William Siebenschuh, and Tashi Tsering

An East Gate Book

M.E. Sharpe
Armonk, New York
London, England

An East Gate Book

Those wishing to make donations to Tashi's school project can do so via the
Boulder-Lhasa Sister City Project
776 Cottage Lane
Boulder, Colorado 80304

(303) 443–9863

Photographs courtesy of Tashi Tsering

Library of Congress Cataloging-in-Publication Data

Goldstein, Melvyn C.
The struggle for modern Tibet : the autobiography of Tashi Tsering /
Melvyn C. Goldstein, William R. Siebenschuh, and Tashi Tsering.
p.   cm.
Includes index.
ISBN 1-56324-950-2 (cloth; alk. paper)
ISBN 0-7656-0509-0 (pbk; alk. paper)
1. Tashi Tsering.
2. Educators—China—Tibet—Biography.
3. Political prisoners—China—Biography.
I. Siebenschuh, William R. II. Tashi Tsering.
III. Title.
LA2383.C52T37   1997
365′.45′092—dc21
[B]
97-4968
CIP

Printed in the United States of America

BM (c)   10   9   8   7   6   5   4   3
BM (p)   10   9   8   7   6   5   4   3

Contents

Preface   vii

Photographs follow pages 88 and 156

Prologue   3

*The Struggle for Modern Tibet:
The Autobiography of Tashi Tsering*   6

Epilogue   197

Index   203

Preface

One evening in December 1963, Tashi Tsering unexpectedly stopped by my Seattle apartment. I had just finished finals and a busy quarter at the University of Washington and was relaxing playing mah-jongg with three Tibetan friends. As a graduate student in Tibetan language and civilization, I knew Tashi well, so I thought nothing of his uninvited appearance. Stopping by people's houses was a normal part of Tibetan culture. With the tiles clicking and banging nonstop, we exchanged greetings and commented on exams and our relief at the quarter's being finally over. Tashi said he didn't want to join the game and stood by the table watching us and talking. He seemed unusually serious, but then I was paying attention primarily to the flow of tiles, not wanting to miss a discard. After about five minutes Tashi suddenly asked the Tibetans whether they had messages they wanted to send to relatives in Tibet *because he was returning home.*

In response to a round of "Oh, don't fool around" and "Be serious, Tashi," Tashi didn't elaborate much. He simply repeated that he was returning to Tibet and would convey any messages his friends wanted him to transmit to their relatives. The mah-jongg game continued nonstop, although our comments quickly turned serious with warnings that he was making a big mistake and suggestions that if it were a question of money we were sure help could be found. But Tashi would not relent. He responded unequivocally that his decision had nothing to do with money. Instead he saw himself as a representative of the common people who wanted to help create a new, modern Tibet. The atmosphere became somewhat tense, since the other Tibetans, who were aristocrats, hated the communists and China and were committed to freeing Tibet from Chinese control. No one gave Tashi any messages, and a few moments later he left. In his wake we discussed what we perceived as his bizarre comments together with the nuances of our current mah-jongg hands. The idea that he would actually go back was too unthinkable to take seriously. None of us really believed he would leave America to return to "Red" China.

I didn't see Tashi again for twenty-two years. Then in 1985, I received permission from China to begin two months of research on a fellowship from the U.S.-China bilateral exchange program (the National Academy of Sciences Committee for Scholarly Communication with the People's Republic of China) and arrived in Lhasa in May. I had reestablished contact with Tashi by mail a few years earlier and was overjoyed to find him waiting for me at the guesthouse where my hosts had booked me. After a joyous reunion, he suggested I move to the Snowland Hotel, a small hotel near his home, and I agreed. It was wonderful to see him so well and yet also painful to hear briefly of the terrible times he had experienced. Thus began the second incarnation of our friendship.

Since 1985 I have made numerous research trips to Tibet and have always stayed at the Snowland Hotel so I would be near Tashi's house. We visited often. Tashi also remembered that I loved Tibetan food and butter tea, so from the first trip he always saw that I had a good supply of the best quality *tsamba* (roasted barley flour) on hand and arranged for a flask of fresh, steaming butter tea to be brought to my hotel room every morning for breakfast. He is that kind of person.

On one of my trips, Tashi surprised me by asking if I could help him publish a book about his life. He thought foreigners needed to know about common Tibetans—that is, Tibetans who were not aristocrats or monastic prelates or incarnate lamas. He felt his life story could play a useful role in assisting both Westerners and young Tibetans born in exile to understand the real—non–Shangri-la—Tibet. I agreed that it was a good idea and told him I would try to help him. As it turned out, soon afterward I was able to invite him to Case Western Reserve University for a few months to assist me on a research project.

Tashi lived with me, quickly settling in on my third floor. One evening not long after his arrival, he again raised the issue of my helping him write a book. As chairman of the anthropology department and director of several research projects, I was very busy at the time but felt I had to agree. Tashi deeply wanted us to work together on his autobiography, and as an old friend I felt obliged (by Tibetan cultural norms) to make the time to help him. However, I insisted that he would have to tell me everything that happened in detail—the good and the bad. As a serious scholar, I told him, I couldn't collaborate on a book that was factually incorrect or self-serving; there were already several Tibetan "Pollyanna" books, and we didn't need another. Tashi didn't hesitate for a moment. He immediately agreed.

And so in 1992 our earliest collaboration on this book began. Every evening after eating and watching the evening news, I joined Tashi and turned on the tape recorder. Tashi talked, and I asked questions while the tape recorder relentlessly rolled for one or two hours. He talked in Tibetan and English, and he spoke frankly about his life and thoughts and feelings. By the time he was ready to return to Tibet, I had almost fifty hours of tapes.

After Tashi left, I had the tapes transcribed but could not find time to start working on them. On my next several trips to Tibet, Tashi always asked politely how the book was coming along, and I always told him I would get to it soon. But, in truth, I was unable to. Then, in 1994, another opportunity arose for Tashi to come to Case Western Reserve University, this time to work on a large dictionary project I was doing. He came carrying the hope that during the year he would be in Cleveland we could also finish the book. So when Tashi moved back into his room on the third floor of my house, I started in earnest to hammer out a draft of his autobiography. When, after a few months, I perceived how long the project would take, I decided to try to find a collaborator who could work with Tashi and me.

One afternoon, while I was sweating away in the university's sauna, a colleague from the English Department, Professor Bill Siebenschuh, sauntered in and sat down. I mentioned the project to him and asked if he knew anyone who might be interested in helping Tashi and me produce a draft. He said the project sounded fascinating and that he would try to suggest some name. The next day he called to say he himself would like to be involved. I was delighted, and so our two-year, three-way collaboration began.

* * *

When I left the university's fitness center after talking with Mel Goldstein, I was already hooked. Mel had given me a brief version—the highlights—of Tashi Tsering's story, and when I got back to my office it must have taken me all of five minutes to decide that I didn't want to try to find other people who might be interested. I wanted to take a shot at it myself.

I began with the pages and pages of written transcripts of the audiotapes Mel and Tashi had made and drafts of the prologue and first two chapters that Mel had already written. The early chapters I submitted met Mel's and Tashi's approval, and by June 1994 we decided we could go at full speed.

By August, the story that kept growing and unfolding had gotten beyond the tapes, and I was interviewing Tashi once a week. On Wednesdays we would meet for lunch at the University Hospital cafeteria, and then go to the lobby of the new Lerner Tower, find a couple of comfortable chairs and a place to write, and get down to business. We usually agreed beforehand on what we would cover on a particular day, and Tashi often came with pages of notes to help him remember and organize his thoughts. Mainly, though, he just talked—so quickly and with such emotion that sometimes I couldn't take his words down fast enough. When we were finished, I would take my notes and his papers back to my office and begin to write, and he would go home to proof and critique any chapters I had just finished. The cycle would begin again the following week.

The project was totally collaborative from the beginning. Every time I finished drafts of a series of chapters, Mel and Tashi would read them carefully, and then we would meet to clarify dates and sequences and to discuss questions of historical accuracy, all counterpoised with Tashi's thoughts and feelings. The process itself caused Tashi to remember things he had almost forgotten, events he hadn't thought about in years, and they, too, had to be sorted, evaluated, and assimilated. We worked hard all through the fall of 1994. By November, Tashi and I were meeting twice a week, while Mel was reinterviewing Tashi on almost every incident in the manuscript, as well as initiating a whole new set of interviews on Tashi's adventures as a Red Guard. By great good luck we were able to complete a draft before Tashi had to return to Lhasa in February 1995. He was able to read every line of the original before he went home.

I have many fond memories of the whole process. One of the most vivid is of a particularly frustrating Wednesday interview. With great emotion Tashi was trying to describe his first impressions of the Changwu prison, and I was having a lot of trouble getting the physical details straight. It was just one of those days. The more trouble I had, the faster he talked; the faster he talked, the more confused I became. Finally, I almost shouted, "Tashi, stop! I can't visualize what you're talking about. I can't see it in my mind's eye, and if I can't see it I can't describe it in the book!" He smiled and said, "Okay." Then he stood up decisively and began to pace rapidly about the lobby, which is large and always crowded. I have no idea what the passing interns, doctors, patients, and visitors must have thought when they saw an animated, sixty-five-year old Tibetan taking large purposeful strides at right angles around the room followed by another man writing furiously in a battered spiral-bound notebook. "Here was where the first wall was," he said as I hastily began to draw a diagram. "The door was there. There was the stairway down, and there—over there in the courtyard—was where the cells were." He absolutely beamed when he could see that I finally got the picture, and I think the image of the whole episode has stayed in my mind because for me it epitomizes the strength of Tashi's commitment to getting details right and his unwavering conviction about the importance of his story. He is a remarkable human being, and having had the good fortune to get to know and work with him, I share his conviction.

Melvyn C. Goldstein
William R. Siebenschuh
Cleveland, Ohio
July 31, 1996

The Struggle for Modern Tibet

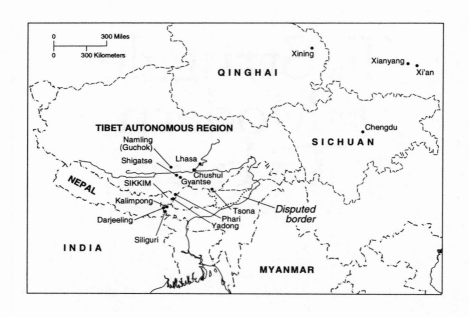

Prologue

Tashi Tsering, step forward."

The year was 1942. I was a thirteen-year-old member of the *gad-rugba*, the Dalai Lama's personal dance troupe, and my legs had just gone weak with fear.

Two days before, I had forgotten to attend an important ceremonial performance at which I was to play the *gyangling*, a Tibetan wind instrument much like a clarinet. Today the whole troupe had been ordered to assemble for a special meeting in the park in front of the Potala Palace where we had Saturday practice. No reason had been given for the unusual meeting.

All the dancers were seated in a semicircle on the dusty ground in front of the troupe's director, a cruel man we all called "Pockmarks" behind his back because his face was disfigured with smallpox scars. He stood there glaring at us, so we all knew he was seething; carefully we kept our eyes focused on the ground to avoid drawing attention. I had been afraid all along that the meeting had something to do with my missing the performance, so I couldn't resist periodically stealing a glance at Pockmarks out of the corner of my eye. To my chagrin, each time I looked up I found him staring directly at me, the anger exploding out from his eyes.

"Tashi Tsering, step forward."

The words rang in my ears, producing a ripple of fear throughout my body. Trembling, I rose and walked forward, my head bowed in our traditional gesture of respect and humility. Though none of the other dancers dared to raise their heads, it felt as if every eye was on me as I took each step. I could almost feel my comrades' inner sighs of relief now that they knew the target of the day's meeting was me, not them.

"You missed your performance without asking leave. How could you do such a thing! Gadrugba are servants of the Dalai Lama and the government and have a great responsibility to serve to the utmost."

The director spoke sternly, his voice rising to almost a shout. I didn't know what to say and struggled to think of some way to explain away my lapse. After a minute of silence that seemed to me to last ten or fifteen, he yelled, "Well, Tashi," and I blurted out:

"I'm terribly sorry. I don't know what happened but I swear it will never happen again."

Pockmarks smirked, his gold-capped incisors glittering, and said, "Oh, is that so. Well, we'll see to that by helping you improve your memory. Take off your trousers, and lie face down!" I thought I saw a hint of sadistic pleasure in his eyes as he turned and ordered some of the teachers to bring whips.

There was now no hope. I was going to be lashed across my bare buttocks with long thin switches made from tree branches. This centuries-old Tibetan punishment was the most painful kind of beating. It was based, I suppose, on the idea that fear and pain make people work harder and obey better. I was terrified in anticipation of the pain I knew was coming.

When I was stretched out on the ground, one teacher held my hands and another my feet while two of the older teachers stood on either side of me and took turns striking me with the switches. At first it was not too bad, but as the number of blows increased and the skin split, the pain became excruciating. I tried to be brave and block it out by thinking of other things, but eventually the agony was so great that I couldn't think of anything else. All I could see was the scarred and smirking face of the director. All I could hear was the explosive swishing of the switches and the popping sound of the blows hitting their mark. When I could bear it no longer, I started to scream.

Then I woke up.

Sweating profusely and unable to stop shaking, for a moment I honestly didn't remember where I was. But as my eyes and then my head cleared, I began to recognize the familiar details of my room. The year was 1962, not 1942, and I was not a powerless child in Lhasa. I was in my own bed in my college dormitory at the University of Washington, Seattle, United States of America.

It was twenty years since that beating, but the memory had extraordinary vividness. I was sure this dream about the cruelty of the traditional society was not an accident. For months I had been debating whether I should give up the comfort and freedom of America and return to try and help my people in communist Tibet. As a critic of the oppressive and feudal aspects of traditional Tibetan society, I felt I should return to work with the mass of common Tibetans to create a new society that was both modern and just, and yet still distinctively Tibetan. But I also knew that I would be taking a substantial risk by returning.

Over and over again I weighed the alternatives. I asked myself repeatedly how I could justify staying in Seattle, warm and safe and comfortable, watching my homeland from the sidelines. "Did I have the courage," I asked myself, "to give up the new life I had found for the unknowns of Lhasa and the Chinese?" The dream seemed a sign sent to remind me of my values and my obligations to my country and people. It seemed to be saying that since I hated the injustices of the old society I should return to help construct a new society. For days I couldn't stop thinking about this mission. I was so preoccupied I barely took notes in class.

My idea of what I might be able to do personally in Tibet was vague. It was also, in retrospect, probably naive and idealistic. But at the same time it was genuine and deeply felt. My whole identity as a person and Tibetan seemed to be hanging in the balance.

Two years later, in 1964, I boarded a ship in Havana, Cuba, and began my long journey home. This book is the story of my early life in Tibet, my political awakening in America, and the hardships—but also the successes—I experienced after returning home.

1

My name is Tashi Tsering.

In Tibetan, Tashi means "good luck" and Tsering means "long life." Looking back on my life now, I believe my name has turned out to be prophetic. For a long time, though, it didn't seem so. But that is getting ahead of my story.

There was nothing particularly unusual about my childhood. I came into the world in 1929—the year of the "iron horse"—in a small village called Guchok in a mountain river valley about a hundred miles west of Lhasa. I was born during what is now called the "old society," although while I was growing up I had no idea there was going to be a "new society." There was simply our traditional Tibetan way of life.

My first ten years were like those of most other Tibetan peasant boys. When I was very young, I ran and played on the slopes and in the meadows, carefree and without many duties or responsibilities. On those wonderful days when it was warm enough in our valley, I sometimes ran around naked with the other children just for the joy of it. Although the country was rugged, the horizons were majestic. There seemed to be an endless expanse of great mountains and beautiful valleys, and I loved the physical sense of freedom.

Guchok was like most other small Tibetan villages. The few hundred inhabitants lived in clusters of stone houses scattered along the sloping foothills of a mountain valley fed by a glacial stream that provided the precious water needed for irrigating our crops. The flat-roofed houses were two and three stories high, and like most families, we lived on the second and third floors, keeping our animals on the first.

Guchok was divided into an upper and a lower village. We lived in the upper village, in the higher part of the valley where it was harder to grow crops but easy to find forage for the grazing animals. Thus not only did we grow barley and lentils, but we kept many yaks, goats, and sheep. Ours was basically a subsistence economy. We ate the produce of our fields and flocks and made virtually all of our clothing—spinning our wool and weaving it on wooden looms. When we needed something we couldn't produce ourselves, such as salt, we bartered to get it, although Tibet had its own coinage, which we sometimes used. Like most villagers throughout Tibet, we were surprisingly self-sufficient.

My family was large, ten of us in all. There was my mother and then my four paternal aunts who, though they were celibate Buddhist nuns, mostly lived at home and provided the family with a significant labor force. There were also my paternal grandmother, two younger brothers, and my two fathers. I say two fathers because it is common in Tibetan society for brothers to take a wife jointly. It was only when I lived abroad that I learned how rare and shocking this marital custom was to Americans and even to other Asians like Chinese and Indians. I never thought about it then, and it does not bother me now. In our culture, it was completely natural for brothers to marry the same woman, and there was no stigma at all about brothers sharing a woman sexually. We saw this custom as an effective way to conserve resources and enhance the material well-being of the family. We believed that polyandry, as this custom is called by anthropologists in the West, prevents fragmentation of the family's land across generations. If each son in a family marries monogamously and brings in a new unrelated bride, we think the family is unstable and likely to split up, with each son and his wife and children taking a share of the land. By contrast, with polyandry, there is only one wife and one set of children, so fission is far less common.

Keeping brothers together was also important for us because not only was all of the work of our household done without machines—by people (and animals)—but our normal activities often involved the need to provide people for free corvée labor. For example, we had to provide animals and people to move goods and commodities for the government's transportation system. The more available the labor, the stronger the whole family unit became.

The older of the two brothers who were my fathers was the one we actually called "father." He also was the head of the household and slept with my mother in a separate room on the second floor of our stone house. My other father, his younger brother, was always called "uncle" in our region. In our household, he slept downstairs, where we kept the animals. I remember now that my mother would sometimes go downstairs to sleep with him, but I didn't think much about it at the time. In our culture the wife played the key role in holding such marriages together. She was responsible for visiting all the brothers regularly and making sure they were satisfied and that the marriage and household functioned effectively. My mother must have done a good job, because there was no friction between my fathers.

We never worried about who the biological father was, and I had no idea which of the two fathers was actually mine. My mother never told me anything, and it never occurred to me to ask. I don't think the brothers knew the truth themselves—or cared. Both "father" and "uncle" called me "son," and they treated all the children equally. To this day I cannot fathom why non-Tibetans find polyandry so strange and even disgusting. In America it is common for one woman to have two or three husbands in the course of her life and occasionally to have sexual relations with more than one man at a time. In Tibet it is the same; the only difference is that sometimes both husbands are there at the same time, and they are brothers. We find this system eminently logical and natural.

My family was relatively well off by local standards, and I had a carefree youth with little or no work until about the age of seven, when I started doing odd jobs around the house. My first major responsibility came when I was eight years old and my father told me I was to work as a shepherd in the summers like the older boys. I was thrilled. My job really was not hard, but I felt great pride. I had to help drive the animals (about three hundred sheep and goats) into the mountains each day, stay with them while they grazed, and bring them back in the evening. In summer the days were long, the skies were immense, and the mountain valleys were beautiful. I loved the feeling that I was doing something that mattered to my family. But I have to admit that it was mainly just fun, because I met many other young herders like myself, and there was always something to do while watching the herd graze. When the weather was hot, we shepherds played in the icy streams. And despite the dominance of Buddhism in our society, with its strong emphasis on the sanctity of life, we often hurled stones at birds and rabbits with our slingshots, and sometimes we even caught fish in the streams with our hands. When we spotted a fish hiding we reached out with cupped hands, careful that no sudden movement frightened it. Then, holding our breath, we would grab as fast as we could. Usually we missed, but occasionally we got lucky and were able to fling a fish onto the bank. We boys thought that was a great feat and would immediately set up a makeshift hearth of stones and dung, which we lit with the flint strikers we all wore. I can still recall the glorious taste of the freshly cooked fish. On quieter days we spun wool on simple handmade spindles or sewed boots for the winter. We ran, occasionally fought, and mostly played and enjoyed the delicious feeling that we were on the way to becoming men while our charges grazed on the mountain meadows! Herding was serious work since our animals represented the major portion of our family's wealth, but for us kids, it was mostly fun.

The way my family and my village lived from day to day, season to season, and year to year seemed a timeless, comfortably repetitive pattern. As I think back about this life after so many years, I find it easy to idealize and to become nostalgic—but only up to a point. Most of the people I knew then had no interest in change. They worked hard to improve their place in the social and economic system but not to change the ground rules. They had no wish to leave the places they were accustomed to or to break the seamless continuity of the traditional way of life. However, even as a young boy I began to realize that I was different. I liked the life I was living, but I also began to feel dissatisfied. As a child I found it hard to put my finger on exactly what was wrong, and I recall feeling more than a little bit confused about my misgivings. Somehow I felt I wanted something more out of life even though I had no words to describe it. I think that this feeling stemmed from my intense desire to become literate.

From as early as I can remember I wanted to learn to read and write. This desire was not common in our village or in the rest of Tibet. There were no newspapers or radios, and although most people were illiterate, that was not a problem for them or for the village as far as anybody could see. In our tradition-bound world there was no need for literacy in the modern sense. The community and the culture told you who you were and what to do. There were clear and prescribed roles for persons of every age and gender, and, therefore, the possibilities open to restless or ambitious individuals were extremely limited. You didn't have to think much and weren't encouraged to question. In any case, there were no schools, so reading and writing were skills possessed only by the rich and by government officials, and of course also monks. Later when I lived in America one of the things that struck me most was the strong value everyone placed on education as a means of social and economic advancement. I, too, felt that education was vital, but this idea was not something village Tibetans thought much about.

I'm not sure what it was that made me want to learn so badly, but I think my desire may have come from watching my father, who was one of the two or three literate people in the village. Looking back, I am not even sure how literate he really was, but I vividly remember how I loved to sit and watch him in the physical act of writing. I was fascinated by his deft, sure movements when he mixed his own ink, carefully filled the inkpot, sharpened the point of his bamboo pen, and then proceeded to create letter after letter. Where did he learn to draw these shapes? How did he know which ones to use? I think the purposeful physical acts themselves became a symbol of some kind of special power that I wanted for myself. I felt the same way when my father was doing arithmetic. Tibetans used a complicated system in which objects like beans, sticks, and stones representing tens, hundreds, and thousands were laid out on a board and moved around to do computations. I used to watch with wonderment as my father magically moved the beans and stones. Of course I wouldn't have put it that way at the time, but as I've thought back the fascination was exactly what I've just described. I was certain that I wanted to know what my father and others like him knew. And that presented problems.

There were no schools in our village, so I remember asking my father and mother to send me to the district center, three or four hours' walk from our village, where a few men offered private tutoring in reading and writing to children. But I could never convince them to agree. I still don't understand why my parents wouldn't send me. They always said, "Yes, yes, we'll think about it." But as far as I could tell, they never did. The closest I got was when my youngest aunt, a nun, taught me the alphabet for a few weeks. Then she stopped, and I wasn't sure why. As I said, people in our village weren't interested in education; they didn't consider it important because they saw little connection between literacy and the physical realities of their daily lives, including their material success. To them, history was a sort of continuous past that was just like the present and would presumably be just like the future. Why did they need to know more than they already knew?

Even though I was very young, I still remember how frustrated I was at having so little control over my own life. Indeed, if it hadn't been for a stroke of luck, I probably would have grown up an illiterate peasant like my playmates. I call it a stroke of luck, but my parents didn't see it that way.

It all began in 1939 when I was ten years old. In that year the Tibetan government needed replacements for the Dalai Lama's ceremonial dance troupe, called the gadrugba. It was the custom for the government to recruit young boys (from eight to ten years of age) from the provinces of rural Tibet as a tax on the better families. The boys selected for the troupe were taken to Lhasa to be trained. They served until they reached the age of eighteen, when they were retired and replaced by a new cohort of youngsters. It was a recruit year, and so in 1939 the Council of Ministers in Lhasa ordered a number of districts, ours among them, each to send two boys to the capital as candidates for the final selection for the gadrugba.

In our village everyone hated this tax, as it literally meant losing a son, probably forever. Parents, therefore, often told lies about the ages of their children to avoid their being candidates. I don't know if my parents tried such deceptions, but if they did it did not work, for one day my father received an order from the district governor to send me for the preliminary examination. This order threw my family into chaos and changed my life completely.

My mother cried, sobbing loudly, when she heard the news. In fact, I recall clearly that the whole family was angry and fearful. The possibility that the son they thought would take over the family farm might be lost was awful to contemplate. Their immediate reaction was to try to find a way to avoid sending me. In Tibet when we want to influence an outcome it is typical to go to a relevant official, give an appropriate "gift," and solicit his assistance. My mother acted immediately, giving a minor district officer she thought might be able to intervene when it came time to choose the boys a present of five large balls of expensive yak butter, and asking him to help the family.

While this action calmed my parents' anxiety somewhat, I had a totally different view of the situation. I was not at all afraid of leaving my home and village. To the contrary, I was excited and eager to go to Lhasa. At night I would stay up dreaming about the holy city and a new life that included learning and knowledge. So despite my parents' unhappiness, I couldn't wait to go to the district for the competition. In fact, I was so eager that on the day we were required to travel to the district center, I got up early and left without waiting for my family. I found out later that my mother looked for me frantically all over the village before learning that I had gone on alone. The district meeting place was three or four hours by foot from our village, and when my mother caught up with me about halfway along, she scolded me severely, I think in part because of her apprehension at the thought of losing me. But at that point nothing could dampen my spirits. This competition, I thought, was going to be my chance!

When we got to the district center, we were called to the governor's castle and told to wait in the courtyard till His Excellency came to examine us. A crowd of about twenty or thirty other boys had already gathered, each accompanied by a parent. You could feel the tension of the parents and the excitement or fear among the boys. The air was charged with electricity, and I couldn't stand still for a minute. My mother, who was still angry that I had been selected in the first place, tugged at my hair and clothing and warned me to stop jumping around. She tried everything she could to keep me from drawing any attention to myself. "Stand still and keep your eyes looking downward," she ordered. But I had never been in a castle before, and far from being intimidated, I was fascinated by it. Full of energy, I ran around looking out of the windows at the town below, trying to imagine what might lie ahead, even looking slyly at the other boys to see what the competition was going to be like.

When the officials assembled, they had all the candidates line up in a row while they walked by and studied us carefully. They seemed to be looking only at physical features, and they asked no questions. I don't know on what basis they made their decisions, but eventually they picked two boys to go to Lhasa, a first choice and an alternate. I was chosen as the alternate from my district. My mother was furious on hearing this, but my heart was racing. My dream was coming true; I was one step closer to a new life.

When we got back to our village my mother went straight to the minor official and demanded the "gift" butter back. I'm told that she made quite a scene—yelling at him and calling him all kinds of names.

He returned the butter but that did not change my situation, and in about a month my father and I were on our way to Lhasa.

From the minute my mother knew the exact date when I was supposed to leave, she asked me to sleep in the same bed with her. Each night we would talk far into the night. One day while we were talking, her voice broke and she said, "*Olo* [a loving name for son], when you leave I may never see you again. You must write to me." And then she remembered, smiling, "I know you do not know how to write. But I will not forget you, and I will see to it that you do not forget me. I will send you dried meat, butter, and warm clothing with the travelers that pass through Guchok on the way to Lhasa."

When it came right down to leaving, I also found it very hard to go. My mother met my fathers and me outside the house and put a ceremonial white scarf called a *khatak* around my neck, as is our custom. Then she gave me a full bowl of *chang* (traditional barley beer) and held my hands tightly together in hers. She scarcely spoke; she didn't have to. Hot tears ran freely from her reddened eyes. When I looked at her familiar, strong, work-roughened hands, the hands that had washed me, fed me, brushed my hair, and held my face, my resolve began to collapse inside. Leaving the warmth and love of my family suddenly seemed enormously frightening. But at this point, my going was a tax obligation and had to be fulfilled whether we liked it or not. We had no choice in the matter.

Finally, my mother touched her forehead to mine, and we set off. She and the other family members stood silently looking after us, tears welling in their eyes. I also cried. I really wanted to go but also felt terribly sad. Try as I might, I could not banish the frightening thought that I would never see my mother and family again.

The first stages of our eight-day journey were difficult. We usually spent the night with peasant families we encountered on our way. We had brought our own food and bedding, and so had only to pay for fuel to cook with. I felt lost and empty inside and viewed the start of every day with apprehension. Fortunately, however, childhood is a time of great resiliency. The journey gave me some time to compose myself, and by the fourth day my spirits had risen high once again.

When we came in sight of the capital city I got my first glimpse of the magnificent Potala Palace. It totally dominated the Kyichu Valley where Lhasa is situated. The view, more grand than anything I had imagined, was truly awe-inspiring. The palace seemed bigger than our entire village; it seemed to cover the mountaintop like a gigantic hat. For better or worse, I knew I had entered a new world.

Lhasa at that time was a city of only about thirty thousand people, but to me, coming from a small village, it seemed immense and I was afraid of getting separated from my father and not being able to find him. Everything we saw was new and exciting, and in many cases downright strange. I was shocked to find many bustling tea shops serving a strange kind of Indian tea that was mixed not with the usual salt and butter but with milk and sugar. My father, however, was very tense and irritable and did not share my enthusiasm. I realize now that while he was not as demonstrative as my mother, he still hoped that because I was only an alternate I would not be chosen for the dance troupe. But for whatever reason, with all the confidence of the very young, I had no doubt that I would succeed.

Not long after we arrived, I was summoned to appear before the Dalai Lama's lord chamberlain, a very powerful monk official in the traditional government. The audience was held at his home, and as we were ushered into the drawing room I had no idea what I should do or say. It was crowded, and I was concentrating so hard that the voice of the lord chamberlain startled me.

"Pick up your head so I can see your face."

He was sitting on a high cushion or throne, and he ordered me and the other boys to stand directly in front of him. I was so nervous I had been afraid to lift my gaze to meet his.

"Tell me your name and age and who your parents are."

I don't remember what I said, but the particulars didn't seem to matter. From his seat on the cushion the lord chamberlain looked carefully from one boy to another. I had no idea what was coming next, but after about ten minutes he said simply, "It will be good if Tashi Tsering becomes a member of the dance troupe."

I could scarcely believe my ears. It had happened just as I had hoped it would. I was about to begin a new life.

I was told to report the very next day to begin an intensive six-month training period. My future, I naively believed, was assured. In retrospect, I can see far more clearly than I could then how lucky I was. My life had been changed dramatically by what amounted to little more than a stroke of luck, a twist of fate. I had been the right person, at the right age, in the right place, at the right time. Had I not been chosen to be a dancer, besides becoming a monk there would have been no other opportunity for a peasant boy like me to break free of the gravitational pull of his village and the traditional peasant life. And therefore without the experience and perspectives that the subsequent events of my life provided me, I think I would simply have been overwhelmed by the events that were to come and change my country and way of life so drastically. But I couldn't know any of that at the time. I had been chosen by the lord chamberlain. I was full of pride and excitement. My time, I believed, had come.

2

You are to move your bedding here. You will eat and live here for the next six months."

We—the new recruits—were lined up all in a row to get our final instructions from the lord chamberlain who stared down at us from his throne, looking very majestic and important.

"Your task will be to learn the twenty-eight gadrugba songs. At night you will learn the words, and during the day you will practice the dance steps. Twice a month—on the holy fifteenth and thirtieth of the lunar month—you will get a day's rest. Otherwise you must work hard and learn well. This is a glorious responsibility. You have all been chosen carefully from good families. From now on you must realize that you are special. The government will give you uniforms that no one else has the right to wear."

He paused and smiled.

"There is a saying among the Lhasa girls. 'Only the lucky girls can get the young men who wear the *jangdi* dress of the dancers.' So it is a great honor to be a gadrugba and to perform in the living quarters of the Dalai Lama. But [the eyes hardened], while it is a great achievement to become a gadrugba, your life will not be easy. For the next six months you will have to study hard and endure many hardships."

I can still remember how keyed up I was. My head was bowed in respect, but my heart was pounding with excitement. I was so proud to have been chosen to receive such an honor. I could already imagine

16

myself dancing for His Holiness, the Dalai Lama. I could also see myself reading and writing in a beautiful hand like my father. Now that I was in Lhasa all things would be possible.

It didn't take long for reality to set in. Almost immediately I went to live with the other boys in a large house near the Potala Palace that was to be our home for the first six months' intensive training. It was like going to boot camp—or prison. There was one teacher for every five students, but the learning process was not at all what I imagined it would be. It wasn't liberating mentally or physically. It was difficult, painful, and demeaning. Not one of us knew how to read, and so the songs had to be learned by rote and with little understanding. We weren't encouraged to think about what the words meant. The teacher would sing, and we would imitate him. Since none of us had been to school, we had no system or previous experience with learning to draw on. And the teachers' idea of providing incentives was to punish us swiftly and severely for each mistake. They constantly hit us on the faces, arms, and legs. They encouraged competition among us to spur us on. When we ran to line up at the beginning of morning, for example, the first boy in line got to punish the later-comers with a slap across the face. Each boy got to punish the one below or behind him. It was terrible. I still have some of the scars from the almost daily beatings. I was shocked by the treatment but soon learned that the teachers' methods had been used for centuries. They did exactly what their teachers had done to them, so these methods were considered perfectly normal and reasonable.

Nevertheless, I hated the way I was being treated and being made to treat others. I tried hard, but it was difficult for me to memorize the words and tunes to the traditional songs, and I felt it was terribly unfair to punish me for mistakes I didn't think I could control. Worst of all was the sense of complete powerlessness. But we simply had to accept the training just as those who went before us had done. Gadrugba training was my first exposure to the harshness and cruelty that permeated our traditional society, and it made a strong and negative impression on me; only later would I be able to articulate my feelings fully.

The six-month training period seemed to last forever, but finally we were told it was over. We were now ready to perform. Henceforth we would practice once a week on Saturdays and perform at the major ritual celebrations throughout the year. Thus the stress of memorizing the songs and dance steps was over and we were full-fledged gadrugba, but there were still some practical problems to be solved. Because our training period was completed we weren't allowed to stay in the old house anymore, and we all had to find places to live on our own. The government paid us no salary, our parents being "compensated" for our loss by a tax concession. Some of the other young dancers' families had relatives in Lhasa with whom they could stay, or a parent or relative was able to stay with them. But neither of these options was available to me, and since I was too young to live on my own, my father arranged for me to stay with a local family who lived just below the Potala in the walled town of Shöl. The head of the family was one of the higher servants of a senior monk official (the *chigyabchemmo*). Although he was a servant, he was more like a steward and in his own right was rich with many milch animals.

The arrangement was straightforward and quite typical in our society. "Now Tashi," my father told me, "this family will look after your needs from now on. You will live with them, and they will give you food. They have said that they will teach you writing, so that is good. I will send some grain up from the village to help out, but you will also be expected to help them by doing chores around the house. From now on you are to obey them and work hard. Do not let us down." All I could say was, "Of course, father." And I really thought that it sounded fine.

However, as soon as my father left Lhasa, I found myself engulfed in a new nightmare that was even worse than the six-month training period. My new "family" treated me like a common house servant. They didn't give me enough food to eat, and what they did provide was of poor quality and very different from the hearty meals I was used to at home in my village. They also always made a point of giving me something different from what they were eating themselves. It was as if they wanted to make it clear at every meal that my status was inferior to theirs. And then they had work for me to do all day long and even at night. I had to feed the animals first thing in the morning and gather their dung, which I carried on my back and laid out to dry for fuel. During the day I had to go and sell yogurt or milk, carrying a large pot on my back. Then in the evening I again had to help with the animals, including the milking. It was hard work that took virtually all of my time, as I was their only "servant." In my village people worked hard, but never like this. I felt powerless and extremely frustrated. My father's last words to me were that I had to help this host family with their work, so I felt I had to do whatever they ordered, although I didn't really understand why they were so mean.

Worst of all, they didn't teach me a thing—not even how to write a single letter. I think I could have shrugged off all the other hardships if I had felt I was getting somewhere with my learning. But I was being treated like a servant and accomplishing nothing. I was trapped in a dreary round of demeaning duties punctuated at regular intervals by the weekend practice and performances with the gadrugba. But what could I do? I was young and they were powerful, and I felt I had to comply.

After two years of living this way, I was so miserable that I began to think seriously of how to extricate myself from this family. I tried to send messages back to my own family, but as I received no response I didn't know if my messages got through. So, after much soul-searching, I concluded that I had to run way. Flight was actually a traditional Tibetan response to oppression and exploitation, but at that time I knew only that I didn't want to continue to exist as the equivalent of a powerless slave and saw no way to change the behavior of the family toward me.

One morning, therefore, I left the house, ostensibly to do chores but went instead to a small monastery in Lhasa where there were always monks willing to exchange room and board for light labor. I found work, but no sooner did I start my new life than the father of the host family where I had been staying suddenly appeared and took me back, giving me a severe scolding and a stern warning not to do such a thing again. He, I learned, had friends in all the local monasteries and through them discovered where I was.

The next few months were a repeat of the past two years, and so I again decided to flee, but this time out of Lhasa to the Drepung Monastery, five miles west of the city. It was a great adventure for me and initially turned out well. There was plenty of work since Drepung housed ten thousand monks and was like a monk city. I immediately met some monks who were happy to let me do chores for them such as bringing water in return for food and shelter. I was still a kind of servant, but it seemed totally different. The chores were easy and occupied only a small part of the day, and, critically, I was in control. I could leave any time I wanted. However, after a few weeks, the father of the terrible host family suddenly appeared and took me back again. I still remember how the kindly monks begged him to let me stay or at least not to treat me harshly, but he did not listen. "You monks know how to pray, but you know nothing about the world," he said with a sneer. "This boy is so full of mischief, he never does our housework properly. Since you don't know what you're talking about, you'd better just shut up."

When we got back I was treated even worse than before, and after the recent taste of freedom my life seemed totally unbearable. Although I was just turning fourteen years old, I now became convinced that if I really wanted to escape I would have to flee far from Lhasa and the long reach of my host family and their friends. Where to go now became the pressing question.

I had heard about Kalimpong, a town in India where many hundreds of Tibetans lived, engaging mostly in trading activities. It seemed the safe haven I was seeking, and I started to find out about it and make plans to flee there. But Kalimpong was a long way away, and ultimately I decided to head south where there were also a number of towns such as Gyantse and Shigatse and Phari that might provide suitable anonymity.

Ironically, while I was deciding where to go, my parents, who had finally learned how miserable I was, had themselves decided to send one of my aunts to Lhasa to rent a house and look after me. But I didn't know of their plan and one fall morning set out to escape. I had no money and only the clothes on my back, but I was determined to succeed this time. Leaving Lhasa, I headed south and west in the general direction of Gyantse and Shigatse and beyond them the rugged Himalayas and vast reaches of India. I really didn't know where I was going; I was only certain that I had to free myself of that household and gain control over my work and time.

The first day I followed a group of villagers driving home a donkey herd since they were also heading south. I didn't talk to them; I just tagged along until we came to the great Yarlung River, the river that flows west to east, bisecting Tibet, and then turns south and snakes down through the mountains into India as the Brahmaputra. At Chushul, on the northern bank of that river, there was just a ferry landing, no bridge. People crossed on a large wooden barge, but I had not a penny for passage. I decided to play on the shore by the boat, getting on and off but pretending I had no interest in crossing. After a while, nobody paid much attention to me and I was able to slip onto the boat and cross unnoticed. After I got across the river, I walked as far as the foot of the imposing 15,800–foot Gambala Pass and there asked a family to give me food and shelter for the night. They saw that I did not even have a bowl of my own and were kind, feeding me and giving me a place to sleep in the corral with the sheep. It was an exciting night for me, for this was the farthest I had ever gone.

The valley was beautiful, and I thought that maybe I could stop here and find work, which I heard would be easy. But then the image of the head of my host family riding up and dragging me back to Lhasa came to mind, and this time I decided to take no chances. The next day I moved on and started the long ascent to the Gambala Pass. Along the way I met some Mongolian monks who were going on a pilgrimage to the Tashihunpo Monastery in Shigatse, the seat of the Panchen Lama. Since that was the direction I wanted to go, I fell in with them and followed them over the pass and a bit beyond, where we stayed overnight. They seemed not to mind my tagging along. In fact they noticed the poor quality of my shoes and gave me an old pair that they didn't need. The trail was stony and uneven, and I was extremely grateful for their consideration. The monks also gave me some tea and tsamba, and I slept peacefully that evening, now two days away from Lhasa.

On the third day, I fell in with a group of muleteers from Lhasa. Muleteers were notoriously rough and extroverted, and, sure enough, they soon began asking me questions. I liked their down-to-earth manners but nevertheless decided not to tell them that I had been in training for the gadrugba, since fleeing from a government obligation was a serious breach. Instead I made up a story about how I was a servant in a noble family who had made a mistake and had run away to avoid receiving a whipping. They believed me, as that was a rather common occurrence in Tibet, and thought I was quite intelligent. In fact, they were so taken with me that they wanted me to join them on their journey to Kalimpong in India. That was vaguely where I had originally hoped to go, and I asked many questions about India. Kalimpong sounded fantastic, but now that it was a real option, I began to have second thoughts. I was getting farther and farther away from both my own village and Lhasa every day, and suddenly I became fearful of losing contact with my roots. I wanted to put as much distance as I could between myself and my host family, but on the other hand I became a bit afraid of where this would all end and began to think that the best solution might be to try simply to go to the town of Shigatse, not so far from my village home. So I told the muleteers the truth about being a runaway gadrugba dancer and asked their advice. Their attitude changed immediately, as they knew they could get in serious trouble for helping me, and they told me to go back to my village and discuss what to do with my family.

I left them when we got to the town of Gyantse, where I found shelter with a well-to-do family. Again, I did various chores for them and they provided room and board. They were, however, interested in my story and inquired who I was and what I was doing. I liked them, so I told them the whole truth. They were a family of government serfs themselves, and they seemed to feel that we had much in common. They weren't at all afraid to help me and told me I could stay with them as long as I wanted. I was grateful for their kindness and the offer of shelter, but after three or four days I got restless and again set off down the road, this time to Shigatse. I had still not decided to return home, since I knew I had disobeyed my father's clear instructions and was afraid of what he would do, but at least I would be near if eventually I decided to return.

Along the road I met a group of Tibetan ladies coming from India with their servants and immediately offered to help them carry their baggage.

They agreed and fed me on the trail. When we got to the city, I looked up a family whose name I had heard from my parents and told them that I was a runaway gadrugba dancer who had been mistreated and needed shelter and food. They allowed me to live in their house, and as before, I did chores to pay for my food and shelter.

As the days turned to weeks, I began to realize that running away was at best a temporary solution, and I became concerned about what was going to happen to me in the long run. I wasn't being badly treated, but I wasn't learning anything and I wasn't doing much more than the tasks of a servant. I was getting nowhere, and I don't know how long I would have drifted if it hadn't been for what at the time seemed like a miracle.

One day after about two weeks, while I was working in the kitchen, I was astounded to see my younger father standing in the doorway. My first reaction was to try to hide myself in one of the cubbyholes where the family kept dung as fuel for the fire. My uncle smiled broadly as he watched me.

"Come on out, Olo. We know all about your troubles. Your father is planning to go to Lhasa to try and straighten things out. I have come to take you home."

"Yes. Yes," I said, and I rushed out to greet him.

I hadn't realized how much I had missed my family until that moment and I hugged my father-uncle till my arms ached. When we had time to talk, he told me that my family had heard I had run away from Lhasa and was in the Shigatse area. My mother was so frantic with worry that my uncle had come all the way from our village on horseback to find me and bring me home. The family I had been staying with seemed happy for me and wished us a good journey. As we started on our way my uncle let me ride together with him on the same horse, and to my great relief, he did not ask many questions. Like all of my family, he was instinctively tactful, and sensing my embarrassment he let the matter of my problems in Lhasa drop. For my part I literally beamed with happiness. For all my brave thoughts and daring plans, I was grateful that my adventures were over for the time being and that I would have a chance to go home.

When we got back to my village I learned that all sorts of rumors had spread about what I must have done in Lhasa and why I had tried to escape. But I told my family the truth, especially about how badly I had been treated, and they were sympathetic. Even the other villagers eventually understood why I had fled. But while the worst seemed to be over for me, it still wasn't clear what my family was going to do. They were glad to see me and very understanding, but my flight had created a serious problem for them. My parents had been compensated for the loss of their son to the gadrugba by a tax exemption for one tax unit of land. The financial benefit from this was substantial. However, because I had run away, they were fearful they might lose not only the tax benefit but also the land itself. In Tibet, the government demanded compliance from peasants like us. So after much discussion, they decided I had to go back, and I reluctantly agreed after they explained they had a good plan that would preclude my receiving any punishment for my actions.

The scheme was simple but clever. My father was to go to Lhasa alone and meet with the head of the gadrugba, telling him he had heard I had run away but that he did not know where I was. He would say he was going to look for me, but that finding me might take some time. However, he would promise that he would bring me back and ask that I be granted leave in the meantime. The plan worked precisely as my father intended. After a lot of talk and the offer of gifts that amounted to bribes, Pockmarks assured my father that when he brought me back he would not beat me.

In the meantime, my parents had sweetened the package for my returning by offering to let me use the month or so it would take for my father to go and return from Lhasa to start learning to read and write. If I wanted, my father said, they would send me to a teacher to study. My troubles in Lhasa had not discouraged me from wanting to study. On the contrary, they had actually strengthened my resolve to learn to write and better myself. So, when my father left for Lhasa to see what kind of deal he could make, I left to study Tibetan with a family in the small town of Khartse. The family took in students, mostly the children of wealthy town families, and I joined them for what ended up three months of intensive work. It was my first real opportunity to learn, and I was enormously excited.

From the moment I arrived in Khartse I knew my time was limited, and I wanted to master as much of the basics as possible. I had a small room where I worked at my lessons day and night. The master was a very kind man and an eager tutor who taught because he knew Tibetan well and loved to teach others to read and write it. He had about ten students, and he taught us our letters by having us write them on an oblong wooden board that had been covered with chalk. When I drew the letters on the chalk they would appear as the black color of the underlying wood. After the teacher corrected my exercise, I would wipe off the old chalk, repowder the wood, and start again. I studied the thirty letters of the Tibetan alphabet on the slate for one whole month. In the second month I studied the complicated combinations of letters that typify written Tibetan; and in the third month I began to write cursive script on paper. I was elated at the idea of myself forming correct letters just as my father had. I think my excitement must have been all too apparent and perhaps a bit amusing to my teacher. But he seemed to understand how I felt. One day when I was particularly proud of myself he told me a famous saying of the thirteenth-century scholar Sakya Pandita: "Writing and reading are the basis of all knowledge and not the smallest instrument for making a living." My teacher seemed to know why learning meant so much to me, and I remember his words and his kind manner fondly to this day.

My resolve to learn to read and write was now more focused than it had been in the village before I left for Lhasa. It had been clear even to me that in the world of the capital city, learning was the key to advancement and wealth. I saw more literate people there than I had ever seen before, and it didn't take long to realize that the ones who could read and write were the ones who were more respected. They were also the ones who became the officials and got the better positions. As a member of the gadrugba, I already had a great opportunity since it was customary that when we became eighteen and were replaced by new cadres of young dancers, we would receive government jobs. But there are jobs and there are jobs. The boys who rose highest in the ranks were the ones who could read and write in a perfect hand.

These thoughts about the possibility of advancement in Lhasa reminded me of a truth about myself that sometimes made me uncomfortable but I couldn't deny. As happy as I was being reunited with my family and starting to study, I still had problems living in our village, where nothing had changed. I had glimpsed other ways of life and broader horizons. Nobody thought the way I did, and people who understood what I was hoping and feeling—like my teacher—were extremely rare. As I felt myself falling back into the old routines and the roles I used to play, I also began to yearn again for the urban life and the possibilities it seemed to hold for me. To be truthful, except for my desire to educate myself, I didn't have a very clear picture of what my future might hold. But I knew what I wanted to get away from.

And so, after my father's successful negotiation with Pockmarks, I returned to the city once again with as much study as I could cram into a few months. My father brought expensive gifts for the dance troupe officials who, in turn, as agreed, did nothing to prevent my return or punish me. Of course I did not go back to the family I had stayed with before, and my father this time found me a suitable house where I lived more or less happily for some time. Then other events began to happen that would change the course of my life.

3

I had not been long in the city again when I was told to deliver something to an important monk official. There I met another monk named Wangdu, who worked as the major-domo of that official. He was extremely cordial, talking with me in a gentle and friendly manner, and I could tell he liked me. It was a pleasant change from the distance usually maintained between superiors and inferiors in Lhasa. I genuinely enjoyed meeting him, but soon forgot about it—until, that is, a few days later when Pockmarks called me to his presence and announced:

"I have been asked to send you to Wangdula [la is a polite suffix added to names], the monk steward you met last week."

That was all he said, but I knew immediately what was meant. Wangdu was asking for me to become his homosexual partner. In the manner customary to monks and monk officials in Lhasa, he had asked my superior for permission to invite me, and now I was being asked. For a moment I didn't know how I wanted to respond, and I stood there speechless, trying quickly to think what to say. Pockmarks became impatient and again asked:

"What do you say? Will you do it?"

The question was firm and couldn't be evaded, but I still didn't know what I really wanted to say. After all the problems I had in Lhasa, I wasn't sure if placing myself in a relationship with Wangdu would bring new difficulties or be the start of an era of success. I could have refused. I had no sexual feelings for him or for men in general. But I had liked him and also understood that having an intimate relationship with someone aligned with power and authority was an opportunity not to be lightly dismissed. So I decided to agree, and hesitantly said I would accept the invitation. It was the start of some of the best years of my life.

My decision and some of its ramifications have often seemed shocking or confusing—or both—when I have tried to explain them to foreign friends whose cultures and assumptions are so different from mine. But I didn't find the invitation strange at all. To see it in proper perspective, you have to understand how the old Tibetan society was structured and what our customs were. For most of its history, Tibet has been a theocratic state. The bureaucracy that ran the government consisted of two kinds of officials—lay officials and monk officials. The original logic behind the creation of a class of monk officials was that as Tibet was a theocracy, monks should participate in administering the country. However, over the years, these monk officials became token monks in the sense that they neither lived in monasteries nor engaged in religious rites and prayer ceremonies. They were really bureaucrats who took religious vows. They wore a version of monks' robes but worked as full-time government officials. Living in houses in the city like other officials, they wielded equal power and status with their lay aristocratic counterparts and were jointly in charge of government administration and its day-to-day operations. However, though they were "token" monks in most senses, they were required to obey the monks' vow of celibacy.

In traditional Tibetan society, celibacy was defined specifically to mean abstaining from sexual acts with a female or, in a more general sense, from any sexual act that involved penetration of an orifice whether with a female or male. Consequently, anal sex with a male was as strictly prohibited as vaginal sex with a woman, and if discovered would mean expulsion from the monk rolls.

However, human nature being what it is, monks over the years developed a way to circumvent the iron law of celibacy. Monastic rules, it turned out, said nothing about other forms of sexual activity, and it became common for monks and monk officials to satisfy themselves sexually with men or boys by performing the sex act without penetrating an orifice. They used a version of the "missionary position" in which the monk official (the active, male-role player) moved his penis between the crossed thighs of a partner beneath him. Since no monastic disciplinary rule was technically violated, this behavior was condoned and rationalized as a pleasurable release of little significance.

The typical relationship was between monks—an adult monk (the male role) and a younger, boy monk—but there were several types of lay boys who were particularly desirable. One was the boys or young men who performed in the Tibetan opera, many of whom played women's roles. Another was the young gadrugba dancers. Thus Wangdula's request was not really unusual.

Obvious similarities aside, this "homosexuality" is quite different from homosexuality in Western terms. First, it was restricted almost exclusively to monks and monk officials and has always been looked on simply as a traditional way to get around a rule. The monks are not considered "gay" in the Western sense, because Tibetans don't see this kind of behavior as the result of gender identity that is somehow biologically or culturally determined. Indeed, as a rule, in Tibet nonheterosexual activity by ordinary people is frowned on. Lay people seldom if ever have same-sex lovers. The monks' behavior is just a fact of the way our culture has evolved. Thus, when the head of the gadrugba made his request, I was not shocked. It did not affect my sense of my own sexual identity, and I knew it would not affect anybody else's opinion of me in that sense.

Agreeing to become Wangdula's lover turned out to be a good decision for me. Though not a government official himself, as the steward of an important official Wangdu was well known in elite circles. I therefore benefited directly from his connections with status and power. Moreover, from the beginning of our relationship, he took an interest in me as an individual. He treated me kindly, frequently gave me presents when I went to his house, and, most important, was concerned about my career, playing a central role in my continuing education and my plans for advancement. Wangdu wrote in the beautiful Tibetan calligraphy of the Lhasa governmental elite, and he both valued education and understood my desire to learn. Sharing my own values and aspirations, he arranged for another official to accept me as a student, and later he put me in contact with two superb teachers who taught me different aspects of grammar and composition. Thus it turned out to be largely through Wangdula's efforts and kindness that I finally got access to the tools I so desperately wanted and needed. But sometimes my life got a bit too exciting.

The Tibetan word for a boy in my situation is *drombo*. In our language the word literally means "guest," but it also is a euphemism for "homosexual (passive) partner." Because of Wangdu's status and visibility, I became a very well-known drombo, and my reputation sometimes caused more trouble than I could handle. For example, once a powerful monk from the Sera Monastery became attracted to me and made several abortive attempts to abduct me for sexual pleasure. The monks of Sera included many famous *dobdos*, or "punk" monks. These were accepted deviant monks who carried weapons and swaggered through the streets, standing out in a crowd because of their openly aggressive manner and distinctive way of dressing. They were also notorious for fighting with each other to see who was toughest and for their sexual predation of lay boys. All schoolboys in Lhasa were fair game for these dobdos, and most tried to return from school in groups for protection against them.

I knew for some time that I was being pursued and had several close calls. But I was always able to escape until one fateful day when that monk caught me after a gadrugba performance in Lhasa and forcibly took me to his apartment in the monastery. He made me a prisoner, threatening me with beatings if I tried to escape or I refused to cooperate with him sexually. It was distasteful, but he released me after two days. The incident, however, reawakened my ambivalent feelings toward traditional Tibetan society. Once again its cruelty was thrust into my life. I wondered to myself how monasteries could allow such thugs to wear the holy robes of the Lord Buddha. When I talked to other monks and monk officials about the dobdos, they shrugged and said simply that that was just the way things were.

Wangdu was frustrated and angry with what happened, but knew he couldn't say or do anything because the monk who kidnapped me was famous for his ferocity and brutality. Despite his position, Wangdula was afraid of becoming the target of retribution. The situation was made worse because this incident was not the only attempt of this sort. Other monks were attracted to me as well, and for a period of time I was in almost constant danger of being kidnapped. On several other occasions these attempts were successful. Each such episode infuriated Wangdula but also solidified the ties between us. He wasn't simply angry at being bested. He genuinely cared about me and my welfare, and while I did not feel sexually attracted to him, I couldn't help responding to his affection and concern. Moreover, I appreciated the good things he had done and was willing to do for me. And I liked him after a fashion. I think because of his sympathy for my desire to learn and because of the many stressful experiences we shared in those early years, a very strong bond developed between us that lasted until his death.

As I say, it has never been easy to talk about these things with people from cultures where the customs and assumptions about sexual matters differ greatly. To such people, for example, it would also be hard to explain the fact that during the years after I knew Wangdula, I had relationships with women. While Wangdula was jealous of other men, he had no objections to my relations with women. And there were times when Wangdula willingly shared me with other officials, and I accepted this arrangement because in spirit it was quite a different thing from the violent kidnappings. Moreover, it was simply what was done in those days.

Strange as this may seem to Americans, during this same period I also got married, at least briefly. My relationship with the woman I married began several years after my relationship with Wangdula started. Communication with my family was difficult and uncertain because there was no mail service, so on one occasion my mother decided to come to Lhasa to visit me and at the same time make a pilgrimage to Lhasa's holy sites. She rented a room for herself, as my own quarters were too small for both of us, and stayed for about three months. During her stay, she met a neighbor who was the wife of a family of minor officials in the service of the Dalai Lama and together they got the idea that I should marry her daughter, a girl named Tsebei. I was eighteen years old at the time but, as was the custom, was not consulted about the negotiations until the very end. I had seen Tsebei a number of times before the marriage but had no real opinion of her. She was a quiet girl, the eldest child in her family. I wasn't at all attracted to her, but on the other hand her family was well off and I thought that perhaps my mother was correct in seeing this marriage as good for me. So I agreed, but without real enthusiasm.

It was not usual for members of the gadrugba to marry while they were still active dancers, but since my term was nearly up the two mothers thought they could bend the rules a bit and petitioned the appropriate officials to make an exception. Tsebei's family, in fact, was on very good terms with the gadrugba leader, and he readily agreed. A few weeks later I moved in with Tsebei's family as her husband and we began to sleep together. There was no real marriage ceremony.

However, Tsebei and I never had much to say to one another, and no particular empathy or affection arose. That was not so strange in Tibet and would not have upset me too greatly had it been the only problem. However, it was not. The attitude of her father and brothers bothered me tremendously almost from the beginning. Though they were willing to permit me to marry their daughter-sister and join their family, they had no sympathy for my desire to continue my education. They seemed just to want me as a new source of labor they could control. My father-in-law, in particular, couldn't understand why I would want to work at my studies as hard as I did, since as far as he could see they would bring me no concrete rewards. "Tashi," he said to me one day, "you are very good at learning, but you can never get a high post. All you'll ever get is a lowly position where you sit all day with nothing to do. So why waste your time and energy on this fruitless activity?"

My new father-in-law was in part correct. The old Tibetan society was very hierarchical and class oriented. Coming from a rural, peasant background, I was aware of the limits to advancement—no matter what my ability. For example, I could never become a full government lay official, as such posts were the hereditary prerogative of the aristocracy. But I also felt that knowledge and learning were important and that I could rise to become a person of substance and status. And there was also the idea of freedom. I couldn't quite articulate it at the time, but I intensely disliked having to take orders from Tsebei's brothers and father. It seemed a regression to my years with the first host family, which I had hated so much. So after three months of snide comments about my studying, I could stand it no longer and decided I had to get out of the marriage to pursue my dreams. Consequently, one day I walked out the door with the resolute decision never to return. For me the marriage was finished.

But leaving was not so simple. Since Tsebei's family was friendly with the gadrugba leader, my leaving had ramifications. At first, therefore, I hid out in Lhasa while I tried to see if I could make arrangements to flee to India for a while, since there I would be beyond Tibetan law. But as I was finalizing this arrangement, my old nemesis Pockmarks learned of my whereabouts and sent people to catch me.

As Pockmarks had originally given special approval for my marriage, he was particularly furious at my running away. He yelled and hit me many times, trying to make me change my mind and go back to Tsebei, but I refused. And in the end I won out, although I paid a price. Pockmarks agreed I didn't have to return, but insisted on first punishing me for leaving. His idea of a reasonable punishment was a full-scale caning—twenty-five strokes of the switch on the bare buttocks. It was painful and humiliating, but when he was finished my marriage was officially terminated.

During this period, my relationship with Wangdula remained stable. He was always a good friend and a kind lover, and he continued to help me with my education and career. His sympathy, support, and approval were crucial, and gradually my spirits rose. I put the episode of my brief and unhappy marriage behind me, and I renewed my studies. Already I was able to read and write Tibetan very well, so well in fact, that the younger students of my teachers envied me, and their admiration gave me much needed encouragement.

Fortuitously, just a few months after the marriage fiasco, all my efforts in studying Tibetan suddenly paid off. The year was 1947. I was eighteen and due to complete my term as a gadrugba in a few months. At that time I would automatically be in line for some sort of lower-level government position, depending, of course, on what was available and appropriate to my skills. The better positions, such as full clerk (or *chola*), were few and far between, and often we ex-gadrugba had to wait years for such an opening to occur. However, I learned from Wangdu that an old monk official who was a clerk in the Potala Treasury was going to retire soon. Because he was a friend, Wangdula felt there was a chance I could secure his job. The problem was timing. Technically, I was still dancing and therefore not eligible to secure a post until my term was up. But this opportunity was too good to pass up, so Wangdula and I discussed the situation and came up with a plan. He was powerful enough to make discreet inquiries about the position and ascertained informally that I had a good chance of being selected. Based on this information, I went ahead and applied for the position without saying anything to the head of the gadrugba.

The first thing I had to do was pass a calligraphy examination—an examination I had in effect been training for all these years. To begin the process, I had to supply the examiners with a sample of my handwriting. In Tibet in those days, literacy and education were in large part measured by one's calligraphic skills, and a good hand was critical for any kind of higher position. Candidates were allowed to look at samples of the previous official's handwriting, and I requested some and studied them carefully. When I had practiced enough I presented myself to the examiners, who made me write a page in their presence. From their reaction it appeared that I had done well and was likely to get the job, but there was a catch. I had to obtain permission from the head of the gadrugba. By this time Pockmarks had died, but his place had been taken by an equally domineering man, who was, not surprisingly, furious when he heard my request.

"How did you get such a position?" he asked angrily.

I told him exactly what I had done and emphasized that it all had been through the proper channels, but I knew exactly how he would respond. Going ahead with the process of applying for the position and taking the examination without first getting his permission had been a calculated risk. But I was already experienced enough to know that if I had asked his permission first, my request would almost certainly have been denied. I had long since learned that if I wanted something important I just had to try to go after it myself—and sort out the problems later. The question now was, Could these difficulties be resolved? The head of the gadrugba seemed truly angry, probably because he felt he had lost face.

"You ask for my approval after you already have the job! That is an insult. You should have consulted with me before you acted," he said angrily. "Now there is nothing to do."

That was, of course, precisely the problem, and I knew that I had to help him save face. So, on Wangdu's advice I went to one of the new director's friends and persuaded him to intercede on my behalf. I even tried to bribe him with a gift of tea, but he did not accept the tea. He was, however, sympathetic, because he also knew Wangdula, and he agree to act as an intermediary. Slowly but surely the balance swung in my favor. The friend persuaded the head of the gadrugba to relent; and finally it was agreed that I could accept the position if I paid a fine to the whole organization of the dancers. It was decided that I should sponsor a tea for the entire group, and I gladly paid for it. Thereafter, for the rest of my term as a gadrugba, I continued to practice and perform part of the time but also went to my office to begin my new duties. I can remember vividly how proud and excited I was, even now.

My office at the Potala Treasury consisted of three chief officials (two of whom were monk officials and one an aristocratic official), about thirty lower-level clerks, or cholas, like me, and three sweepers. It was responsible for supplying the Dalai Lama's daily requests for things like tea, butter, and ceremonial scarves, and much of the staff did what amounted to manual work, although there was written work to be done as well. As many of my co-clerks were illiterate, I was among those given the more sophisticated tasks that involved writing. I recorded the day's business, what was transacted and among whom, and I kept records about taxes and saw to it that regulations were followed.

As you can imagine, I was extremely pleased, not only because it was a position for which I was qualified, but also because I could still remember what it had been like to carry dung, feed the horses, and eat scraps in the home of my first hosts in Lhasa. I really felt I had moved up and now had a secure status in society. Not the least of my pleasure was due to the fact that the job was one of the first tangible signs that my efforts to better myself were having some effect.

The working conditions themselves were quite comfortable. We clerks would have yak butter tea in the mornings, and sometimes when there was not much work we just sat around and made small talk. The office closed at four o'clock in the afternoon, and we used to have tea at closing time as well.

Life was very good for the next year or so, although sadly my relationship with Wangdu came to an end. The official whom Wangdu served got posted outside of Lhasa, and Wangdu had to accompany him. Our parting was difficult, but Wangdu again helped me, this time finding a new relationship for me with a very prominent monk official who lived in a big house right in front of the Potala Palace. My new host was rich and powerful, and I lived very comfortably with him. I had a small room of my own and joined the rest of the household for dinner in the evening when there was a joint meal.

But good things seldom last; and before long my life was to take twists and turns that I could never have imagined, even in my dreams.

4

In 1950 (when I was about twenty-one) Radio Peking announced in a New Year's broadcast that the People's Liberation Army's tasks for the coming year would include the "liberation" of Tibet, Hainan Island, and Formosa.

The war between China and Japan had ended. The communists had defeated the Guomindang, and—driven by the new political, social, and military agendas—they were ready to move outward. By May 1950, Chinese troops had begun to assemble on the banks of the upper Yangtze River, on Tibet's eastern border. Continuing the position of previous Chinese governments that Tibet—which was then functioning as an independent polity with its own government and army—was a part of China, they now were ready to "liberate" it. After attempts to persuade our government to send negotiators failed, in early October the invasion of eastern Tibet began. Within a month, most of Tibet's tiny and inadequate army had been destroyed or neutralized. There was little or nothing standing between the Chinese armies and the capital city of Lhasa.

Mao Zedong wanted to liberate Tibet peacefully, however, not simply conquer the country by force. Consequently, after its initial victories, the Chinese army stopped its advance and tried to compel the Tibetan government to accept "peaceful liberation"—that is, to acknowledge formally that Tibet was a part of China. The Tibetan government sought help from the United States, India, and Great Britain, but after receiving none, it reluctantly sent delegates to Beijing to try to negotiate with the Chinese. The result was the Seventeen Point Agreement for the Liberation of Tibet, signed in Beijing in May 1951. According to its terms, Tibet agreed that it was part of China but the traditional government of the Dalai Lama was allowed to remain in place—at least until the people agreed to reforms. For a while our lives went on as before.

We all felt certain that change was coming, though. We had heard that the communists were atheists and the sworn enemies of the rich and prosperous. Rumors of all sorts flew everywhere; some even said that the Chinese were cannibals. There was no end of guessing what the Chinese might or might not do, but we didn't have to wait long to find out. By September 1951 Chinese troops and officials began to appear in Lhasa.

My own life changed very little at first. My term as a gadrugba had ended by the beginning of 1950, and I had settled comfortably into my new job in the Potala Treasury, where I began to have more of a social life than I had ever had before. Like other young men, in the evenings I used to love to go to the tea shops, which were really more like open-air cafes than American restaurants. "English tea" laden with milk and sugar and British Indian–style cakes were served to us as we sat outside at communal tables. We didn't need money every night; we would run a tab and pay at the end of the week.

The camaraderie was delightful. Crowds of young people gathered to play mah-jongg and other games and talk the kind of nonsense young people talk. But they also talked about ideas, and these discussions were a relatively new experience for me. I began to meet the sons of merchant families who traded in India, people with experiences quite different from my own. Naturally they talked a lot about India and the British, and their different ways of doing things, and their discussions soon got me interested in learning English. They were extremely friendly and happy enough to teach me what they knew. They weren't professional teachers, of course, but they were eager to please, and I learned the English alphabet while sitting in tea shops, where I also learned about the St. Joseph's School in Darjeeling, a place where a few wealthy Tibetans went to study. I couldn't help but be struck by how different these young men's general attitude was about learning, especially in contrast to that of the people in my village or my temporary father-in-law. My wanting to know more made perfect sense to these young people; it seemed completely natural. Although I didn't realize it at the time, these discussions were among my first encounters with what I would call a modern attitude about education.

I was very enthusiastic and very malleable then, so much so that I'm sure I must have amused many of my new acquaintances. I got extremely excited about the new ideas I encountered, whether in the books I read or in conversations at the tea shop. I remember reading one religious book that affected me so much that I became a vegetarian for a while. I began to meditate two hours a day and used to carry a Buddhist rosary in my hand and intone the prayer *Om mani padme hum* as I walked in the street. Finally friends convinced me that I needed meat to work effectively and that my behavior was becoming excessive. I learned more during those years than in all the years before then, and the more I learned the more I wanted to know, the more questions I wanted to ask. And then my life suddenly started getting complicated, and I had a lot less time for reading.

One of the complications was that I fell in love. It so happened that a beautiful young woman named Thondrup Dromala regularly came to get milk at the house where I was staying. She was eighteen years old, very shy, and I was attracted to her from the moment I set eyes on her. I started thinking about her all the time. She used to go to the well to get water and to the same houses everyday to get milk. I learned her routines, and I used to try to meet her "coincidentally" whenever I could. In this way we became accustomed to seeing one another and talking, and after a while I was able to get her to come to the house where I was staying. Eventually, she let me kiss her and then kiss her more regularly. But even this intimacy took a long time to achieve, because she was shy.

I could invite Thondrup Dromala over only during the daytime, because her family was very strict. Her father was dead, and her mother was watchful and suspicious. Her brother, who tried to play the father's role, was even stricter. Eventually, however, we began sleeping together, and after that, not surprisingly, the affair began to become a matter of gossip. When our relationship became public both the brother and my mentor decided that something ought to be done. And so negotiations about a possible marriage began, lasting for some time.

During this period Thondrup Dromala and I became very close. It was not at all like my earlier "arranged" marriage. This time I was head over heels in love, and the feelings were strong on both sides.

Because our relationship was now acknowledged, it became a bit easier to be together. Sometimes we would leave the city and go to a place where we could eat and spend the day. When the weather was warm we would sometimes bathe in the rivers. In the colder weather we had to stay inside. I often skipped work to spend the day with her. I wasn't quite a high enough official that I had to be at work every day, and it was surprising how easy it was to sneak out. I would usually just send my boss a message that I wouldn't be in that day. There was seldom, if ever, a problem.

For a while things looked promising, and I became quite attracted to the idea of marriage. Besides the fact that I loved Thondrup Dromala, her brother, the head of her family, was a *tsidrung* (a monk official), and he was rich. I don't think I ever admitted it to myself at the time, but I can see now that the idea of becoming part of her prosperous family was definitely attractive. Though I was better off than I had ever been, I still was by no means wealthy, and in the old Tibetan system I could never move up to become a full-fledged government official at a rank equal to that of her brother's. I might become a senior chola, or clerk, in the treasury, but in our system all the lay officials were selected from the aristocracy. And I could expect no significant financial support from my own family, as they had already done what they could. On the other hand, Thondrup Dromala's family had a huge house and plenty of money, so the prospect of becoming a son-in-law in this family could not have been more pleasing. But it was not to be.

It seems that while I had been quietly planning to join the household of the woman I loved, her mother and brother had ideas of their own. Because of my peasant background, I wasn't exactly a prize catch. I was poor by their standards, and what would have been a big social and financial step up for me would have been a step down from their point of view. And there were other factors as well. The brother had another candidate in mind for a son-in-law—someone he'd had his eye on who would be both husband to Thondrup Dromala and his sexual partner at the same time. And so the negotiations for our marriage came to a standstill.

I found out later that the mother turned against me as well. She said she learned that there was another woman pursuing me at the time, a woman a bit older than me but with a large estate in Phembo, just north of Lhasa. When this woman began to become aggressive in her pursuit of me, openly sending me presents of food and butter, my prospective mother-in-law made an issue of it. Even though she knew that the woman and I were not sleeping together, even though I did not agree to a relationship with her, even though I was true to Thondrup Dromala, her mother turned against me and did everything she could to divide us. I think she probably used this other woman as an excuse. The fact seemed to be that neither the mother nor the brother wanted me as a member of their family, and that was going to be that.

But nature has a way of taking its own course, and while relations between me and the family cooled considerably, Thondrup Dromala and I drew even closer together, and it soon became all too obvious that she was pregnant. Having a child before marriage was an embarrassment to the family as well as to us, and we were frantic and didn't know what to do. From that point on things just went from bad to worse. The family forbade her to see me, and so we had to meet secretly. When I think back about it, I am amazed at some of the things I did during this time. Of course the family couldn't keep us apart. Sometimes she would come secretly to see me. At other times I would sneak into her house and stay the night. The house was so big that it was easy to enter and equally easy to stay hidden until nightfall. She kept me concealed until everyone else was asleep, and then we would come together. We met this way many times both before and after the birth of my son (in 1953).

Eventually, of course, our luck ran out. Thondrup Dromala and I had been sleeping together in various places, taking whatever chance or opportunity offered. One night after the birth of my son, the three of us were asleep and the mother found where we were hiding. She woke us up at midnight and made a terrible scene, screaming at her daughter, ordering her to stop seeing me, calling me all sorts of names. She worked herself into such a state of anger that she pulled her daughter out from under the covers and began to beat her mercilessly. Since I was not her husband, I had little or no power to prevent it. But I pleaded with the angry mother. At last the beating stopped and she left us in peace for the rest of the night. I left the house in the morning.

Eventually the relationship became impossible. After catching us in the house, family members were doubly on their guard, and they made it difficult for me and Thondrup Dromala even to meet. And the more I learned about the relationship between the brother and the mother, the less I liked them. The brother was full of himself, arrogant, and treated his mother disrespectfully. In his anger he actually shouted at her and called her names, and his behavior bothered me a great deal. I believed strongly in our tradition of respect for one's parents, and the more disrespect I saw, the more I realized that this was not a house I wanted to join. Meanwhile they continued to make it clear that they wanted no part of me.

For a while Thondrup Dromala and I considered living together on our own. We really loved one another, and we thought about it carefully. In the end we decided against it because we knew that without the support of her family and only my salary to live on we would be poor. It wouldn't be the kind of life that either of us wanted. Inevitably we began to drift apart, though I did everything I could to care for my son and support him. These times were extremely painful.

Meanwhile, there were strong winds beginning to blow in other quarters. If my private life had been filled with the turmoil of my relationship with Thondrup Dromala and the birth of my son, my intellectual and social life had begun to be equally complicated. By 1952—a year before my son's birth—the Chinese were more of a presence in Lhasa. The first troops had appeared in the city in September 1951, but initially they kept a low profile. However, as their numbers increased, they became more active and visible. I became fascinated by the ways they did things, which were so different from our own. They fished in the rivers with worms on a hook and set out to become self-sufficient in food by using dog droppings and human waste they collected on the Lhasa streets for the new fields they opened in a swampy area along the river. These were things we would never have thought of doing and, to be honest, found revolting. The Chinese wasted nothing; nothing was lost. So despite the revulsion, I was also overall fascinated by the extent of their zeal for efficiency and their discipline. They would not even take a needle from the people.

The bureaucracy I had become a part of was very different. It worked slowly and inefficiently, and there was much corruption. In my office, for example, I had worked in my new job long enough to see how wasteful and inefficient our system could be. While, as I said, the work was sometimes very pleasant, I had become increasingly aware of how greedy many of my colleagues were and how the system encouraged bribery and corruption. Already I knew that some senior clerks sent to distant estates to collect revenues for the government kept a good bit of the money for themselves, while the directors of the treasury turned a blind eye. I also knew of clerks sent to India to buy goods for the treasury at Lhasa who used the pack animals supplied by Tibetan peasants along the way to transport goods of their own for sale. Or sometimes they simply sold the animals and kept the money. There were many other examples of this kind of petty—and not so petty—graft in our office. I'm sure the three chief officials in my office knew about many of these activities, but they never did anything to stop them. It was just the way things were done in those days. Watching the Chinese at work was the first time I finally had a basis for comparing our system with someone else's, and I must say I was attracted not only by their efficiency and energy but also by their apparent idealism.

The Chinese worked tirelessly and with a sense of dedication and purpose. Soon after arriving, they opened the first primary school in Lhasa and a hospital as well as other public buildings. I had to admit that I was impressed by the fact that they were doing things that would directly benefit the common people. It was more change for the good in a shorter period of time than I had seen in my life—more change, I was tempted to think, than Tibet had seen in centuries.

The Chinese also established a radio station and set up a loud-speaker in the Barkhor, the central market area, so we could listen to the broadcasts every day. The propaganda was very low key at first. The Chinese didn't try to force themselves on us too quickly. But even so, new ideas were everywhere. You couldn't avoid them. Our old, traditional, essentially static society was suddenly being bombarded with strange terms like "socialism," "capitalism," "communism," and "feudalism," the meanings of which I wasn't at all sure. Our language had no words for these concepts, and it is arguable that even if we had technically had the words themselves most of the people wouldn't have known about them, because there were no schools in Tibet that taught such subjects. As it was, new words had to be created so we could express these concepts in Tibetan, but the correspondences between our versions and the originals were rough at best. The new Tibetan word for "socialism" literally meant "common assemblage system" and for "capitalism," "capital system." Of course, nobody understood these words at first, but we soon began to learn what some of them meant, and that in itself was significant. Until then, education to me had meant mainly learning to write in a beautiful hand and doing simple arithmetic. In my recent conversations at the tea shops I had begun to sense how much more there might be to learning and the extent of knowledge, but I had no understanding of history, or science, or social science in the modern senses. If I had understood anything that could have been called politics, it was most certainly the old, traditional politics. Intellectually and politically, therefore, it is almost fair to say that I was a blank slate just waiting to be written on. But unlike most of the older officials I associated with, I was not just waiting. I was eager.

Predictably, the new concepts and ideas we were now being exposed to were attractive to some, frightening to others. The whole country was unsettled—especially the people of Lhasa, the center of Tibetan civilization and government. On the one hand those who felt they were being treated badly by the traditional society believed that any change would benefit them. The wealthy, the aristocrats, the bosses would be punished for their sins. Those who were suffering now believed they would be rewarded. On the other hand the people in power—those who had something to lose—saw the coming of the Chinese as a threat from the beginning. The class orientation, however, was not clear-cut, because virtually all religious Tibetans were hostile to change. They feared that the atheistic communists would destroy their beloved Tibetan Buddhism and the old theocratic state that perpetuated it.

Yet one category of better-off, younger men I knew were genuinely excited by the prospect of changes. Some were young traders, others were forward-thinking aristocrats, and still others were monks who did not see social change as a threat to religion. They became early supporters of the Chinese and their ideology of reform and egalitarianism.

The Chinese encouraged Tibetans to broaden our education, and of course they wanted to educate us in the "right" way themselves. They said they were going to change things for the better in Tibet, and we could help. They were offering a chance to learn about the ideas and concepts we were hearing about daily from the loudspeaker in the marketplace. Study groups they called "units" were being formed, and I had friends who joined them and invited me to come along. Because I could see the immediate changes, like the new roads and the school, with my own eyes, I was beginning to believe that bigger, more profound changes were really going to happen in our extremely conservative, geographically isolated society. And when I thought about the brutality of my training in the gadrugba, the abuses of authority, the strict limits on advancement for people like me from a common background, and the lack of opportunities for education, I began to think such changes might be exactly what Tibet needed.

However, I was not particularly attracted to communism. Indeed, at the time I'm not sure I could have told you what communism was. And I really thought that Tibetan Buddhism was the greatest religion in the world. But I now began to have a much clearer sense of what I thought needed to be changed in our traditional society, and the Chinese presence seemed the most likely impetus.

There was a problem, however. Gyentsenla—the monk official at whose house I was living—and all of the other monk officials who had supported me and were my friends and patrons were dead set against the communists and the changes. They had always had my best interests at heart and would have viewed a decision to accept the opportunities or adopt the examples offered by the Chinese as an act of disloyalty to them. I was terribly torn. Some of my younger friends from the tea shops and the office were pressing me to join one of the new groups. A part of me wanted to do so, because I was eager to learn about concepts like socialism and feudalism. But when it came right down to it, I couldn't, because at the time I didn't have the courage to defy my patrons or reject my longtime friends.

Since I felt I couldn't just stand still and accept things entirely as they were, I had to consider another alternative. India was the obvious choice. The talk in the tea shops about the school in Darjeeling had stayed in my mind, and I had in fact been thinking about the possibility of going there for some time. I wanted to continue to learn and grow, and I wanted to know more than just calligraphy. I wanted to know what "socialism" and "imperialism" meant and what the history of the rest of the world was. I was beginning to feel that there were things about Tibet that ought to be changed, and I felt sure that the only way to create change was to break with tradition and look at things in new ways.

The plan I came up with was simple. I would go to study in India for three years. That seemed plenty of time to learn English and the ways of the world outside Tibet. To do this, however, I would need money, so I decided to try my hand at trading. I took a leave from my office at the treasury and borrowed as much money as I could from my friends, paying them only the interest at first. With the money, I bought as many salable commodities as I could in Lhasa and then I resold them at a good profit in villages around my home area. Then I also bought local foodstuffs from around my home village and took them back with me to sell in Lhasa. At that time there were no taxes on trade in Tibet. There were no licensing fees or tariffs, and my practical experience working for the officials in Lhasa served me well. I actually hired people to help me move my goods. I sold grain, barley, cheese, butter, and peaches in Lhasa and made a decent profit in the first year. And then unforeseeable events took control of my life once again.

After about a year of trading in and around my village, I came home one night to learn that my father had been physically beaten by a rival family. Though I had been unaware of it, it seems that while I had been living in Lhasa resentment had been growing toward my family back in our village. The tax exemption my family received because of my service as a gadrugba resulted, as was customary, in the burden of our taxes being passed on to the other villagers. The Tibetan custom was for the tax to be the responsibility of the whole village. So when my family got an exemption, the others had to do what had previously been our share. Many in the village felt this added burden was unfair, and a number of them had begun to ostracize the members of my family, scarcely even speaking to them. It all came to a head when Dorje Tseden, the son of a family that was our great rival, and some friends of his set upon my father and beat him severely. When I learned about it, I was wild with anger and immediately went to the authorities to make a complaint. I told them the whole story and asked them to give my family justice. They listened patiently, and then nothing happened. It was extremely frustrating. Dorje and his family had friends among the district officials. I had no chance of a fair hearing, so I decided to take things into my own hands. I felt the honor of my whole family was at stake.

Just after the new year in 1956, I asked Dorje Tseden to meet me halfway between his house and mine. I was determined to avenge my father on the spot. But Dorje must have guessed my intentions, because he tricked me. When we stood face to face, he was extremely polite and deferential. He admitted that he had made a terrible mistake, asked me to forgive him, and promised that he would be good to my family from then on. Foolishly convinced by his courtesy and apparent sincerity, I decided to let the matter drop. However, a few days later I found out that after disarming me with his clever words, Dorje went to the district officials on the sly and accused me of threatening him physically. The result was that we were both summoned to the district headquarters to sort the matter out. I decided that I didn't want to wait or put my trust in official justice a second time. I had a gun that

Wangdu had given me. I took it and called some friends I knew would be willing to help, and then we set a trap.

To get to the district headquarters, Dorje and I both had to follow the same trail through the mountains. He must have suspected I was up to something, because he rode ahead of me, and I could see that he had brought some friends with him just as I had, possibly armed as well. As we wound our way through the mountain passes, the tension began to mount. I stayed behind but always kept him and his party in sight. He never looked back, but he knew that my men and I were there. What he didn't know was that I had sent one of my companions on ahead to wait at a particular spot where the trail was very narrow and dangerous—the river on one side and a sheer cliff on the other.

When Dorje reached the spot just a little way ahead of us, my henchman blocked his path.

"Dorje Tseden. We are all friends," he said. Why don't you stop, rest your horses, and have some chang with us?"

The words were polite, but the manner was quietly menacing. We were closing in now, and I could see Dorje's mind working swiftly. I think he sensed exactly what was happening, but at that point there was nothing he could do. The trap had been sprung. His path was blocked before; and my men and I were approaching from behind. As we closed, Dorje and his companions turned to face us. They had short swords as I suspected they might, and now they drew them. But when they saw my gun, they also saw that there was nothing they could do. I didn't waste any time pressing my advantage.

"You have had your way until now," I said to Dorje. "You have been able to hide behind your friends in the district. But it's just you and me now. You are a toady and a coward. You attacked my father, and now I'm going to beat you within an inch of your life!"

I ordered Dorje's companions to drop their knives and tie his hands behind his back. Then after we secured the companions as well, I whipped Dorje till my shoulder hurt and I was out of breath from swinging the stick. I was so tired I had to find a place where I could descend to the river and get some water to refresh myself. When I had rested for a while, I began beating Dorje once again. He shouted and cried at first, but he eventually passed out. When I could see that he was utterly defeated, I finally felt that the matter was settled.

"I have had my revenge now," I said, when he regained consciousness. "As far as I'm concerned, this business is finished and you have nothing further to fear from me. You can go about your own business now."

But he couldn't go anywhere at the moment. Scarcely able to move, he was not able to go on to the district headquarters. The last I saw of him that day was when he headed back home to the village. He was not able to sit upright in the saddle and had to lie over the horse, like a sack of grain.

This episode was by no means the end of the affair, as I had hoped it would be. Both the village and the district were abuzz with the story of my beating Dorje. Some people were on my side and thought Dorje got what he deserved. Others, of course, saw it differently. But the district officials were not amused. They said I had taken the law into my own hands—and thus the authority out of theirs (though they didn't put it quite that way). They called it a highly serious affair. They ordered me to go to the court at Lhasa itself, immediately! I learned later that the only reason they didn't send officers of the law after me was that they had heard I was armed. They were afraid people would get killed if they tried an outright attack. So they sent me a stern official notice that I was to appear in Lhasa and wait to see what would happen.

I guess I had been extremely naive. I never thought the matter would be taken so seriously by the government. Until then, my real worry had been that Dorje's own people would take vengeance on me directly. As I saw it, the matter was simple enough: Dorje beat my father, and I beat him in return. But Lhasa was involved now, and I felt I had little choice but to return quickly to the city. I knew that the government was allowing me to save face by asking me to come of my own free will rather than sending officers to try to take me from my village by force and in front of my neighbors and family. So I went back to Lhasa, and my court case began.

All the principals were there—Dorje and my father as well as my-self. The trial was quite an event. And it was expensive. My father had to rent an apartment to live in for the duration, and the proceedings lasted a long time. To my dismay, one of the presiding officials was a man whom I knew sympathized with Dorje Tseden, and this official made things very unpleasant for me during the course of the questioning. He made me tell my story and explain my reasoning again and again, and he always treated me with contempt. He claimed that my father had falsified the extent of his injuries, and he questioned both my motives and my story. I confronted him with my suspicions about his preference for Dorje, but my claims only made him angry and harder on me.

The intermittent questioning dragged on into the following year, until March 1957. It seemed as if it would never end, and I wasn't optimistic about the possible outcome. So when the verdict finally came down it was both a surprise and a relief. I was required to pay a fine (of 750 *sang*) in lieu of a whipping (at the time, a sang was worth about six cents). Dorje Tseden had to pay a fine of 500 sang to cover my father's medical expenses. My father only had to pay an even smaller sum. I was elated. Dorje was the real loser. He got a physical beating (from me) and still had to pay a fine. He was also embarrassed in our village and in the district capital. The judgment against me was little more than a slap on the wrist. I was grateful, but even so I knew that I had come to a kind of watershed.

The more I thought about what had been happening in the past few years, the more I felt I had to get out of Tibet and continue my education. Until I was interrupted by the beating of Dorje Tseden and the prolonged court case that followed, I had been successfully putting money aside with the general idea of pursuing my education in India. I decided that if I was going to act, now was the time.

It wasn't easy to leave, though. I had put down more roots than I thought. I had been living apart from Thondrup Dromala for several years now, but I had continued to support my son. She had married and now had two children by her new husband, but in my heart I felt that I was wrong to leave my son behind, and I felt very guilty about it. There was also my family back in our village. Leaving my family and friends behind to go to another country was far more intimidating than leaving my village to go to Lhasa. And the incident of the beating had reminded me of how strong my feelings for my father really were. I still feared for my family's safety in the village. But by this time I felt that for me the die was cast. India was where I believed my future now lay, and I turned sadly but resolutely toward the mountains to the south.

5

When I left for India in 1957 I had the equivalent of more than 20,000 Indian rupees, or about $5,000. These were the profits from my trading plus a small personal loan from Wangdu. I didn't want to have to carry that much cash all the way to India, so I approached the Chinese trade office, which was always working with Tibetan traders to arrange for purchases in India. The terms were that I would buy agricultural equipment, mainly shovels and picks, and transport them back to Lhasa. In return the office agreed to pay for these items in advance, although I had to secure the guarantee of two high Tibetan officials that I would keep my part of the bargain. Critically, the Chinese also agreed to take my private Tibetan money and give me a check, which I could convert to Indian rupees at the Hong Kong and Shanghai Bank in Calcutta.

The plan I had developed was simple: my second brother would accompany me to India, help me buy the goods, and bring them back to the Chinese to satisfy the terms of the agreement. I would remain in India to study, supporting myself from my private funds.

When I had gotten all these financial matters taken care of, I asked my superiors at the Potala Treasury for leave to go on a pilgrimage to India, and they agreed. Then I went to the Chinese Foreign Affairs Office and asked for exit documents to visit India. This office also said yes. It was surprisingly easy.

We traveled light. Taking only the banker's check for the money, some clothing, a good watch, and the small pistol Wangdu had given me, my brother and I began the trip south through the mountains. We jolted along in a truck southwest from Lhasa to the town of Gyantse and then south to Yadong at the border of Sikkim, a Tibetan kingdom that was a protectorate of India. At Yadong the road became impassable to trucks, and we continued on horseback, following a centuries-old trade route that snaked through the high mountain passes between Sikkim and Tibet. After a few more days of travel we reached the goal of our trip, the town of Kalimpong.

Kalimpong is in the foothills of the Himalayas and at 4,100 feet above sea level is relatively cool compared to much of the rest of India, but it was much warmer than I was used to. The heat sapped my energy and at first I felt sleepy most of the time. The food took some adjustment, too. I liked the Indian fried rice and vegetables and the British-style bread, particularly the toast. But I couldn't get used to the meat. I think it was all in my head, but it smelled bad, especially the goat meat. I couldn't stomach it.

For ages Kalimpong had been a major center of Tibetan trade with India, and there was a well-established Tibetan community there, perhaps numbering as many as a thousand. There was even a Tibet trade commission staffed by the Tibetan government. I had friends among the members of the delegation, and I stayed with them for a month, making the best use I could of the time by hiring a Nepalese instructor to begin teaching me a little English. But I couldn't stay long. I had to exchange our money for Indian rupees, and to do that I had to go to the Hong Kong and Shanghai Bank in Calcutta, which was where the Chinese bank in Lhasa had its accounts. So before too long my brother and I caught a train at Siliguri and headed south for the city.

Calcutta was exceptionally hot, more so than I had imagined. I thought that this must be what our horrendous Buddhist hot hell is like. Everything in Calcutta shocked me at first; I had never dreamed there could be so many people milling about in one place, let alone so many thousands of beggars lying and sleeping in the street. There were throngs of coolies—people who carried things for a living—running every which way pulling rickshaws in the dense and slowly moving mass of humanity. To tell the truth, I was frightened of getting lost, of getting swallowed up in that ocean of Indians. Since I couldn't make myself understood or even read signs or directions, I asked a Tibetan trader friend in Kalimpong to write the address to which I was to be taken on a piece of paper. Without speaking a word I showed the paper to the driver of a rickshaw and, with great trepidation, let him take us to a guesthouse near Calcutta's small Chinatown that was owned by a Chinese man who had a Tibetan wife. Much to my relief, we arrived safely. With the help of the Tibetan wife and several other Tibetan traders living there, I was able to exchange my check for Indian rupees and buy the supplies my brother was going to take back to Tibet. After about a month, when our work was finished, we returned to Kalimpong, where my brother quickly hired some muleteers and left for Tibet with the goods. I remained and began my education.

Tibetans of all kinds lived in Kalimpong. Some were businessmen who had established a base of operations there, while others were individuals who had fled Tibet to escape impossible situations at home—as I had once contemplated doing. There were also political types. Indeed, Jawaharlal Nehru once called Kalimpong "the nest of spies." And there was a very poor criminal class, too. Of these, the men were usually engaged in petty crimes, and the women typically became prostitutes. The single largest group, however, was the mass of transient traders and muleteers. They were the backbone of a substantial bilateral trade that brought Tibetan wool to India and the United States, and took Indian and Western goods back to Tibet.

I was surprised to find Tibetan prostitutes in India, though I suppose I shouldn't have been. I didn't normally go to prostitutes, but once while I was in Calcutta, a Tibetan merchant friend took me to a brothel where there were Indian prostitutes and one beautiful Tibetan girl. This was a fairly high-class and relatively expensive place. I hired the Tibetan girl, who said she came from Shigatse, Tibet's second largest city. I stayed with her and talked for a while, just a short visit. I was really shocked at first by how different the prostitutes acted in India in general. It was all money and business with them: "How much? How much?" Tibetan prostitutes at home are much subtler; their style is different. Obviously they're doing it for the money as well, but they don't make the affair seem so crass and commercial. Though I went to the prostitutes only a few times during my stay in India, and mostly for social reasons—with friends I had made—the conditions of the Tibetans I saw there gave me a lot to think about. I can still recall a very poor and run-down brothel in Calcutta where again I found Tibetans. The house was dark, lacked electricity, and was filthy. The poverty shocked me. I talked with the girls a bit; I felt so sorry for them. Then I gave them some money and walked away. I also met a prostitute in Darjeeling whose husband was a man I actually knew in Tibet. They were poor, and the man was too proud to reveal the fact that his wife was selling herself. Though I can't say that I had a historically aware or fully developed social conscience in the Western sense at that time, the pain these people suffered touched me.

But I don't mean to give the impression that my life was simply one diversion after another. These stories are from the whole time I was in India. From the time I got back to Kalimpong after exchanging the money in Calcutta, my first priority was to begin my education. My sense of helplessness at not knowing the language and having to trust a rickshaw driver to take me where a written message said made me even more committed to learning English.

Of the money I had brought back from Calcutta, I kept 3,000 rupees to live on—to support myself and my studies. That meant I still had about 17,000 rupees left, a sizable amount in those days, when 250 Indian rupees was enough to live for one month and pay tuition at one of the schools. If I did nothing, I estimated that the money I had left would be enough to last for more than five years. But I had thoughts of stretching the money even further by investing it, perhaps even being able to live just off the interest. I approached Lobsang Gyaltsen, a former high monk official, for advice and help, as we had mutual friends. We decided I would leave the money with him, and he would invest it for me. As the former head of the trade commission, he knew all the relevant business people. He was also a wealthy man in his own right, well known in Kalimpong, with a wife, a house, and a car. So I trusted him—and, sad to say, lived to regret it. But at the moment I thought I had provided the financial foundation that would support me for the duration of my stay. Now it was time to see about a teacher.

I soon made friends with another Tibetan countryman—Gyalo Thondrup—who would affect my life in a dozen different ways while I was in India. Gyalola, as we called him, was the Dalai Lama's older brother. He had been a student in China at the time of the Chinese communists' victory and had fled the country in 1949, ending up in India. As I was to learn later, Gyalola was part of a small group of aristocratic Tibetan activists who were organizing anti-Chinese activities in northern India. Gyalola helped me take the first concrete steps toward learning English by putting me in touch with a retired British army officer by the name of Cumming.

Mr. Cumming lived in Darjeeling in the Chorasatha area, where most of the Europeans stayed. Darjeeling was one of the old hill stations to which the British escaped to avoid the summer heat of the plains. And although the British had granted India independence in 1947, there were still plenty of Englishmen and other Europeans living there. When I met him, Mr. Cumming lived in a large house, which he was managing for the owner, who spent much of the year in Calcutta. Darjeeling wasn't very far from Kalimpong as the crow flies. Both cities were on the sides of steep hills that faced one another. I remember that when I went to Mr. Cumming, the taxi went down and down the steep hill to the river at the bottom and then laboriously up an equally steep incline on the other side.

My arrangement with Mr. Cumming was that I would pay him 200 rupees a month for my room, board, and his daily instruction. Mr. Cumming was not a teacher by profession. Though he spoke some Nepalese, he did not speak Tibetan. But as I think back about it, his method of teaching was rather charming, and it helped get me started very nicely.

We had a set routine that started in the morning. First, Mr. Cumming would get up and listen to the BBC. Then he would bring me a cup of wonderful Darjeeling tea. I would drink it, wash my face, and we would have a formal breakfast together. Then we would begin studying. First he would give me some exemplary sentences to listen to and practice writing. Then we would take walks along the mountainside, and he would teach as we walked. For example, if we saw someone on horseback he would say things like, "That is a *horse*. And that is someone *riding* a horse. And that is a *tree* that they are passing." When we were in his house he would systematically tell me the names of things: "This is a *paperweight,* that is the *bookshelf*," and so on. After we took our daily walk, he would go back to his office to work, because he was still the manager of the house and estate. Meanwhile I would go to my room and practice writing the short sentences I had been given and the new words I had learned. At lunchtime we got together again. After the cook served us our lunch, Cumming would correct my lessons. Then he would write out what he thought were the most important sentences and I would practice them in his presence and try to make new sentences of my own. An old battered dictionary was our bible and our judge. It was an English-Tibetan dictionary compiled by a Sikkimese lama in Calcutta in 1904, and we used it to answer questions and settle disputes.

I stayed at Mr. Cumming's house for about seven or eight very pleasant months. My will to learn was so great that I was criticized sometimes for my excesses. I once heard Tibetans talking about me: "He stops Englishmen on the road and starts asking them English words," they whispered. I was probably overeager, but my desire to learn was strong—so strong, in fact, that I finally decided that I wasn't learning fast enough. Though I loved the day's routine at Mr. Cumming's, I wanted to progress and improve more quickly. Eventually, through some new Tibetan contacts in Darjeeling, I found a way.

One of the Tibetan friends I had met was a student named Sonam, who was studying at St. Joseph's (both a high school and a college) in the North Point section of the town. Sonamla was sympathetic to my wish to become better educated, and he took an interest in me. He had a wealthy and established brother, a Mr. Lhawang, who was well-known in Darjeeling, and at Sonamla's request, Mr. Lhawang agreed to try to help me get into St. Joseph's school. I knew it wasn't going to be easy, because I was an unusual student to say the least. I was already in my twenties, had no formal schooling, and was just in the process of learning English, so I needed some kind of special permission—and also some kind of string to pull. I was hopeful that Mr. Lhawang's influence would be such a string. And so it was.

I don't know ultimately who said what to whom, but it was quickly arranged that I would have an interview with the dean of the school, Father Stanford. Part of the interview was a tour of the facilities, and I still remember how amazed I was when I learned how many subjects an education could include. I was taken around by Father Stanford—a religious man—who actually taught secular subjects like science, mathematics, and history. (I had a similar eye-opening experience when I came to the United States and was struck by the sheer availability of education. I remember meeting an eighty-year-old woman in Seattle who was just finishing her B.A. in night school. It couldn't have been more different from the world I knew in the Tibet of my youth.) Father Stanford was very nice, and when our tour was over and we had talked for a while, he smiled and said, "Well, Master Tashi Tsering, we are going to give you special permission to live here in the hostel and audit classes." I was extremely grateful but confused at first.

I knew nothing of the English custom of rather loosely calling someone "Master" and could only understand the term literally, which didn't make much sense. Whose master could I possibly be? Needless to say, my confusion didn't last, and I soon began to attend St. Joseph's College.

It was in 1958 that I moved into a hostel in North Point near the college. I had a small room and ate at the public dining hall with about 170 college students, some African, some Tibetan, some Burmese, and the majority Indian. I paid the sum of 300 rupees for board, lodging, and the services of an Anglo-Indian private tutor in English. Besides the private tutoring, I audited classes in English and history.

I made a point of mingling with the other students as much as possible, so I could listen to their conversations. I didn't accost people on the street anymore, but I made use of every opportunity I could. I remember envying the other students for their fluency and trying very hard to catch up, which often led to humorous mistakes—like my problem with the phrase "Master Tashi." For example, I used to have afternoon tea in the public dining hall, which was just above the hostel. One day I was sitting next to a Burmese student who was having a bun with his tea. Suddenly he looked at me, pointed at the bun, and asked, "Mr. Tashi Tsering, what do you call this in Tibetan?"

"It is a *bom*," I said. "Bom" was the sound of the Tibetan word for that kind of bread. But they all thought I had said "bomb." It made everyone laugh, and I didn't know why.

"And what do you call this?" he said as he sliced the bun and chopped some green chilies into small pieces, which he added to the bun.

"That is a bom chop," I said proudly.

The table was delighted, and from that day on I became known affectionately as "Mr. Bomb Chop." And the nickname stuck. (Indeed, not long ago when a relative of the Sikkim royal family was passing through Cleveland, Ohio, I met her. The first thing she said when she saw me was, "Hello, Mr. Bomb Chop!") Such are the joys of trying to learn a new language.

My days spent at St. Joseph's school were extremely pleasant and productive, and I remember them fondly. Like so many things in my life, however, they were not to last. And as would increasingly be the case in the next decades, the gravitational pull of larger political and historical forces began to alter the plans that I had made.

Events in Tibet were worsening as a Tibetan guerrilla movement began to attack Chinese convoys and outposts in the summer of 1958. And in March 1959, after I had been at St. Joseph's school for about a year, the Lhasa Uprising occurred. The revolt was the end result of a process of disintegration, and what had been disintegrating was the rather uneasy peace between the Chinese and the Tibetans. The first five or six years after the Chinese entered Tibet in 1951 had been a sort of honeymoon. The Chinese tried to influence us but without using harsh measures or anything that could really be called strong-arm tactics. They allowed the Dalai Lama and the government to continue to exercise internal authority and did not try to curtail religion or the life of the monasteries. They courted the country with roads, bridges, schools, and hospitals—that is, with easy-to-see results and attractive promises of what our future might be like if we accepted their presence and embraced their ideas.

But as the decade wore on, tensions increased. In 1956, the Chinese launched social and agrarian reforms in some of the ethnic Tibetan areas located in Sichuan Province to the east of Tibet proper, and that's when the troubles started. The changes angered the regional landowners and the lamas, and they rose up in arms. The Chinese sent troops to suppress them, and the result was a bloody rebellion in which several monasteries were bombed and many Tibetans killed. It also resulted in many of the Tibetan rebels fleeing from Sichuan to safety in Lhasa. Although no reforms had occurred in Tibet per se, the whole episode raised the larger issues of what the Chinese presence might eventually mean to our Buddhist religion and to the integrity of the native cultures—to our traditional way of understanding and dealing with the world. What kinds of changes were acceptable, and what were not? How much was too much? How fast was too fast? These were the sorts of questions that swirled like gusts of wind through our rugged mountains.

Though a number were of several minds—like me—and saw good possibilities for change as well as bad, the monks and most aristocrats and even most common Tibetans knew exactly how they felt; they wanted no changes. It all came to a head in 1959, when the Chinese invited the Dalai Lama to see a special dance performance at the military headquarters in Lhasa. The people believed that the invitation was a trap and that the Chinese were planning to take the Dalai Lama forcibly to Beijing. They took to the streets in huge numbers to block his visit. Anti-Chinese sentiment gathered momentum rapidly, and from this relatively small beginning came a major popular uprising. Within a week the situation was so serious that the Dalai Lama decided to flee to India for safety, and while he was in full flight, serious fighting broke out in Lhasa and soon a full-scale rebellion erupted and spread to other cities and other parts of the country.

Of course it was to no avail. The Tibetan rebels were no match for the resources, training, and military leadership of the battle-hardened Chinese troops, and the rebellion was quickly quelled. Aristocrats and monk officials poured out of the country to join the Dalai Lama in northern India, and because of my connection with Gyalola, and because some of my own plans had already begun to go badly awry, I was drawn inexorably into the orbit of the expatriate Tibetan activists.

The first thing that happened was that my schooling came to an abrupt halt. When the Tibetan refugees began to pour into northern India, my friend Gyalola asked me to help our people by going with him to one of the refugee camps in Assam. He wanted the world to know how the Tibetans had suffered at the hands of the Chinese and said he needed me to help him collect the narratives of the refugees so that we could tell their story to the world. I was to interview as many people as I could and write down what I learned. I knew it would mean scrapping my plans to continue learning English for a while, but I liked and respected Gyalola because he had been kind and taken me seriously when I had first met him in Kalimpong. I was grateful for his help in directing me to Mr. Cumming, and frankly I was flattered that he was now asking me to help. I felt I could scarcely refuse.

We flew to Assam and visited a huge refugee camp at Mussamari, a town on the Tibetan border near the Tsona area. When we were on the ground and I had a chance to look around, I was shaken by what I saw. The people seemed in a state of shock; they looked extremely tired and haunted. Many had left their homes in such a hurry that they had nothing except what they could carry on the run. They also suffered badly from the heat and lived in the most primitive conditions. They slept in tents or bamboo-stick huts; sanitary facilities consisted of pit toilets; the food was minimal; and the only thing they had to drink was greasy mineral water that had a film on the top and left a bad taste in your mouth. They were ordinary people, too. Looking at their defeated, exhausted faces, I found it easy to imagine my parents or the people in my village in their places. If it hadn't been for the support offered by the Indians and other world relief organizations, many more would have died than actually did.

At Gyalola's request, I spent about two weeks in the camp going from tent to tent interviewing everyone I could. I tried to get as many eyewitness accounts of the uprising and flight as possible, taking careful notes in Tibetan. But it turned out to be more difficult than I expected. Most of the people I spoke to were illiterate and did not have an orderly or logical way of controlling and expressing their thoughts. Moreover, their experiences were quite varied. Many had not even seen the actions of the Chinese army in Lhasa. They had simply been a part of the general panic that gripped the country, and their stories were of the sufferings they had incurred on the journey through the mountains, not at the hands of the Chinese. I had a hard time getting concrete evidence of Chinese atrocities. But I collected as much as I could, and when I had done so Gyalola took me to Delhi, where we organized and prepared our findings. We stayed at an Indian vegetarian hotel, and for the next few months we translated all the stories I had collected from Tibetan into English. We put the materials we were translating together with similar eyewitness accounts from other refugee camps, and eventually they were presented to the International Commission of Jurists in Geneva, Switzerland, in 1960. The commission wrote a famous report condemning the Chinese for their atrocities in Tibet. But in the end no one intervened, and the world went on about its business, as it always does. As for me, I continued to be pulled further and further away from the plans that I had originally made for myself. I had enjoyed working with Gyalola, and I soon found myself embarked on another project involving the fortunes of the newly exiled Tibetans.

In 1950, when it had seemed like a Chinese invasion was imminent, the Dalai Lama's substantial stocks of gold and silver had been transported out of the country to safety in Sikkim. During the 1950s, though the Dalai Lama himself was in Tibet, the gold and silver remained in one of the storehouses of the maharaja of Sikkim. The Chinese had asked for its return but had not made an issue of it at the time. Following the Lhasa Uprising and the flight of the Dalai Lama, they claimed that the money was not the Dalai Lama's personal fortune but belonged to the country—which they now considered to belong to them. At that point the Tibetan leaders decided it was time to secure their treasure more permanently and farther away from the border; and because of my association with Gyalola, I found myself involved. It was quite an operation.

The gold and silver were in the form of coins and ingots. When I became involved, the gold and silver were being hand-loaded onto trucks in Gangtok, the capital of Sikkim, and driven south to Siliguri, the location of the nearest airstrip. At the airport the literally millions of dollars' worth of gold were loaded onto Dakota cargo planes and flown to Calcutta. This treasure was eventually to provide the core of funds that would support the Dalai Lama's government-in-exile.

When this precious cargo reached Calcutta, the gold was immediately put into the banks. But for a while the silver was stored in a single room on the third floor of a trusted Tibetan merchant's house. It was my responsibility to stand guard over it, and for nearly a month I stood sentinel in a silent room full of coins and odd pieces of silver. It was one of the strangest experiences of my life. The only action I experienced was when we went to melt the various small pieces of silver into ingots. Other than that, and a little time spent away from the room when I went to eat, I kept my watch alone. I did a little studying, but not much. Gyalo Thondrup had trusted me to guard the silver and that's exactly what I did. After about a month's time, final decisions were made about disposing of the silver, and my job was finished, but not my association with Gyalo Thondrup.

For a variety of reasons, I found I was becoming increasingly dependent on Gyalola and his projects. Partly our relationship grew because I genuinely liked him; he was someone I could talk to, and I valued his friendship. Partly, the projects themselves were interesting and made me feel important in the sense that I felt I was actually doing something to help Tibet. Partly, too, the reasons were financial. I was running out of money.

The initial 3,000 rupees I had set aside to live on was now more or less exhausted by the cost of Mr. Cumming, St. Joseph's in North Point, and my expenses in Calcutta. I was living at the moment on a stipend from Gyalola. I wanted to continue my education, but I needed more money to do so. And then I had a more serious setback, which made my difficulty more acute.

Beyond such employment as I got from Gyalola, the only large source of income I had left was the money I had given to Lobsang Gyaltsen to invest. That was my safety net, or so I thought. But when I contacted him, I learned there was a problem. Lobsang Gyaltsen was so terribly sorry. It seemed he had lent my money to another Tibetan trader. He had written receipts and produced all the proper documents, which stipulated that the trader agreed to use the money to buy Indian goods and sell them at a profit in Tibet. He would then return my money with interest. In theory it was a very good idea, but in practice, a disaster. I was told that the trader had made several trips across the border, but that the Chinese eventually caught him and confiscated all his goods. He managed to escape back into Kalimpong, but my money was gone. At that point there was nothing I could do. I was given a receipt for the full amount, which I kept for years. (When I was imprisoned by the Chinese in the 1960s, they confiscated the receipt and I lost it forever.)

To this day I don't know whether Lobsang Gyaltsen told me the truth. I understood my own situation, though. I had been wiped out. Without my even knowing that my money was in danger, it had simply vanished, and I was devastated. I had worked very hard to accumulate it, and, worst of all, a portion of the money wasn't even mine, and I felt terribly guilty. Most of the money was mine, though, and it was a fortune to me. It was the most I have ever lost in my life. It was also my guarantee, I had hoped, of years of study in India, and I couldn't continue my education without it. When I realized how hopeless the situation was, I cried in frustration and anger; what I thought I saw was the destruction of all my dreams. But I was still young enough to hope, so I had a talk with Gyalola. He was as helpful as he could be, but with limits. He was pleased by the assistance I had given him in the past few months, and he said he could continue to pay me if I worked for him and the growing circle of Tibetan activists. But he was not made of money, and he couldn't support my education for years. (At the time I did not know that he was the chief Tibetan working with the American Central Intelligence Agency and really had substantial financial resources.) Basically, what he offered was the chance to continue working for him and the causes in which he was involved.

It was a tempting offer. I had always liked to think of myself as a good, loyal Tibetan, and I had to admit that my work in the last few months had been exciting. But there were problems as well, because now there were two Tibets—the one forming itself in exile in India and the people still at home living under Chinese rule. The members of the old Tibetan government now in exile were increasingly determined to fight. Though many who fled the country were extremely pessimistic,

Gyalola and his friends were by no means convinced that the cause was lost. They were politically aware, busy, doing things all the time. I had enjoyed helping Gyalola in the camps; it had made me feel good about myself, especially the thought that in spite of my humble beginnings in a mountain village I was actually working with the Dalai Lama's older brother. But Gyalola was not entirely representative of the attitude of the old-line aristocrats who now constituted the government-in-exile. And among them it wasn't at all clear what my role was going to be if I decided to stay and help. Or maybe the problem was that in fact my role was all too clear.

I felt that Gyalola was different from most of his colleagues. Although technically a Tibetan aristocrat, in reality he was a commoner whose whole family had been ennobled when his younger brother was selected as the Dalai Lama. Thus his life had been very different from that of the old-line Lhasa aristocracy. Moreover, he had gone to China to attend one of Chiang Kai-shek's best Chinese schools and thus was the closest thing I had yet seen to what I would call a "modern" Tibetan. He had surprisingly democratic impulses, and treated me very graciously. I was honored to be able to help him. The others in his group among the exiled government were different, though. They were aristocrats and monk officials of the old school, and they had little use for me inside their circle. I could run errands and take down narratives, but I wasn't one of "them." From their point of view, I never could be. I remember that after we first heard the news about the Lhasa Uprising, a special meeting was called at a private house in Kalimpong. Gyalola and all the other aristocrats and monk officials were invited, and I went, too. But when they went inside to talk, I was told to remain outside. It was the way it was always done. Whether literally or not, there was always a door—the door of class and caste—and I feared I was always going to be on the outside of it.

The incident made me extremely angry—as if I wasn't a Tibetan, with national pride and feelings just like theirs! It hurt my feelings. The impression I still have is that someone didn't quite trust me to do or know certain things, but I didn't really know why. What had I done? At one level, it was a subtle kind of discrimination, very hard to put your finger on or to confront directly. At another level it was very easy to see and understand, because it was nothing more or less than the traditional Tibetan class attitude. I remember one day in the hotel in Delhi when I was helping Gyalola translate some refugee accounts from Tibetan to English. We were discussing the proper English word to use, and I guess it made Gyalola think of something else, because suddenly he said,

"In Tibetan society, there are only two types of people—the kind who'll eat tsamba, and the kind who'll eat shit."

At the time, I more or less understood him to be making a distinction between good people and bad ones. It would only be later, and in another country, that I would encounter Marxist theories about classes and exploitation. But as I remember the moment now, I see that it was a good indication of the strong class attitudes present in the old Tibetan society and the way they were continuing to affect my life. I was still afraid that what my first wife's father said was always going to be true and that because of who I was and where I came from I would only be able to rise so high and no higher—no matter what my wishes or abilities. I wasn't ready to accept such a prescribed role. I had been doing a lot of thinking during these last several years, about what was likely to happen to Tibet and what my own feelings were. It seemed to me that after the Chinese invasion, the days of the old unchanging traditional society were over, whether we liked it or not. The appropriate questions now seemed to be, What other sorts of changes lie in store?

When I left Tibet, I remember thinking that if the Chinese began making wholesale changes, I would probably not want to try to go back. Go back to what? I didn't want to see my country radically transformed. But I also remember holding onto the hope that the changes that lay ahead would not be too radical, that they might be for the better and something we all could live with. I had a lot of problems with the old way of doing things and the old attitudes that limited people like me. I wasn't like the mass of aristocrats and the monk officials. I wasn't afraid of change. I was still excited by the schools and hospitals the Chinese had begun to build. I was just dimly beginning to see what a long way Tibet had to go to catch up with a modern world that seemed more and more likely to influence its fate whether we liked it or not. And so though I felt extremely loyal to Tibet, I was beginning to fear that I might eventually have to make a choice between the Tibet at home—meaning the people still living there—and the Tibet in India. I hoped desperately that it would not come to that. This was a choice I did not want to have to make. So I tried to secure loans to continue my education.

I spoke to Lobsang Gyaltsen and also Gyalola, but both of them turned me down. I was extremely angry and frustrated. If I just kept on working for Gyalola and his colleagues, I could live a life of safety and even service to my country on a limited scale. But this wasn't what I wanted. I still felt that the only way I could achieve my dreams for myself was to continue my education. I often discussed the matter with Gyalola, and when he saw how my mind was working he began to put pressure on me to stay and help him. He was a very clever man, and I think he had begun to see that I had reservations about committing to his and his friends' vision of the future of Tibet. Whatever the reason, he wasn't at all sympathetic to my wish to continue my education. He told me point blank that I didn't have to go to school any more, by which I believed that he meant I didn't have to go to school any more to do the kinds of things he and his friends would be asking of me. It was one of the few subjects we disagreed about, and we had some angry exchanges. We saw a lot of one another in those days. We would go to the cinema together or to the bars, and everywhere we went the subject would rise up between us. One day it got so bad that some strong words passed between us and he called me a bad Tibetan, by which he meant, I believe, simply that I disagreed with him. But I thought to myself that I was every bit as good a Tibetan as he was!

It was hard for me at that time. Gyalola was a good friend who had done a lot for me. Besides, he was the brother of the Dalai Lama, and I was just a peasant boy from the mountains. But I knew what I thought, and I knew what I wanted. I was even beginning to think I knew why. In our old society, Tibetans were of two types—upper class and ordinary. The two groups had very different points of view, different ways of handling their affairs, but in the old society the upper classes' point of view was the only one that mattered. I was becoming convinced that all points of view ought to be respected. Gyalola, of course, didn't see it exactly that way. But even though he was the Dalai Lama's brother, I felt I had a right to disagree with him, because I felt I represented not only myself but a whole class of voiceless Tibetans. I just didn't feel that I had to give in on this point. It would be wrong, I think, to say that at this time I had what could be called a philosophy of any kind. But I knew what I had seen. I was still disillusioned and angry about what I had seen going on in the treasury office in Lhasa. The ordinary people sent their taxes and tribute in the form of money and goods, and both monk and lay officials just took what they wanted. There were ledgers filled with accounts of tea bricks, butter, cloth, gold, and silver. I saw the records that showed that the more powerful monks, especially those from aristocratic families and the Dalai Lama's household, "borrowed" any of these things they wished and never returned them. There was no overall record, no auditing. The officials and their friends and family could come in and take anything they fancied. I saw them doing so with my own eyes. I felt that going to work for the exiled aristocrats and monks would have meant going to work to restore the same old system. It would have meant helping to preserve the traditional attitudes. And that would have meant that people like me would stay in the same old place—outside the door—while "they" decided how my country was going to be run. I didn't want to leave Tibet for good, and I didn't want to change everything. But I thought that there was plenty of room for reforms that would make life better for the common people and that there were surely ways to achieve reform without destroying or seriously undermining the religious and ethnic integrity of Tibetan society.

These were fine thoughts, but because I had no money I don't know what they would have come to or what exactly I would have done if it hadn't been for a sort of miracle that came in the unlikely form of an American from Texas.

Late in the year 1959, while I was working with Gyalola, I was staying in a hotel in Delhi, where I first met Robert Dunnam. The way the hotel was set up, we had adjoining rooms and naturally got acquainted. Robert, a student at Williams College, was the son of a wealthy Texas businessman. He was on leave from Williams and was taking what amounted to a world tour. After his stay in Delhi, he was on his way to Tokyo, where he planned to work for about six months and then return to do graduate work in America. We hit it off right away. He was interested in hearing what I knew about the Tibetan uprising and about the old society in Tibet, because it had been much in the news of late. I told him about many of my experiences and about the stories I had heard at the refugee camps. Soon we became good enough friends that I felt I could tell him about my wish to continue my education and a bit about my troubles. We discussed these things for weeks, and suddenly one day, to my delight, he expressed real sympathy for the plight of the Tibetan people. To my true amazement, he also offered to help me get to America to continue my studies.

Much of the process involved in accomplishing this plan was hidden from me. Phone calls were made. Hopes were raised. Then there was a lot of silence and waiting. Just before he left, Robert wrote a letter to Williams College recommending me for a scholarship. Nothing happened immediately, but he and I corresponded for the next several months, at the end of which time I was told that Williams would offer me a Baldwin scholarship. I didn't know what that was, but it seemed to be a scholarship intended specifically to help foreign students. Obviously, I didn't need to know all the details. All I needed to know was that the appropriate committee had met and decided to give me the award.

However, after the initial excitement died down, all I could see were more difficulties. I wasn't sure how I was going to get a passport or whether I was going to be allowed to leave India. More important, the scholarship did not include the considerable funds necessary to pay for my transportation to America. For a time it looked like a kind of cruel joke: my hopes had been raised only to be dashed. But to my surprise and great relief, my luck held. I managed to get "stateless" papers from the government of India documenting India's agreement that I could return—a passport for the stateless. These papers allowed me to secure a U.S. visa. And the Tolstoy Foundation agreed to pay for my airplane ticket to New York. (I was to learn later that Tolstoy himself had been an officer in the Office of Strategic Services, and in 1943 had been part of a special mission to Tibet. I'm happy to say that I got to meet him in New York and thank him personally for helping me get to America.) So my dream was still alive. Twenty-five years earlier I had been running around naked in my native village, catching fish in the mountain streams and waiting for the time when I could be trusted to tend the family's flocks. Now here I was about to leave for America in pursuit of an education that would lead me who knew where.

I worked for Gyalola until very near the time I left for America. He didn't approve of my going, but what could he do? Not long before my departure he sent me with a letter to the Dalai Lama himself. It was a long trip, some 200 miles by train from Delhi, and then a taxi to Dharamsala, the Dalai Lama's home base in exile. When I got there I was granted a private interview, which was very rare indeed. It was a great privilege, and I think Gyalola may have had a hand in sending me in order to appeal to my loyalty and patriotism.

After all my years in the gadrugba dance troupe, I knew the protocol by heart. When one had such an audience, the formal behavior was prescribed. When one entered the Dalai Lama's presence, one prostrated oneself three times. Then one offered a khatak—a special ceremonial scarf—by extending it to the Dalai Lama with both hands. After I had entered, I offered it so to the Dalai Lama. In traditional fashion, he accepted it from my hands and placed it upon my shoulders. Then our interview began. He asked me why I had come. I told him about the letter from his brother. He then asked me about my plans to go to America. (I was surprised at how much he seemed to know about me.) In particular he wanted to know what I intended to do afterward.

"I am going to do something to help Tibet and Tibetans. But at this time I cannot tell you exactly how." It was as honest as I could possibly have been at the time.

The Dalai Lama was thoughtful and kind. (I believe he remembered me from the time that I was a dancer.) Then he looked directly at me and offered three suggestions.

"Be a good Tibetan," he said. "Study hard. And use your education to serve your people and your country."

The interview was at an end, and I had much to think about.

I fully intended to study hard, as the Dalai Lama had urged. And I wanted badly to be considered a good Tibetan and to use my education to serve my people and my country. I just wished I could be more certain that those powerful words and phrases—"good Tibetan," "my country"—meant the same things to both of us. At that point it was hard to say for sure and easy to assume the best, and so I did. I ended the audience with a formal bow and a kind of inward smile. In a short time, I was on my way to America.

6

On the first leg of my journey, I took an Indian Airlines domestic flight from Delhi to Bombay. Then, for the first time in my life, I boarded a Boeing 707, which took me from Bombay to Cairo, then from Cairo to London with stopovers in Rome and Paris, and from London to New York. Much of the flight was over the Atlantic Ocean. It was breathtaking to realize how far the plane was above the clouds and, when the clouds broke, to see the dazzlingly clear blue of the ocean far below. It was not the first time I had been on a plane, of course. While I was living in Kalimpong, I sometimes flew to Calcutta, and I had flown to the refugee camps. But those were small planes, and I had never seen anything as big as a 707 before.

It was also the longest flight I had ever made. We touched down at La Guardia on June 30, 1960, some seven hours after we had left Heathrow and sixteen hours since Delhi and Bombay. The international student group that had been helping me knew when I was coming and had sent someone to meet me at the airport. He collected my luggage and then introduced me to a student aide, who helped me catch a city bus and accompanied me to my hotel.

I still remember my first bus ride in New York. While we hissed and jolted through streets crowded with cars, I tried to see everything at once. It was confusing and disorienting, hard to register what I was seeing, because I had so little context and didn't know what to expect. Of course everybody knows about America and talks about it, even in Tibet, but I didn't have specific or concrete images to anticipate, nothing I was confident I would see. I focused mainly on things that were different from my previous experiences. For example, I was struck immediately by the sheer number of cars, trucks, and buses. There were so many vehicles running in groups both parallel and perpendicular to one another that it was like observing the movements of large schools of fish or flocks of birds. My memory of the Indian cities that I knew was that they were more crowded with people—and dirtier! In New York the roads were both cleaner and wider. The people on the streets also were cleaner and better dressed than those I had been used to seeing. And of course I was surprised by the size and number of tall buildings. As my bus entered the heart of the city, the giant skyscrapers on every side actually reminded me of the mountains in my home village, so high that they sometimes blocked the sun. There had been nothing like that in Calcutta or Delhi.

My helper took me to the New York YMCA, where the student group had booked a room for me for two nights. I was on the twenty-seventh floor, and when I looked out the window, all I could see were tall, faceless buildings that looked glass-covered because of all the windows. I felt very lost and lonely. In India I was always in places where I could easily find other Tibetans, even friends or acquaintances. Being in New York on that first day was almost like being on another planet. Fortunately, however, I didn't have any time to sit around feeling sorry for myself, because I had practical problems to deal with.

My immediate concern was to find a job. Starting in September my major expenses at Williams College would be taken care of. But it was the beginning of the summer, and I had only 400 Indian rupees in my pocket (about $80) and several months to go until classes started. So I needed to make some money. This was the famous "Land of Opportunity," I reasoned, and I never doubted that I would be able to find work. It was extremely foolish to assume so, but luck is sometimes better than either knowledge or experience, and I was very lucky.

Almost immediately after I had gotten settled in my room, I went to visit two of my benefactors, Mr. Raymond and Mr. Tolstoy. Mr. Raymond was the director of the international student organization that had supported me and facilitated all my communications with Williams College. I visited him in his office, where he welcomed me to

America with a warm handshake. I had a good talk with him during which he told me that of the thousands of foreign students his office handled I was the only Tibetan. "I hope," he said, "that you will make the best of your American education." I told him I was determined to study hard and that I knew I would have to work harder than most because I had so little background compared to American students. Mr. Raymond was kind and encouraging, and when I told him about my immediate need for money to get me through the summer he supplied me with a list of addresses where I might find a job.

Next I went to see Mr. Tolstoy, the man whose foundation had paid for my plane ticket to America. I found him in his apartment and was eager to tell him how grateful I was for his foundation's support. I even made him the present of an Indian tie. He seemed pleased with my gift and thanked me quite cordially. Then he took me around the apartment and showed me a box full of black and white pictures he had taken in Tibet. There were some beautiful shots of the Potala Palace and the Jokhang Temple. And there was even one of Mr. Tolstoy himself, on horseback in rich Tibetan fur clothing in front of some tents and piles of supplies. The snapshot was taken when he traveled through Tibet and China during World War II. When it was time to leave, Mr. Tolstoy said, "Well, Mr. Tsering. I am happy to be able to help you. Your country is under communist control now, and I think you need plenty of help." I felt much better after speaking with Mr. Raymond and Mr. Tolstoy, and on the very next day (my second day in America) I took the list Mr. Raymond had given me and began exploring the streets of New York.

The borough of Manhattan is logically organized, and though I walked a lot of streets and rang a lot of doorbells, I was able to find my way around. The city began to seem a bit less mysterious and ungraspable. On the second day of my job search, as I was running around from address to address, I found myself on the west side of Manhattan at about Ninth Avenue and Forty-sixth Street in front of a six-story, red brick apartment house. It wasn't one of the numbers on my list. I don't know what made me do it, but I just decided for no particular reason to knock on that door to see if I could get any work. Maybe I just wanted to see if I could find something on my own? A silver-haired lady in her sixties answered my knock.

"Hello, what can I do for you?" she asked.

"I am Tashi Tsering from Tibet. I have just arrived in New York, and I'm looking for a job for the summer."

The lady smiled. She looked me up and down for a minute and then said, "I don't have any jobs to offer, but you're welcome to stay at my house as a guest."

I was delighted by her kindness and her offer and I accepted immediately.

The lady's name was Miss McPeek; and the apartment building, which was apparently part of a larger estate, was now being run as a sort of boarding house or hostel. (To this day I don't know whether Miss McPeek was the owner or just the manager.) I ended up staying there for the rest of the summer (about two months) at a cost of only $2 a night. And Miss McPeek made me feel at home right away. There were about forty small rooms available in the building and about twenty other boarders when I came. We ate by ourselves at breakfast and lunch, but we dined family style at dinner, where we sat together at a long table. Sometimes Miss McPeek did the cooking herself, sat right at the table with us, and passed the food to everybody. Her kindness was a godsend in those first weeks in America, which were very hard for me. I don't know what I would have done without her, because she helped me in so many ways. She even got my job back for me!

The day after I had moved into my new quarters, I got a job in the laundry room in the same YMCA where I had stayed at first. My hours were from six in the morning till three in the afternoon, and I suppose I made about $65 a week. What I was doing was simple enough. I would accept and bag the incoming laundry, mark it with an identifying tag, and when the people came back to pick it up, I would find their bag for them and collect the money. I also checked people's luggage and returned it when they asked. We wore special uniforms that the YMCA provided, and at the times when we had a lot of business, things got pretty hectic. You couldn't just lie around. I had several co-workers. They were a Hungarian, a Latvian, and our supervisor named Ralph, a gruff man who smoked heavily and used terrible language.

One day after I had worked at the YMCA for more than a month, a reporter from the *New Yorker* magazine came to talk with me on my lunch break. Miss McPeek had told him about me, and he wanted me to tell him about my early life in Tibet and my experiences in India. I gave him a rough sketch of my life, which was actually published sometime that fall. But it took me a while to finish the story, and I was late getting back to work. We punched a time clock in and out, and so when I returned there was no hiding the fact that I had missed some time (I think about an hour). Ralph was furious. "You can just turn around and go right back home," he snarled. "I don't want you working here any more."

I didn't know what to do or say, and so I simply went back home to Miss McPeek's. When I told her what had happened and why, she was furious. Since she had arranged the meeting with the reporter, she felt responsible for my losing my job. She called Mr. Johnson, the general manager of the YMCA, and told him what had happened and why I had been late. She was magnificent. I remember that she even gave the manager an earful about how important it was for people in this country to learn more about Tibet. Americans had a right to know about such things. She felt perfectly justified in arranging the interview for me and what was the problem? So what if it made me a little late for work—was that worth losing my job over? The general manager was no match for Miss McPeek. He caved in almost before she had finished talking. I was to go right back to work that minute, he said, and he met me there himself and smoothed the way with Ralph. "Well," he said, "this sometimes happens in America. It's all right this time—but don't let it happen again."

Miss McPeek was one of the kindest people I have ever met. At the Christmas break I returned to New York from Williams because she had called and said, "Wherever you are, whenever you're in New York, you are always welcome in my home." I have taken her up on her kind offer many times, and she has been as good as her word. She always had a room waiting, and she wouldn't hear of my paying her. When she died not many years ago, I was extremely sad. She was a wonderful friend.

When my job and my living arrangements were finally secure, I actually managed to make some friends and explore the city. For example, I discovered that Lobsang Samden, another brother of the Dalai Lama, was a student in New York, and I visited him in the apartment where he was staying. We would sometimes cook Tibetan food, drink American beer, and talk long into the night. I found that he agreed with my idea that Tibet had to change its social system, that church and state needed to be separated, and that Tibetans needed a modern education.

I also met a Mongolian monk named Geshi Wangyela, who had studied at Lhasa's Drepung Monastery and received the top monastic degree of *geshe* there. He lived across the Hudson River in Farming-dale, New Jersey. He invited me to his house on several occasions and always served traditional Tibetan butter tea and mutton. At that time, he had ten novices who were studying Buddhism with him.

Geshela took quite an interest in me. One day he was talking with me and said that since I was not a monk and didn't have any relatives here I needed a real home. It turned out that he had ideas of perhaps arranging a marriage for me here and giving me a home in that sense. I soon learned that he had a particular Kalmuck Mongol woman in mind, and he even took me to meet her and spend a day with her family. The woman's name was Barbara and she made a few visits to the city to see me. But my long talks with Gyalola and the parting audience with the Dalai Lama were still very much in my mind. I had come to America to get an education and eventually use it to help my countrymen in Tibet, so there was no way I could agree to such a match. The offer was very kind, but in the end I made it clear that my plans were so uncertain that I did not wish to pursue the relationship.

As I think back about it now, I saw quite a bit and met quite a few people in that short summer before I began my studies at Williams College. When I had sold some small Tibetan items and jewelry to make some extra money, I took the occasion to go to see the famous Statue of Liberty. I had a Buddhist friend named George whom I visited in Greenwich Village. I went to museums and especially enjoyed looking at paintings from different "schools." In fact I was particularly impressed by the modern expressionist paintings! Before the summer was over I went to see a Broadway show, to the famous nightclub called the Latin Quarter, and to a few American movies— among them *Gone with the Wind*. I also made a point of going to see the United Nations. I was glad I had seen it up close, because this was the summer when Nikita Khrushchev attacked the policies of the United States and banged his shoe on the table for emphasis. Having actually seen the United Nations Building, I found it easier to imagine the impact of Khrushchev's gesture. I also took the opportunity that summer to go to the top of the famous Empire State Building. Of course I was impressed by the view from that height. But the view also made me think of the achievement of the builders of the Potala Palace. The Empire State Building was higher, but the Potala had been built by hand, centuries ago, without benefit of modern technology or construction materials. Thinking of its construction reminded me that while Tibet badly needed to modernize, it also had valuable traditions and achievements to be proud of.

At the beginning of September, it was arranged that I could get a ride to Williams with a current student who lived in the New York area. It turned out that Steve, the young man who drove me to the school, was my new roommate. When we arrived, I met my old friend Robert Dunnam and got myself settled in a dormitory. And then I was ready to begin my studies, which turned out to be a lot harder than I had thought.

Soon after I arrived at the college, I had an interview with the dean of students. Among other things he asked me what kinds of courses I would like to take. I told him I wanted to study philosophy and economics, but when classes actually began my ambitions outran my abilities and I found myself in trouble very quickly. For a while, in fact, I was almost lost in my classes. I had only studied English for a few years, part of the time just walking around with Mr. Cumming. I was really not so far away from the "Mr. Bomb Chop" who amused my fellow students at St. Joseph's school in Darjeeling. And here I was thrown into college-level classes with extremely well-prepared American students. Though I found that I could understand most of the things my teachers were saying, I had a lot of trouble taking usable notes, and the reading assignments nearly killed me. It was simply too much reading—much of it highly sophisticated material—for someone with as little knowledge of the language as I had.

I studied like a crazy man. My roommate and friends studied hard, too, of course. But they could take weekends off, go on dates, run around with their friends. I stayed in most of the time except to visit with my friend Robert Dunnam. Other than that, studying was all I did. I would get up in the morning at seven and go to bed after midnight. I got myself a tutor to help me learn to read and write English more effectively. But as I see it now, I was obviously trying to do too much too fast. If I'd had more knowledge and perspective at the time, I probably wouldn't have even made the attempt, so I'm glad in a way that I didn't know any better! I just squared my shoulders and plunged ahead as best I could. And my papers continued to come back to me covered with so much red ink that I could scarcely see what I had originally written. My courses were in English, history, and economics, and the grades I got were never higher than Cs and Ds. But I didn't get discouraged, because everyone was as helpful as they could be.

(The dean himself was the one who found an English tutor for me—his son, who worked for free.) And even though my grades were poor, I was encountering ideas that had a profound effect on me.

In my history and economics classes I made my first contact with medieval European history, the French Revolution, the American Civil War, and the theories of Karl Marx and V.I. Lenin. The revelations started when I began to read about medieval history, because as I began thinking about Europe in the Middle Ages—about the cathedrals, the monasteries, the feudal system, the aristocrats and monks who had all the power and land, and the close connection between church and state—I saw parallels to the old, theocratic, and essentially feudal Tibetan society of my youth. It was a shock to realize that the huge social and economic gap between the Tibetan aristocrats and the peasants, the ownership of the land by a small minority, the extremely close relationship between the leadership of the church and the secular rulers were by no means unique to Tibet, as I and all Tibetans had been accustomed to believe. Today's great European nations had in the past been more or less like Tibet. Yet they had been able to change and eventually modernize.

As generally well known as these facts of history are to most Americans and Europeans, they were a revelation to me because all my life I had assumed that the old Tibetan way of life was the only possible alternative for us, the traditional theocratic government the only possible form. And because our government, our religion, and our culture were linked so inseparably, I had become used to thinking that there was no way we could make significant changes without hopelessly tearing the fabric of our religion, national culture, and ethnic identity. But now I realized there were other possible models. Many European societies had managed to change and become powerful and competitive modern nations without serious damage to their culture, values, or essential nature. I felt a renewed sense of hope that similar changes could occur in Tibet, and I worried less that my hopes for change were somehow disloyal or subversive. It seemed much clearer to me now that this movement from a theocratic and feudal society to a more modern industrial society was the common trend of modern history. These realizations weren't instantaneous, of course; they were part of a gradual but steady process, and the courses I was taking were the key. The more I learned about the history of other countries, the more ideas I began to have about possible futures for Tibet.

The year 1960 was a very exciting time to be in America for a variety of reasons. It was a presidential election year, and John Kennedy was running against Richard Nixon. Like everyone else, I followed the campaign closely. It was my first introduction to how American politics were conducted, and in particular I watched the debates with as much interest as a citizen. I remember I thought that Nixon lost, at least the second contest, because Kennedy asked him a lot of questions for which he didn't seem to have answers. Of course I didn't understand a lot of the subtleties of the issues they were talking about, but the larger subjects came through clearly. I reacted mainly to the surface drama—the human drama—which was exciting enough. And I remember being both surprised and excited by the idea of the debates themselves, because the spirit of public argument and free exchange of ideas was so different from what I had been used to. Here were important people openly discussing—and disagreeing—about what was best for America and its future. It was the last thing that would have happened in my own country at that time or in the past. I had of course seen democratic elections in India, but even there I hadn't seen anything like the debates and the free exchange of ideas that they represented. I thought it was fantastic. Though in my classes I read slowly and wrote imperfectly, the books I was reading and the events that occurred around me during the two semesters at Williams opened my eyes. And the following years I spent in Seattle at the University of Washington completed my political awakening.

After that first year at Williams, I went to Seattle for a number of reasons. For one thing, I had gotten only a one-year scholarship to Williams College. For another, my friends at Williams were concerned about the difficulties I had been having trying to catch up to my American classmates with so little educational background or support. We decided it might make more sense for me to continue my work at the University of Washington, where there was a large Tibetan project. Money was available to pay my major expenses, and there was a small but established Tibetan community already there, which would make me feel more at home.

So at the end of the summer of 1961, I got on a bus in New York and traveled 3,000 miles in six days and six nights to Seattle, Washington. I took the bus because just before I had left New York I had asked Miss McPeek what would be the best way for me to see America, especially the vast agricultural heartland. "You must go by bus, of course, Tashi," she responded. "You are the most inquisitive person I have ever met. You are always after something new to learn about America. We native Americans often take the facts of our country for granted and sometimes don't appreciate them. You come from a country that is having changes in its way of life forced on it by the Chinese. I think you will appreciate what you see here." I was glad I took her advice.

To begin with, I was extremely impressed by the roads themselves. American highways were the best I had ever seen. I was struck by the size of these American highways. They were four- and six-lane thoroughfares on which cars traveled in both directions at once and at speeds of 70 miles per hour and more. The roads in America seemed to go everywhere and offer convenient and inexpensive transportation to even the most ordinary families and common people. The few roads built by the Chinese in Tibet in the 1950s seemed backward and primitive by comparison.

The bus became a traveling home. We slept and ate at regular intervals at the bus stops. As we crossed the incredibly fertile farmlands of the Midwest, I was interested in the farms and farming I saw. I saw farms—some of them huge—and a lot of cows but not nearly as many sheep as there would have been in the Tibetan plateau where my village was. As in New York City, I was struck by the number of machines and buildings—tractors, gleaming harvesters, huge combines, enormous barns and silos, and the machinery for irrigation. And to my surprise, there were almost no actual farmers to be seen. Very few people were working in the fields. I think the absence of large numbers of farmers and farm workers struck me the most, because it was so different from what I was used to seeing in Tibet and India and because it confirmed what I remembered reading something about in my classes. In an agriculturally advanced country like America, a relatively small percentage of the population is able to supply food and other farm products not only to the rest of the country but to the rest of the world. In more agriculturally and industrially backward countries, a very high percentage of the population works in the fields but can barely supply the home country with enough to eat. All the more reason, I thought to myself, that Tibet simply had to modernize!

When the bus got to Kansas City, I took time out to visit a Trappist monastery. It was only a few miles from Kansas City and was home to about seventy completely silent monks. They all worked together on a farm the order owned, and their labors supplied most of their daily needs. The monks ate in common in a large dining hall but maintained strict silence—even through the meals. I had been invited to the monastery by Father Stanley, who had been inspired by the story of the life of Milarepa, an eleventh-century Tibetan hermit saint who had led his whole life in meditation. Father Stanley told me the story, which I enjoyed very much and made me glad once again that I took Miss McPeek's advice about how to see the country.

When I finally arrived in Seattle and made my way to the university, I was greeted warmly by Professor Terry Wylie, who told me he hoped that I would feel more at home with the fellow Tibetans I would find there than perhaps I had felt at Williams College. In many senses I did feel more at home. The university's Far Eastern Studies Department, which had provided the scholarship, had also found me a summer job translating ritual ceremony manuscripts from Tibetan to English.

When classes started in the fall, I took courses in Far Eastern history and Tibetan history and then added courses in political science and philosophy over the next year and a half. This time around my academic difficulties were fewer, and my grades were a lot better.

I reencountered the writings of Marx and Lenin that I had first read at Williams College, and I read some of Mao Zedong's works as well. I was not then and I am not now a Marxist in the ordinary sense of that word. But I was attracted by the aspect of their philosophy that involved greater power and opportunity for peasants and workers. I was struck by their notions of the cycles or phases of history, the idea that religion could sometimes be used to enslave or hinder the common people, and the importance of revolution in the history of most of the modern European states. I read biographies of Marx and Lenin and was especially interested by the troubles Marx had because of his political views—the way various governments put pressure on him and how he was exiled for a time. In Lenin's biography I was fascinated by the account of the Russian Revolution of 1917 and how the workers rose up and overthrew the tsar. And I remembered the French Revolution that I had studied the previous year—how the peasants sent King Louis XIV to the guillotine. In short, I was struck simultaneously by the importance of revolution for these countries and by the violence of the events themselves, which I found a little frightening.

It was during this period that I think I really began to think of myself as a new, "modern" Tibetan. I was no longer blinded by the self-serving religious ideology that had so effectively masked the total domination of a small religious and aristocratic elite over the mass of poor peasants and held back all attempts at change. I thought it was time for some kind of revolution in Tibet, too, although I didn't wish for any of the violence or the bloodshed of the sort I had been reading about. Yet it was hard for me to imagine how such changes might be made to occur under our old society in any other way. Moreover, the Chinese were in control now and developing their own governmental structures in Tibet. And although I was still apprehensive about the Chinese presence and long-range intentions, I began to think that perhaps what Tibet had been living through for the past ten years might in fact be the answer in the sense that the Chinese invasion of our country might have done something that we could not have done for ourselves. It had provided a revolution for us. It had swept away the old guard and its exploitative institutions and made participation by the common people in government possible for the first time in Tibet's history. As the quarters sped by at the University of Washington, my mind was filled with a welter of such ideas.

To support myself for the summer I took two jobs. Part of the time I worked in the university cafeteria. Part of the time I worked as a cook's assistant in a tavern called the Red Hand. And in what time there was left, I wrote a book in Tibetan. Writing things down helped me clarify my thinking, so I decided to record my impressions of America. I didn't really do any research; I just expressed what I had seen, heard, and thought about since I had been here. I talked about the many positive things. I felt that in terms of pure wealth and material things America was a sort of heaven on earth. I had never seen a place where there was so much apparent wealth, there were so many creature comforts and so many opportunities to find work. I wrote about the openness and generosity of the people I had met and the relative class-lessness of American culture. I talked about the very high literacy rate, the accessibility of schools and libraries, and what I thought was the amazing availability of education to people of all classes and ages.

But I didn't paint an entirely positive picture. The 1960s in America were extremely volatile and turbulent times, the more so, of course, as the decade wore on. And I had seen what I had seen. I wrote about the problem of racism and the situation of blacks in American society. If America was a land of tremendous material wealth, it was also a highly materialistic country, excessively so I often thought. I tried to record my thoughts about the divorce rate, the sheer amount of violence in the culture, and the many other social problems that were getting more public attention as the 1960s wore on. When I had finished, I sent the manuscript to my countrymen in exile in India, and it was published in Tibetan in Darjeeling in 1963 under the title, *My View of the American Way of Life*. I didn't actually see a copy of the book until much later. I mention it here mainly as an indication of the level of intensity at which I was thinking and feeling during the course of that summer, a period in my life that raised far more questions than it answered.

The main question and by far the hardest was, of course, What was I going to do? Was I just going to sit around and think about abstract political ideas, or was I going to try to make some sort of concrete personal commitment to help my country? What role could I play? What specific steps should I take? These were not easy questions.

In the midst of this, my personal life changed. During the past year, a young Tibetan woman in Seattle whom I knew and liked had an affair with a Tibetan monk and became pregnant. The monk, however, refused to marry her, and a potentially embarrassing scandal was looming. The woman's name was Tsejen Wangmo Sakya (she was a member of the ruling Sakya family), and as the affair dragged on she became despondent and contemplated suicide. I had great respect and empathy for her, so when her brother asked me if I would be willing to pretend to be the child's father and marry her, I agreed. The wedding took place at the King County Court House in Seattle, and when we took the oath I put a diamond ring on her finger. In a few months, the baby was delivered at the same hospital where I was then working as a dishwasher in the cafeteria. (I actually used some of the money from my salary to pay for the medical expenses.) The child was a beautiful boy she named Sonam Tsering. Although I hadn't planned any of this, I suddenly found myself in a serious relationship. Tsejenla and I grew to care for one another quickly, and the pressures on me began to become immense. If I was going to take any action because of my new convictions about the situation in Tibet, I had to act soon or not at all. I could see that if I stayed much longer I would inevitably put down roots that would make it too hard to go home again.

As I look back, I can see that there were three turning points in my life, three decisions I made that had enormous consequences. The first was my decision to leave Tibet and go to India. The second was the decision to leave the relative security of India and come to America.

And the third and by far the most difficult was the decision to leave the safety and material comforts of America to go back to China and Tibet. My conscience told me that I ought to go. The more I thought about it, the surer I became that the Chinese invasion of Tibet provided a once-in-a-lifetime opportunity for Tibetans and that I wanted to become part of the process of change. I knew that Tibetans who didn't like my views would be quick to say that I was a Chinese sympathizer and nothing more! I knew I had already disappointed some of my fellow Tibetans in exile just by coming to America and that returning to "Chinese Tibet" would only make things worse. My close American friends thought I was crazy to consider going back. They couldn't understand why I would want to leave the comfort and security of America. And they feared (quite rightly, as it turned out) that I might be in some danger from the Chinese, who might consider me a spy for either my own people or for the Americans. The pressure to decide what to do increased almost daily.

In a curious way, President Kennedy helped me make my decision. Of course it's not that he even knew of my existence. But one of the books I had read in America was his *Profiles in Courage*. I had always remembered a line from that book: "Man does what he must in spite of difficulties, obstacles, and dangers, and that is human morality." I think that particular idea had jumped out at me when I first read it because it was so relevant to what I had been thinking for most of the time that I'd been in America. Whatever the reason, the words came back to me now and gave me courage. Within a short time I wrote a long letter to my friend Gyalola in which I told him of my decision and tried to make my feelings as clear as I could. Although he was part of the government-in-exile and also the old system, I felt that he would at least understand what I was trying to do and might even have an open mind. I told him that I felt Tibet must be modernized, and to do so the old political domination of religion had to end. Modernization would not happen with the government-in-exile, so I explained that if we were ever to modernize we had no choice but to see that it could only happen under the aegis of the Chinese Communist Party. It was not easy for me to do it, but I went on to tell him that after much deliberation I had decided to accept the presence of the Chinese and the communist system so that I might be allowed to use the education I had acquired and help Tibet become a more modern nation. Patriotism in exile wasn't going to be enough for me. I felt that the only way I could help my country was by being there. I had to go back to the high plateau and rejoin my people. I had made up my mind.

I left Seattle with a heavy heart on December 10, 1963. By that time, President Kennedy had been assassinated. America was in a state of shock and mourning. The activity in Vietnam, still only a small cloud on the horizon, was getting larger and larger. It seemed a particularly ominous time.

Saying good-bye to Tsejenla and leaving Sonam behind were among the hardest things I have done. Before leaving I went to see all of my friends, some of whom still couldn't believe I was actually going. "He is in his early thirties, full of vigor, and has worked hard to succeed here in America. And now he wants to go back to China?" said one. "Take care of yourself," they all warned. Professor Wylie asked me if I was being fair to the Dalai Lama by going to China and therefore not serving him directly with the education I had acquired. That, of course, was the crux of the matter. The obvious way to help my country would have been to join the government-in-exile and work with it. But for all the reasons I had been agonizing about for months, I felt I could not take that course. All I could say to Professor Wylie was that I had made my decision after thinking about it for a long time, that I felt it was the right path for me, and that I would always remember everyone who had helped me with my education.

I left Seattle the way I had come, by Greyhound bus. Although in some senses my leaving was a sad occasion and my future uncertain to say the least, this trip was one of my best experiences in America. Instead of its taking six days and nights, as when I had come west from New York, this trip lasted a month. I had planned it carefully so that it allowed me to visit several American cities and see friends and also simply stay with American families willing to take foreign travelers into their homes.

At the beginning of the trip I talked with Gyalola in person. His travels had brought him to the United States and he was staying at the Mark Hopkins Hotel in San Francisco, one of the first major stops the bus made as it wound its way south down America's rugged Pacific coast. When he knew my plans, he got in touch with me immediately, and we agreed to meet.

I arrived in the city on December 21, 1963. The tour allowed a stopover of several days, and so I stayed in a small hotel and spent the better part of two days talking with Gyalola, sometimes at meals, sometimes in the lobby of his hotel, and sometimes—when the conversation got serious or emotional—in the privacy of his room. I knew he had gotten my letter, and of course I knew that he would not approve of much that I said. Though glad to see him, I was full of anxiety because I had not expected to have to see him face to face so quickly. My ideas and convictions were new and still quite vulnerable, and I knew it would be extremely difficult to deal with his opposition. And so it proved to be. We didn't waste much time in small talk; these conversations with him were the longest, frankest we had ever had. They couldn't have come at a more crucial time in my life. Though at times our discussion was both painful and difficult, it was an extremely valuable experience because it helped me continue to clarify my thinking. The meeting was so important to me that I remember the details with amazing clarity even now.

Gyalola's arguments were clever. He knew how I felt about many of the abuses in the old society, and in September he had sent me a letter in which he was at pains to dissociate himself from the more reactionary and old-line Tibetans in exile. He had suggested then that we—he and I—represented the younger, more progressive thinkers who would have to carry on the battle against the Chinese. He felt I was making a bad decision; he wanted to convince me to return to the Tibetan community in India, and as we sat in comfortable chairs in the lobby of the Mark Hopkins Hotel, he began to make his case in the strongest possible terms, presenting his arguments slowly and with great care.

At first, Gyalola talked with pride about the current situation of the Tibetans in exile in India—many of them the refugees whose plight I had helped him chronicle several years ago. Their condition and prospects were much better now, he told me. A trusteeship had been established for them. Some of the Dalai Lama's gold had been invested in Tibetan-owned factories in India, and the profits were being spent on the settlement of the refugees and on their education.

Gyalola said that in general, the settlement of the Tibetan refugees was going well. The oldest people were the hardest to place, of course; and some had already migrated to other countries. But thousands had also been settled in areas like Mysore and Madhya Pradesh. And for the children, the future of any country, things looked even better. He said that among Tibetans in India there were about eleven thousand children under the age of fifteen. Of those, at present there were about five thousand already studying and learning in a variety of schools established either by the Indian government or by the Tibetan government-in-exile. He conceded that to educate the whole eleven thousand was a hard task, but he was extremely optimistic that it could be done, and he was especially enthusiastic about what the result would be. These newly educated children will be, he said proudly, "the leaders of the next generation. They will be the doctors, lawyers, technicians, and teachers of the future. And if they can never return to Tibet, they will become the core of a highly successful Tibetan community here in India. In the meantime, while we are waiting to see whether we can return to our country, they will render valuable services to the Indian government, which can also use young professionals of this sort. All will be good. You will see."

And then our conversation took the turn that I'd always known it was going to take. (By this time we had retired to the privacy of his room.) He finally asked me directly what I intended to do, and I told him emphatically that I had decided not to work for the Tibetan government in India and that I was seriously considering returning to Tibet. I said I felt that the relative minority of Tibetans living abroad had no right to assume that they represented the majority of Tibetans who were still living at home—and who were "Tibet" as much as or more than the exiles.

"We have every right to represent Tibet," he said quickly. "We represent over 10 percent of the population, and we did not leave the country of our own free will. We were driven out by the Chinese!"

"No," I replied just as quickly. "I cannot feel justified in working for a small minority of Tibetans who are no longer in direct touch with the majority of the population still living at home under Chinese authority."

Gyalola was angry now and spoke sharply.

"Tashi Tsering, you have no idea what you're saying. You won't even acknowledge the existence of the problems you will have to face if you seriously attempt to return. For one thing, the Chinese are the most suspicious people on the face of the earth. They won't trust you no matter what you say or do. I have lived for years in China and know them. I have seen them in action. At one point if I had been willing to collaborate they told me that I could have a high position in the government they set up. Mao Zedong actually invited me to Beijing. They cheered my so-called leftist thoughts. But I knew what would happen if I trusted them. You simply don't know what you're doing. You will end up being used by the Chinese. They won't kill you. They will use you!"

I had trouble meeting his eyes for a moment, and so I stared out the window at the heavy fog that was rolling in off the vast Pacific and slowly blanketing the bay. Gyalola had become so agitated that he had stood up and was now pacing nervously as he spoke. The room was so quiet that I could hear his shoes creaking as he took each angry step. Perhaps he felt he had become too hostile, because suddenly he sat down again and took another tack.

"I must tell you that personally, I have no real objection to the decision you've made. Other Tibetans whom we both know might be shocked, but I am not. You show tremendous courage in wanting to go home again, and I for one admire you for it. None of us denies that there are serious problems and challenges that must be faced if Tibet is to be saved. But I urge you to consider how much progress we—the government-in-exile—have already made. Under the leadership of the Dalai Lama we are far better organized than we were when you were last in India. Three years ago, when the refugee camps were full and we and our countrymen were in chaos, it was because we lacked experience; we had few educated people to help us; we simply didn't know how to respond to the situation of our sudden exile. The Dalai Lama, though in India, is not emotionally remote from our people. He has spent vast amounts of his own personal treasure to help resettle and begin to train them for whatever the future brings. We are making headway in our efforts to take our case to the international community, and the Indian government will continue to help us until the Dalai Lama himself can return to Tibet. Please consider that the best way to help your country is to help our cause." It was an appeal hard to ignore. And then he made an even stronger push.

He offered me a job as a director of the Tibetan House in India—and at quite a good salary. He told me that the house would eventually become both a museum for the preservation of Tibetan artifacts and also something of a trade center whose business would be to facilitate the sale of Tibetan products. The idea was both to preserve Tibetan ethnic and cultural traditions and also encourage more international commerce in Tibetan-made goods. By the time he had finished describing the project, Gyalola became almost poetic. If you accept this position, he said, "your achievements will become known not only to the Dalai Lama but also to your friends in America who will be proud of you and proud of the results of their decision to support your education. I hope you will consider this offer carefully," he said finally. The fog was so thick now that I could see nothing but white cotton. Looking out the window was like looking into the center of a cloud.

Even as he had been describing the attractions of his offer, I knew that I wasn't going to be able to give him the answer he wanted. I temporized. I said I would do anything I could to help my countrymen if it could be done without working directly for the exiled government whose interests represented the old guard, not the mass of poor Tibetans. I said again that I wanted to work for myself and for all Tibet—not just for a relatively small group of exiles.

Gyalola's response was sharp and unhesitating.

"Everything to be done for Tibetans goes through His Holiness the Dalai Lama and his exile government. There is no separate job for you. There is no separate Tibet. When you say that you do not want to work for the government-in-exile are you also saying that you do not respect the Dalai Lama as your leader?"

What could I say? I replied that outside Tibet there is no alternative for Tibetans but to follow the Dalai Lama.

"Very good, then." Gyalola was pacing again. "The Dalai Lama wants me to tell you that you should come back to India and work with your fellow Tibetans if you genuinely have their best interests at heart. But he also wants you to know that we can do without you if we have to. Others will serve as well." He then offered me another choice—to work in the Tibet House in New York City for at least a couple of years before doing anything else. I said I would have to think his offers over very carefully. I felt that such a decision would affect the course of the rest of my life, and when I made it I wanted to do so without any regrets, without looking back. I said that I felt my decision not only affected me personally but also the way in which I might help all Tibetans. At this Gyalola lost his temper completely.

"That is ridiculous," he said with flashing eyes. "You aren't thinking of the Tibetans at all. You are thinking only of yourself. I know you. I know your nature. When it comes right down to it, you won't be able to stand up to the Chinese. You have courage but how much ability do you really have to help anyone? Please forgive me for being so blunt."

And then the momentary rush of anger drained away. For all intents and purposes, it was the end of our debate. I could see that Gyalola felt he had gone too far. I knew that his genuine affection and respect for me had overcome his anger, and I was moved and tried to conciliate.

"It doesn't matter that we don't see eye to eye on this," I said with some emotion. "It is important to me that we can talk. You are surprisingly broad-minded, really. You have never tried to forbid my return. You have helped me many times in the past. I know that you are trying to help me now, and believe me I appreciate it. I also appreciate the fact that we can talk so freely and that I can be so frank with you. There are few people I can talk to in that way." I said these things and he responded as the good friend he is, but I think it was clear to both of us that we would always be on opposite sides on these issues. His loyalty was to the Dalai Lama's government-in-exile; mine was to the Tibetan people still at home, and if that meant working with the Chinese, so be it. That was simply the way it was going to be. It was late by then; we were both drained; and so we went to bed for the night.

The next day the talking was easier. By the time our long breakfast was over, the morning fog had burned off and the day was exceptionally clear. We sat again in the comfortable chairs in the lobby, and now that the strong words were over we were able to exchange ideas more peacefully. I tried to tell him why I thought that using the presence of the Chinese was our only chance. He did not become angry, but said somewhat wearily that I should not be fooled. The roads, the hospitals, the schools were just for propaganda purposes. Didn't I realize that all the important positions were held by the Chinese—and would always be held by them? "They're not interested in Tibet," he said. "They're interested in China." I told him I had heard that as many as three thousand newly trained Tibetan technicians had returned to Tibet after being trained in China. "Most of them," he said with a wave of his hand, "trained as political leaders."

I changed the subject and tried to tell him about the way my reading of Western historians and philosophers had affected my thinking. He listened thoughtfully and surprised me by saying that he was not absolutely against communism. "The original theories are good," he said. "But it is far easier for me to talk to communists from India or the United States than the ones from China or the Soviet Union." As I was thinking about what he had just said, he suddenly looked at me directly.

"Since your feelings are clearly a matter of principle, maybe it is best that you do return to Tibet. We, however, will never surrender to the Chinese. We will fight for our cause wherever we can and try to cause the Chinese as much trouble as possible in the meantime—especially in the United Nations."

"What exactly are you trying to accomplish?" I asked.

"I would like to make Tibet a neutral nation," he said thoughtfully.

"And with the assistance of both China and India, I would like to see it become a modern democratic society. I see it as becoming a good friend and neighbor to China but also as being part of the larger, international community."

I have to admit I was surprised. I had never heard Gyalola talk this way before. Having shared the turbulent experiences of the night before and in this new mood of conciliation, we talked long into this day as well.

After lunch we went to his room, still in a mind to talk. But the time to part had come, and I think we both knew it. We talked about increasingly neutral subjects, and as I was about to leave, he said, "Take care of yourself. I hope I will see you in India. Whatever the case, let me know your final decision and your plans as soon as you can."

I went to my own hotel room with a heavy heart and momentarily felt my resolve weaken. I was surprised by the level of affection I had for Gyalola. My emotions at the moment were far harder to deal with than any of the arguments he had advanced. I believed that his ultranationalist feelings prevented him from seeing the genuine good that the Chinese had done in the past and could do in the future. I knew that he thought I would end up becoming a "yes man" for the Chinese, but I felt he did not see that since the exiled Tibetans were essentially powerless in India, they were already "yes men" in their own way. But intellectual positions are one thing and emotions are another. In a diary that I kept in those days, I wrote that night that "I earnestly do not know what to do at this moment. I hope in the coming days I can think more clearly and make a final decision on the basis of principles and not emotions." I think the thing that helped me keep my resolve was a phrase Gyalola had used when he talked so eloquently about the children as the future of our country. "They will be the doctors, lawyers, technicians, and teachers of the future," he had said. *"And if they can never return to Tibet, they will become the core of a highly successful Tibetan community here in India."* Those were the words that I couldn't get out of my mind. Gyalola could accept the idea that the Tibetans of tomorrow might have to live permanently outside of Tibet. Maybe it was because he was born in the ethnic Tibetan part of the Chinese province of Qinghai rather than Tibet proper, or maybe it was because he had lived most of his life outside of Tibet. But I couldn't accept such an idea. Tibet to me wasn't just an idea, an abstraction; it was a place—my home. It was the mountains, rivers, the flinty landscapes, and the villages I knew as a child. Somebody else's mountains and villages simply weren't the same. There was no acceptable substitute. As shaken as I was then, I knew in my heart that going back was the only answer for me.

I think it was a good thing that the meeting with Gyalola took place at the beginning of my bus trip. As powerful as his words and affection had been, their effects began to diminish and come into perspective as the excitement of daily new experiences began to vie for my attention. And my own convictions, which had been battered but not destroyed, had plenty of time to recover and grow stronger once again. I left San Francisco on December 23, 1963.

Our first stop was Los Angeles. On the trip south, the coastal mountains and the farmlands of the central valley reminded me a little of my own country. When we arrived I stayed the first night with a family who were used to entertaining foreign visitors. Until now in my travels I had been mainly sightseeing. On this trip I got a close look at the rhythms and commonplace details of American life—the lives of ordinary people—and I couldn't help being fascinated. I arrived just in time for Christmas Eve and enjoyed watching the traditional celebration of this important Christian holiday. While I was there I also saw some of the famous movie studios and the Hollywood Bowl. But I was also interested in the things that interested my hosts. Even at this holiday season there was still much talk about the recent assassination of President Kennedy, about what was going to happen next, and about the racial politics that were beginning to intrude on the private lives of everyday people. Even during the eating of the traditional turkey dinner, the people I visited couldn't entirely get their minds away from more serious thoughts. I spent New Year's Day in Las Vegas, Nevada, the gambling capital of the United States, and was very impressed by a side trip to see the magnificent Hoover Dam. In Colorado Springs, I got to visit the campus of the Air Force Academy.

The best thing about the bus was the pace—very slow—so that not only did I get plenty of chances to see the enormous variety of sights America offers but I also had plenty of time to think. Partly, thinking was very painful. When I thought about my wife and the child I had left in Seattle I was sometimes overwhelmed by the cost of my decision and what I was leaving behind. But the time to think was very helpful when it came to dealing with my anxieties about all the things Gyalola had said or implied. Given some time to think rationally, outside the orbit of his powerful presence and friendship, I was able to regain my confidence in my decision once again.

As the bus rolled along, we visited Chicago, where I was especially impressed by the Museum of Science and Industry and the other buildings built for the famous Colombian Exposition, and also with the vast industrial plants, especially the steel mills. We went through Buffalo, New York, near which I got to see Niagara Falls. We stopped in Boston, Massachusetts, and New Haven, Connecticut, where I got to see the famous campuses of Harvard, the Massachusetts Institute of Technology, and Yale University. Eventually we wound our way to Washington D.C., then back up to New York.

In New York my friend Robert Dunnam supported me, as he always has. We had several long conversations, and he told me, "Tashi, it is good for you to go back and help your fellow Tibetans there." While I was waiting in Havana for the ship that would take me to China, I wrote a long letter to Gyalola in which I tried once again to explain the reasons for my decision more fully and concretely, and I got a strong letter in return. His response was, I suppose, to be expected. "You are an opportunist," he wrote. "We say it is good if you want to serve the interests of Tibet and Tibetans and a pity if you serve the Chinese interests instead." And Mr. Tolstoy from the foundation that sent me the money to come to America wrote, "You must keep your own integrity and not listen to the communist barbarians."

The voices continued, but I knew that the die was cast. I traveled north to Montreal where, after a two-week wait, I sailed for Havana, Cuba. I had gotten a Cuban visa through the Swiss Embassy in Washington, D.C. In Havana I spoke to the third secretary at the Chinese Embassy, where I sought permission to return to Tibet. After two months' wait the permission was granted, and I sailed for Canton and whatever lay beyond.

Tashi with Robert Dunnam at Williams College in 1960.

Tashi with first wife Tsejin Sakya in Seattle in 1963.

Tashi (left) with friends in Seattle in 1963.

Tashi working part-time as a dishwasher in the cafeteria of the University Hospital in 1963 while a student at the University of Washington.

Tashi in Beijing with his school's Red Guards in August 1966 at Tiananmen Square.

Tashi (left, back row), in costume as a member of the Dalai Lama's dance troupe (gadrugpa).

Tashi in front of Mao Zedong's memorial hall in 1978 during his flight to Beijing to petition the State Council to redress his case.

Tashi with his wife Sangyela in 1981 in Xi'an City.

7

The voyage seemed endless. After leaving Cuba the ship crossed the Caribbean and the South Atlantic, plodded across the Mediterranean, negotiated the Suez Canal and the Red Sea, and slowly worked its way through the South China Sea to Canton. There were only ten other passengers besides myself, and all of them were old and seemed to be going back to Canton to die. We were fifty-seven days at sea, and I was alone most of the time.

I spent part of my time writing. While I was in Havana waiting for the ministry in Beijing to approve my passage, the secretary from the Chinese Embassy who found a hotel room for me had brought me between twenty and thirty books to keep me busy. They were all in English and on a variety of subjects: China, the history of the Chinese Communist Party, ideological tracts, and foreign policy. Alone in a strange country, I had plenty of time on my hands, and so I did quite a bit of reading just to pass the time. Now that I was trapped on shipboard, I needed to keep myself occupied and organize my thoughts. So I decided to write something, because as I discovered when I set down my impressions of America, writing is one of the best ways to discover what you think. And so as our ship rose and fell with the monotonous swells of the open sea I wrote an article about Tibet and China's foreign policy. The physical act itself helped keep my spirits up, although not entirely.

As you may imagine, I still had plenty of second thoughts about my decision to go back. It was too late to change my mind now, but I couldn't help occasionally second-guessing myself. The ship's captain was Swiss, and he and his Austrian engineer were no help. They were both very negative about China, and when they learned where I was going they told me flatly that I was making a big mistake. "Tashi," the captain said, "if you go to Communist China you will lose your freedom." They just couldn't understand my point of view. I knew that many of my American friends and supporters couldn't understand me either, and I worried that they would think I did not appreciate the efforts they had made to get me to the United States. I feared they would think I wasn't grateful.

To strengthen my resolve, I kept returning to the arguments I had framed when I had written to Gyalola after our emotional conversation in San Francisco. The main points still seemed valid. I thought that my generation of Tibetans—and perhaps my class—had a special responsibility. We had not created the Tibet of the past. Historically, the responsibility for the old society lay with the ruling classes—the aristocrats, the monks, and the heads of the monasteries. From exile, these former rulers were now seeking Tibetan independence, and it would have been easy enough for me to have joined them if I had wished. As I tried so hard to explain to Gyalola, however, I did not think their efforts were what would help our country most. I was afraid that independence now, even if possible, would only mean going back to the old ways. I felt strongly that before we sought independence we needed to catch up with the twentieth century and that to do so we needed to accept and even embrace the opportunities the Chinese communists offered. Making sacrifices, taking chances, were, I thought, the responsibilities of my generation, our mission, if you will. The question of Tibetan independence was best left to the next generation. In fact I thought it should be their decision: if tomorrow's young people were comfortable continuing under communist rule, then that was fine. If they thought they were being oppressed and wanted to rise up in revolt, then so be it. That could be their mission. My own mission was here and now—in China and Tibet.

These were brave words, and I believed them absolutely. But they didn't keep me from feeling both isolated and a bit fearful. One of the things that bothered me the most was my sense that there ought to have been more alternatives than I seemed to have. My only choices seemed to be to join the government-in-exile and appear to endorse everything it stood for or to return to Communist China and appear to approve of Chinese policies. I hadn't been able to find any middle ground. The closer we got to our destination, the more apprehensive and full of self-doubt I became.

To be honest, I had felt more than a little vulnerable from the time I boarded the ship. I had to surrender my passport to the secretary from the Chinese Embassy in Havana. The embassy kept the passport and replaced it with a letter, which an embassy official gave to the captain of the ship. There was nothing necessarily amiss in all this. Where was I going or what borders was I likely to be crossing while on board ship? But it made me nervous all the same.

There was one moment in particular that made the implications of my decision to return especially real to me. Just before we docked at Canton, our ship hoisted a Chinese flag. I had seen the new communist standard in Lhasa in the 1950s, but when I saw the real thing again and actually heard it snap in a crisp breeze it made me realize that I was really there—in the People's Republic of China—for better or for worse. And then I got my first real jolt. I was not allowed to disembark! Nobody told me why. Nobody told me anything. The captain gave my letter (the one that had replaced my passport) to the frontier police, and I was put on a smaller ship and simply told to wait.

I was not allowed to leave for several days and felt puzzled—too much like a prisoner to feel comfortable. To be truthful, I was a bit frightened and spent a lot of time wondering why the Chinese were restricting me. Then on the third day I got a surprise visit from four people. Two were from the Canton Branch Office of the Political Consultative Conference. They had come to receive me on behalf of the local government and had brought me a bundle that contained a cotton padded quilt for sleeping and a set of denim clothing to wear. The other two were an older Chinese gentleman and a younger man who also looked Chinese to me. The young man, however, was actually a Tibetan from eastern Tibet who had come to interpret. He stunned me, therefore, when he suddenly said (in accented but perfectly understandable Lhasa Tibetan), "Mr. Zhao [the Chinese gentleman] and I were sent to greet you by the Tibetan Minority Institute of the city of Xianyang in Shaanxi Province [in northwestern China]." I was astonished not just by his Tibetan but by what he said. "Who are you again?" I asked. "Where are you from? The city of what?"

This was an early lesson in how the Chinese worked. Apparently plans had begun to be made for me as long ago as the time when I was waiting in Havana and had first asked for permission to come home. I remembered now that the embassy secretary had asked me a lot of questions about why I wanted to return, what my plans were, and so on. I had told him that I wanted to return to Tibet to help my people, but that first I hoped I would be allowed to continue my studies at a Chinese university, I hoped at Beijing University. It was clear to me now that though nobody had said a thing to me, decisions had long since been made about where I would go and what I would do. I was not to be sent to Beijing as I had asked, but rather to one of the new minority institutes designed to train Tibetan cadres and teachers—the new leaders of Tibet. Because of the time I had spent in America and my experience in American schools, I was to be trained as a teacher.

Now that Mr. Zhao had arrived, I learned I would soon be allowed to leave the ship, and within a day or two Mr. Zhao, the Tibetan interpreter, and I moved to a hot, stuffy hotel near the docks. The heat was oppressive and the only amenity was the mosquito net over each of the beds.

I had brought a few possessions: a calculator, a Minolta camera, two watches, and two boxes of clothing. But I had no Chinese money and there was no easy way to get any, so Mr. Zhao took care of all my expenses. We stayed at the hotel for a couple of days while he made arrangements. In the evenings he tried talking with me a bit through the interpreter. He told me he knew that I had been out of Tibet since 1957, and suggested that perhaps I wasn't aware of what had been going on either there or in China. He proudly listed what he called ten great construction projects that the Chinese had undertaken in the last few years. I listened politely, but I remember thinking that it wasn't "great" construction projects that a country needed—at least not a country like Tibet. I had done a lot of thinking since the days when I marveled at the roads the Chinese built so quickly in and around Lhasa. My courses at Williams College and the University of Washington had enlarged my perspective, and I felt now that Tibet needed to establish a basic and competitive agricultural and industrial base and a modern infrastructure. Above all, the population—especially the ordinary people—had to become literate in the Western sense. Then Tibet could worry about luxuries like great construction projects. I didn't say any of this openly, but I hadn't come all this way and taken the risks I had taken without knowing what I thought. So I listened politely and said little.

On the following day, we boarded a train that would take us 800 miles northwest across the very heart of China to the city of Xi'an. The journey took days as the train wound slowly through the Chinese heartland: through Hunan and Hubei provinces, across the Yangtze, and ever north and west into Shaanxi Province, the western wilderness Mao Zedong had made his headquarters in the early days of the Chinese Communist Party. Finally we arrived at Xi'an, one of the oldest cities in China, and slightly beyond it was Xianyang, which was to be my home for the immediate future.

I'll never forget my first impressions when we arrived. The railway station in Xianyang was just a short walk from the college, and the available student housing consisted of a few rows of simple brick buildings. I was given a single, small room in one of them. In it were one broken chair, a battered desk, and a wooden bed. There was a dim light, and the only window was cracked badly. Coming as I was from the comparatively plush dormitories of the University of Washington and the relative opulence of America, the contrast was stark. I had thought long and carefully about the political and moral aspects of my decision to return. In those respects I knew exactly what I was doing and why. But I now realized that I hadn't given much thought to what it was going to be like living in Communist China day in and day out. Sitting in this barren room in the middle of what at the time seemed like nowhere, I couldn't help wondering for the thousandth time if my choice had been wise. I had always seen myself as going to Tibet, even though my plans included study in China. When I pictured myself it was always in Lhasa, being welcomed, doing good work. Now I saw that when or if I was able to get home was not entirely in my control. I would get to Tibet when and if the Chinese wanted me to and not before. I tried to take comfort in the thought that since they were sending me to the minority institute for Tibetan cadres and teachers, they obviously were thinking about eventually letting me return to Tibet when my training was over. And I liked the idea of being trained as a teacher, so I could use my education and also help others do the same. But I saw now that my situation at Xianyang was little different from what it had been aboard ship. Now that I had fully committed to the journey, I couldn't get off until I reached my final destination, wherever that turned out to be.

The name of the school I had been sent to was the Tibetan Minority Institute, which I learned had been established in 1957. There were about twenty-five hundred students at the university, almost all Tibetans. My unit, the Department of Education, numbered about five hundred, most of whom were the children of poor peasant families. We did many things together, but of course when we studied we were divided into smaller classes. Mine met on the third floor of the building where the Department of Education was housed. It contained forty Tibetan students in all, about half of them from the Chamdo area, near the border with China in eastern Tibet. They were more literate in Chinese than the rest of us. The other half were mostly from the Tsang area, much closer to my own village, and we were more literate in Tibetan. Everyone in my group was, I found, fairly well prepared compared to many of the other students, some of whom were nearly or completely illiterate. Whatever our background or state of preparation, however, our mission was clear enough. We were there to be trained as teachers and then sent back to Tibet to teach others.

Our days followed a strict routine. The school's sense of discipline and order was like the army's, and in fact I learned that many of the teachers had come from the military before being assigned to the school. On a typical day, we woke up early, washed in a common washroom, and then participated in group exercises. We had three meals a day at the school canteen. Breakfast followed the exercise period, and going to classes followed that. We didn't go from room to room as in America. Once we were assigned to a class, the students belonging to that class stayed in one room—a kind of homeroom—and different teachers came to lecture us at various times. There were teachers who taught Tibetan for those students who needed help learning to read and write their own language. Then we also had to learn Chinese. (It was so important that we learn Chinese quickly that some students—I was one of them—were given private tutors to help speed up the learning process.) There were four classes in the morning from eight to twelve and then we broke for lunch. In the summer we were allowed to rest after lunch until one-thirty, after which we went back to the classroom again, usually for political lessons. This went on until it was near time for dinner.

Adjusting to life in the Tibetan Minority Institute was difficult for me. Coming straight from America, I found the regimentation overpowering and the food and the hygiene poor. The food we ate was coarse and plain—blandly cooked vegetables, rice or steamed buns, and noodles. And we normally drank boiled water rather than tea. The state of the bathrooms also disturbed me. They were foul smelling and never clean. It puzzled me why it didn't seem to bother the others as much as it bothered me. Sometimes I even tried to clean the bathroom up a bit myself, but it was no use. In the end the hardest things to swallow were the political lessons, which were interminable. I realized gradually that the Chinese had a political approach that made studying very different from studying at American universities. Here political ideology was more important than subject matter. There was no such thing as critical thinking and questioning. There was the party line, and it was correct! We were there to learn it, not weigh its utility vis-à-vis other ideologies. Hatred for the old feudal society was continually conveyed, and we were constantly exhorted to value collectivism over individualism and the needs of the group over the needs of the individual. Although this message was repetitive and boring, I accepted that it was necessary to ensure that all the future leaders in Tibet understood the goals and ideas of socialism.

In their way, given the standard of living in China, the Chinese took good care of their potential new crop of teacher-leaders. Counseling services were designed to help these new recruits, many in their late teens and just out of farms and villages. If students were homesick, had to deal with news of difficulty or tragedy at home, or simply began to fail in their courses and become despondent, there were both teachers and student monitors to provide assistance and support.

Each group, in fact, had a special "political monitor." Ours was a Chinese woman named Ma Ximei, who met with us every afternoon. It was her job to control and train our minds ideologically, to make sure our political development went smoothly and correctly. She talked to us about Mao's thoughts. She gave lectures on Communist Party history. Sometimes she would tell us stories about communist martyrs and heroes—people who had fought in the revolution or who had died in battle or serving the cause. As I said, there was never any class discussion or debate as in American schools. Ma Ximei just lectured for what seemed like hours and hours. In some ways this ceaseless political dialogue with endless terminological jargon was simply numbing. But at times it could be surprisingly moving. Sometimes Ma Ximei got so involved in the telling of one of her stories that she began to cry. At these times the students would often begin to cry as well, as if they had picked up her mood by contact. And though I was much older than most of the other students and had traveled the world, I wasn't immune. Sometimes I think I just got caught up psychologically in the group's emotions. But sometimes I found the stories of individuals making great sacrifices on behalf of the people moving, and tears came to my eyes also.

I also had a problem controlling what I said. For example, I remember clearly that once at dinner during my first weeks in Xianyang I said—completely without thinking—that boiled water was harder to get here than milk in America. I really didn't mean it as an insult to socialism; it was just an observation that popped into my head, but the other students responded coldly and incredulously in a way that told me I had made a mistake. Saying good things about America, the great imperialist enemy of the People's Republic of China, was not acceptable, true or not. After a couple of similar mishaps, I realized that open expression of deviant ideas, let alone criticism, was not acceptable in China, and I had to learn to be very careful.

I also found that I had to be careful using some of the material items I had brought with me from America. For example, once when I took my American toilet kit to the common washroom and laid out several American jars of skin cream and hair oil, a student said, "Hey look. Capitalist goods." At first I responded honestly that these were very simple, and nothing compared with what the Americans had. But they immediately rebutted this saying, "Oh, you are siding with America." It was said partly in jest, but it was obvious that it had a serious side. Similarly, although almost all my classmates knew that I had come from America, they seldom if ever asked me about it or my experiences there. It was as if there was an invisible rule disallowing such talk. I guessed that they were afraid that showing too much interest in America might make others suspect their motives.

One of the biggest social adjustments I had to make was how to handle my private life, or more accurately, the lack of privacy and freedom to decide what to do. There always seemed to be people watching what one did and said, and everybody knew everything. Given that I had just come from America, I realized that I was being watched particularly closely. It bothered me a lot at first.

Generally speaking, our social interactions were as highly regimented as any of the other activities. Even though there were both boys and girls at the school, there was no such thing as dating in the Western sense—at least in theory. Of course people are people, and the men and women sometimes got together. But the school had its own ideas about what they should be doing with their evenings, and that was studying political ideology. Sometimes Ma Ximei would have evening meetings at her house during the week to which students of both sexes were encouraged to come for political discussion. Couples were also allowed to pair off for intimate consultation and discussion, but the idea was that they would be exchanging political opinions and solving hypothetical problems in the approved way. There were weekly lectures given at the Department of Education, and there were movies every Saturday evening that you had to attend, too. But they were always in Chinese and always full of politics. You never got away from it.

There was another regular activity that by comparison made the routine of the dormitory and the classroom seem pleasant and easy. It was called "labor transformation." What it meant was that periodically we all had to go and work in the fields on nearby farms. It was party policy that even—perhaps especially—groups like teachers and intellectuals should engage in good, hard manual labor. The idea was that this "labor" helped "transform" such people by increasing their understanding and sympathy for the proletariat and decreasing their sense of social distance from them. It was also supposed to humiliate the more intellectual types by reminding them who and what were really important! It all made sense in theory, although it turned out to be very hard for me in practice. Several times a year we were sent to villages for a work stint of a few weeks, usually in June for the early weeding and irrigation and then once again toward the end of September for harvest. And we were sometimes sent back to support the farm laborers in the winter. The school made all the arrangements and then told us when and where we were going. Most times the whole five hundred of us in the Education Department went.

We had plenty of work to do because though the soil in the region was rich, there was never enough water. Irrigation was a constant problem, and the wells were extremely deep. Often you had to lower a bucket 50 feet before you could fill it and bring it back. I never really felt comfortable. During the first summer I remember I tried wearing some of the clothes I had brought from Cuba, and the other students got a good laugh at the way I looked. And those of us who weren't from farms provided quite a sight as we learned to use common tools. I remember that the peasants of the region used a particular kind of sickle to harvest the wheat. It was a clean, powerful instrument if you knew what you were doing, but it was by no means easy to master. I had a lot of trouble getting the hang of it, and I'm not sure I ever did. In the winter we were sometimes sent out to help with projects, but we didn't stay at the site. We would leave early in the morning and return to the school the same evening. I remember these excursions mainly because the weather was often freezing cold and we had to hack at the frozen ground with shovels and pickaxes. Not only was the work hard but the living conditions were harsh as well. When we worked at the farms we all slept together in large barns or in what they called "community houses." The food the peasants ate was scarcer, coarser, and more primitive than anything we had to eat at the institute. It made me realize that, relatively speaking, we were eating well in school.

All in all, during my first year the "labor transformation" stints were the hardest things I had to deal with. They exhausted me, but I never got discouraged. I felt that this period was simply a passing stage I had to go through to achieve my goal of going back to Tibet. I considered being a student at the Minority Institute a wonderful opportunity to learn the skills that would help me become a part of the great revolutionary wave that was going to transform Tibet as well as China. So despite the physical and psychological hardships, I was thrilled to be studying at an elite institute that was preparing the future leaders of Tibet. The plan was that our class would graduate in 1967, so I worked as hard as I could to succeed in my studies and graduate with it.

At one point during this time my confidence in things in general was temporarily shaken by some startling news from home. I had had no communication with my family since the Lhasa Uprising in 1959 and so was surprised to get a letter from them here at the school. When I read the contents, I was stunned. My parents had been denounced as reactionaries. Their property had been confiscated, and they had been sent to Mani, a small nunnery not far from our village, with just a few basic utensils and clothes. They were in permanent exile now, with just enough land to exist on.

Their troubles had begun because of a foolish act of my second brother. From my father's letter I learned that when I sent my second brother back from India in 1958, he kept the handgun I had asked him to return to Wangdula and hid it in our village. At some point, the Chinese found the gun and accused him of being a reactionary counterrevolutionary. That was all the opportunity my old enemy Dorje Tseden needed. He was still smarting under the embarrassment of the beating I had given him years ago and the court's decision that hadn't gone in his favor. He had lost a good deal of face in the local area because the affair was so notorious. (I still meet elderly people from the area who remember the trial and the events that led up to it!) Now it was his chance to get revenge, and he took it. At a political meeting in our village called a "struggle session," Dorje arranged for others to denounce—struggle against—my parents and family for crimes against the revolution. Dorje himself dragged my mother around by the hair, pulling her by her braids, as a result of which she suffered from back trouble until her death in 1992. Dorje also abused my father. I was shocked to learn of these events. The thought of what my parents must have endured made me sad and furious, especially because I was so far away and powerless to do anything.

At the time, however, I saw my parents' sufferings as an isolated incident, more a personal problem than a portent of things to come. Even though my heart ached whenever I thought of them being beaten and humiliated, and I was frustrated by my inability to go to them or help them directly, I didn't connect what happened to them with anything that might happen to me. My second brother had been foolish to keep the gun, and my parents had to pay for it. At the moment, there was nothing I could do. Later, when I returned to Tibet, I swore I would try to right the wrong. So I went back to my studies and tried to put these events out of my mind. Little did I realize that a year later there would be struggle sessions in my own school.

8

At the beginning of 1966, I was feeling quite comfortable and optimistic about my new life because things seemed to be working out more or less as I'd hoped, despite the physical difficulties. However, unbeknownst to me, a major conflict was erupting within the highest circles of the Chinese Communist Party that would reach out and touch my life far sooner and more directly than I could ever have imagined.

My classmates and I didn't become aware of the size and ferocity of the gathering storm until the summer of 1966, when we began to hear a great deal about a campaign called the "Great Proletarian Cultural Revolution" in which students in Beijing were playing a major role. Mao Zedong felt that the Chinese communist revolution was in danger of stalling and stagnating because many government officials running it still harbored old prerevolutionary values and attitudes and were passing these on to the youth who would become China's future revolutionary leaders. Mao, therefore, launched what he called a Great Proletarian Cultural Revolution to smash those in authority and replace the old ideas and attitudes they held with a new proletarian culture. It became the duty of the proletarian class, particularly the young students who were not yet indoctrinated into the old values and culture, to smash all remnants of bourgeois thinking in the government and in intellectual and cultural spheres such as art, education, and literature.

Such class struggle was to be the engine that drove the revolution onward. Of course, we now know that Mao also was locked in a serious contest with other top leaders for control of the Communist Party and that the Cultural Revolution was part of his strategy to destroy his enemies, but at the time, my fellow students and I took it at face value. There were hidden "capitalist roaders" lurking in institutions and offices and hindering progress, and it was our task to uncover them and bring them down.

I never felt in danger myself. While it was true that I had been a clerk in the old regime and had lived and studied in India and America, I was not really a part of any old ruling elite, and I was certainly not someone in authority. The people who were being singled out were lifetime bureaucrats, senior officials, senior teachers, and administrators. I was a peasant from a mountain village in Tibet. Mao's call was not for action against people like me. Moreover, I was highly critical of the old feudal society and genuinely wanted revolutionary change. I became caught up in the enthusiasm of the hour as fully as any of my classmates.

We started to hear that students in Beijing were putting up huge posters that criticized the leaders of the university and demanding that hidden enemies of the revolution—colorfully called "ghosts" and "monsters"—be destroyed. And in August, Mao himself wrote that it was necessary to "Bombard the General Headquarters," and "Learn Revolution by Making Revolution." Soon the Beijing student disruptions and attacks on those in authority began to spread to other cities, and we heard about these events on the radio and in newspapers. Every day the school broadcast the Beijing news loudly over the public address system so the word quickly spread all over the campus. In my case, I also had a small shortwave radio that I had obtained in a trade for a Swiss watch I had brought from America, so I listened avidly to the reports of each new exploit.

Like other students, I found the reports from Beijing amazing and hard to imagine fully. The idea of students turning on their teachers and other authority figures seemed almost unthinkable, given my experience with the hierarchy and regimentation of life in Xianyang. But precisely because it was so unthinkable it was also exciting. Students like me were in the vanguard of continuing the revolution in China! I guess it appealed to my romantic sense of myself as a radical and revolutionary, even though I still couldn't see how these powerful political movements in the big cities could directly affect us here. There were no bourgeois counterrevolutionaries at Xianyang, no enemies of the state that I knew of. Everyone I knew seemed totally committed to the revolution.

All that changed dramatically one sweltering night in late June. I was sitting in my dorm with the windows and door wide open, carefully practicing my Chinese characters and trying to keep cool. At about nine or ten, I heard unusual shouting, and ran outside to see if I could find out what was going on. I was amazed to see students from all over the campus walking quickly toward our large soccer field where the lights were shining brightly. I joined them, curious to learn what was going on, and as I neared the field I could see that hundreds of students had already gathered there and more were streaming in every moment.

The sight at the sports field was astounding. A large brightly lighted stage had been set up, and on it were forty of our school's most important teachers and administrators, including Wang Jingzhi, the president of the institute. I pushed toward the front to get a better view and soon realized that this was not some standard political lecture. The leaders of our school were standing there hunched over, each adorned with a tall conical paper hat filled with large characters spouting derisive labels like "Capitalist Roader" or "Counterrevolutionary." Twenty or so student activists, almost all of whom were Tibetans, were controlling them. I later learned that these students had orchestrated the entire demonstration because they felt that it was time for our school to heed Chairman Mao's appeal to "make revolution."

It was unbelievable seeing the leaders of our school standing humbly with their heads bowed listening to what seemed like thousands of voices screaming slogans and mocking them. Sometimes the student activists would walk right up to one of these "hidden enemies," stand very close, and shout derisive slogans in his or her face. One student, for example, would jump up on the platform and scream, "Down with Mr. Wang who is leading us on the capitalist road." Another would say, "We are defending Mao's thoughts," or "We are the vanguard of Mao's proletarian line and the driving force in Mao's Great Cultural Revolution." The students leading the demonstration were utterly sure of themselves and strutted around the platform like victorious gladiators, completely confident about what they were doing. In a single moment our school's world had been turned upside down. The students now lorded over the teachers. They thought it was natural and right for them to be the ones to revolutionize their elders. All the students, myself included, collectively savored the emotion and power of this first act of "making revolution," although I still found it hard to believe that these leaders were all really capitalist roaders.

The struggle session—that's what it was called—broke up after an hour or so, at which time we students led the subjects in a degrading procession around the campus. One of the things that made the most vivid impression on me was that even Ma Ximei, our class's political ideology teacher, was made to beat a big drum in front of her and chant, "I am Ma Ximei, and I committed mistakes in my political teaching." At this time, none of the "authorities" was actually detained; they were all permitted to return to their homes. And yet it was clear to everyone that the Cultural Revolution was now here—not in Shanghai but in Xianyang, not at some vague future date, but now. For us at the institute, that amazing night was the beginning of a decade of chaos and destruction.

From the next day onward our school ceased to function as an institute of learning in any ordinary sense. We spent our time making revolution—writing slogans, planning more struggle sessions, and putting up huge posters all over campus. In my class of about fifty students, a few activists did all of the planning and the rest of us helped put the plans into practice.

During the next few months I attended many more struggle sessions, and all of us were engaged in what we called "digging in." To carry out class struggle, you needed both revolutionaries and "objects of revolution" against whom to battle. "Digging in" meant digging more deeply into the backgrounds of individuals suspected of being antirevolutionary. In our institute, the most obvious potential "objects of revolution" were the older individuals, the senior administrators and teachers who were raised in the old society. We poured over any information we could find about their backgrounds in their otherwise secret personnel files, trying to uncover evidence of their past involvements with the antirevolutionary Guomindang government of Chiang Kai-shek or any other form of exploitative activity. And students searched their memories for suspect comments and criticisms that teachers had made in the past. These were reported to the student activists and examined closely to see if they contained any evidence of counterrevolutionary sympathies.

I was not a member of the student leadership, but I participated. I am ashamed of that now, but, to be honest, at the time I identified totally with the students and Mao's cause. I felt that if Chairman Mao had called on us to be the vanguard of the revolution, then we should respond, and I did whatever I could to prevent the revolution stagnating as Mao had warned. Mostly my activities involved lugging around an iron bucket filled with paste and sticking up the revolutionary posters that seemed to shout slogans from every wall. I also volunteered for work in the kitchen. Others whose Chinese calligraphy was especially good wrote the striking red or black characters on the posters, and the activist leaders spent most of their time planning new strategies and demonstrations and opening lines of communication with other schools and work units engaged in similar revolutionary activities.

And we began to engage in what was called "revolutionary learning." This activity involved students traveling to other regions of the country to share experiences and learn from one another. Sometimes individual students and sometimes entire schools packed up and went on the road. The most popular location for such trips was Beijing, where Mao himself occasionally gave mass audiences. Individual students who wished to make such "revolutionary trips" could do so quite readily in the new climate of the Cultural Revolution. All they needed were ration coupons for the period they would be gone, which they could easily obtain from the school's Food Requisition Office. Nobody at our institute—or in similar situations elsewhere—dared to forbid travel or to try to tell the students what to do, because that could be taken as a sign of counterrevolutionary thinking. By now, the proletarian students were running the show and made their own decisions.

In early September it was our turn to board the trains and go to see Mao. In Beijing we stayed at the National Minorities Institute, living for a week in tents which we had brought with us from Xianyang. We created a gigantic tent city in the midst of their institute. Along with all the other students, I was extremely excited. I was not a fully accepted Red Guard in the sense that I was not permitted to wear the red armband, but I felt that I was a good revolutionary and as fully committed to Mao and the party line as any of my classmates. Therefore, it came as a shock when the two student activist leaders of my class—both of whom were Tibetan—told me on the day before our scheduled mass audience that I would not be permitted to accompany the rest of the students to Tiananmen Square to see Mao. They didn't accuse me of any counterrevolutionary activities; they simply said it wasn't appropriate for me to go. I was furious because I thought I had very obviously demonstrated that my sympathies were with the revolution and my loyalty was beyond question. Hadn't I given up an easy life in America to serve my people and country? I had worked hard since coming to the institute and did not deserve to be publicly singled out as not worthy enough to see Chairman Mao. It was unjust. It's hard to imagine now that I really felt that way, but at that time, being accepted by the mass of revolutionary students and joining the audience to see Mao were extremely important to me. And I did something about it.

I first tried to persuade the activists that I should be allowed to go, arguing that I had nothing to do with the exploitation of the old society and in fact was a victim of its exploitation. I reminded them that I was from a peasant family and had been compelled to go to Lhasa as a feudal tax. I also tried to convince them that I loved Chairman Mao and his socialist system and that I had every right to be allowed to see him when my classmates did. I used to refer to Mao as "Comrade Mao" rather than "Chairman Mao," because I really thought of him as a friend and comrade in a common struggle. But all my efforts were to no avail. The student leaders let me have my say, but in the end they just stared at me impassively, shook their heads, and told me once again that they had decided that it was not appropriate for me to go. That was all they would say.

I have always had a stubborn streak, and I was so angry at their stony refusal that I did something rather risky. All over China, new administrative offices called "Revolutionary Committees" had been created, and I knew that there was one for the Beijing National Minorities Institute where we were staying. I decided to go over the heads of the student leaders and plead my case there, and I told the activists I was leaving to do that. They were shocked and told me that was impossible, but I was really angry and stormed out saying that I was going whether they liked it or not. When they saw they couldn't stop me, one of them followed me all the way to the office.

The head of the Revolutionary Committee was very gracious and invited me to tell him my story. I did so with the student activist sitting in the same room listening in stony silence. I talked for some time, emphasizing my early days as a tax recruit to the Dalai Lama's dance troupe and the fact that although it was true that I had lived in America, I had rejected the views of the Tibetans in exile and returned to

China. I talked about how hard I had worked since I had come to China, how deep my commitment was, and how loyal I had always been. I was, I told him, a good and dedicated revolutionary who should be permitted to see Chairman Mao. The student activist scowled at me angrily the whole time, but he had nothing of any substance to add to the discussion as no one was charging me with any crime or concrete act of disloyalty. I really must have been quite emotional because I talked nonstop for about an hour. Finally the officer from the Revolutionary Committee raised his hand to stop further discussion. He looked directly at the student activist and said, "It is all right. Let him go. It doesn't matter. It doesn't matter." I was exultant and felt totally vindicated.

Our audience with Chairman Mao was scheduled for the following morning, and I was so energized by my success that I had trouble sleeping. We were all excited, but I think I was even more so because of the difficulty I had to overcome. We got up before sunrise, between four and five, even before the birds were stirring. The air was cool when we lined up for our march to Tiananmen Square, which was about 15 miles from where we were staying. It took us between four and five hours to reach the square, but I don't think any of us was aware of the time or distance. We knew, of course, that we weren't actually having an audience with Mao alone and that there would be many other students from all over China (official figures later placed the total that day at 1.5 million). We would see Mao only at a distance. But to us he was the guiding force behind the revolution, and even a distant glimpse of the man himself was a great honor.

We didn't arrive at the square until between nine and ten o'clock. I still remember how struck I was by the immensity of it and the sight of so many tens of thousands of students in rank order waiting patiently like us. As one group finished another would begin to march past the high balcony on which Mao stood, and we all had a sense of being part of a vast, unified endeavor. When they told us it was our turn, we marched proudly beneath the chairman's gaze, holding and waving the little red book of his writings and shouting revolutionary slogans like "Long Live Chairman Mao." He had a distinctive silhouette and was relatively tall, so he stood out prominently on the reviewing stand. His steady gaze passed over wave after wave of chanting students, but I honestly had the feeling that he looked right at us—right at me—when we passed. And so it didn't matter that we could get no closer to him.

He had noticed us; we were part of his revolution. I remember being highly conscious of the drama of the moment, of the fact that I was in the heart of the new China, playing an important part in the creation of a new order. This was why I had returned to my homeland. I didn't ask, but I think all of us felt much the same way.

The next morning we returned to Xianyang, and for the rest of 1966 we continued to pursue the Cultural Revolution in our own school and surrounding areas. Then, near the end of the year, the decision was made that our school should go to Lhasa to share our revolutionary experiences with Tibetans there. We knew that the Cultural Revolution had already begun in Lhasa because individual students from our school had already made revolutionary visits and reported back to us. I was overjoyed both to be going home and to be going as a part of the revolutionary vanguard.

We had received permission from the military headquarters in Lhasa and made preparations for several thousand of us to depart. We traveled by train from Xianyang to Lanzhou and then to Golmud, the last train stop on the northern route to Lhasa. From there we drove south to Lhasa in military trucks, a journey that took about seven days.

It was December and the road from Golmud traversed Tibet's vast Northern Plateau, an area that averaged more than 16,000 feet in elevation, so it was freezing in the open trucks. We traveled all day, stopping each night at military truck stops, where we got food, fuel, and lodging. Then, as soon as it was light again, we rumbled on. On the seventh day we reached Lhasa in the late afternoon, the golden roof of the Potala Palace glittering over the valley as it had when I had departed a decade ago.

Because the size of our group was so large we divided into two sections, one group (mine) staying at the guesthouse at what had been the Ramoche Temple, the others in Kundeling, in what had been the monastery of a famous Tibetan lama. Not long after we arrived, General Zhang Guohua, the leading Chinese official, came to see us at the guesthouse. He welcomed us warmly, telling us that we were the pioneers of the Cultural Revolution. "You are," he said, "the best vanguard, the Red Guards who are defending Mao Zedong and his views." I was impressed by how seriously he was taking us and struck by how many different things can happen in one person's lifetime. I had first come to Lhasa nearly twenty-five years ago as a dancer for the Dalai Lama, and now here I was back in Tibet but this time part of a vast national movement committed to sweeping away all vestiges of the very society I had once served. If anyone had tried to tell me that such things were going to happen when I was a youth, I would have told him he was crazy! And yet, here I was.

We stayed in Lhasa for four or five months, from December 1966 till sometime in March 1967. A decade had passed since I left Lhasa for India, and a great deal had changed. As I initially looked around, I was struck by the many new houses, buildings, and roads. The size and scope of Lhasa had increased dramatically. I was particularly impressed with the many trees lining the highways, and thought this was a wonderful addition. However, I quickly learned that physical changes weren't the whole story.

I still had friends in Lhasa, and when I went to see them I got quite a different picture. One of the biggest changes in the city itself was the absence of the lively central market. There was nothing for sale on the streets any more. Gone were the cramped booths heaped full of wares, the voices of salesmen and customers laughing and haggling, and the many tea and beer shops I used to frequent. In their place were a few poorly stocked government stores.

It also soon became clear that the people weren't very well fed, either. Food was rationed, and there was almost no meat or butter or potatoes. I had lived in the old Lhasa for many years and was under no illusions about its shortcomings. However, there had always been a lot of food, and if you had any money to spend at all you had quite a bit of freedom and choice. Now the food was rationed at low levels. Each month people got 1.1 pounds of butter and 26.5 pounds of our staple tsamba—and not very good quality tsamba at that. In addition, they got only a small ration of flour. One could subsist on this, but not well.

Perhaps the most striking difference I saw was that people in general seemed dispirited and sullen. They appeared forlorn, as if they had just lost a close friend or relative. And on a more personal level, I was shocked by the fate of one of my closest friends from the old days. Söpela had been one of the early Tibetan "progressives." He was a clerk in the old government who, like me, did not like the old feudal system and had long dreamed of a modern Tibet without serfdom and class exploitation. He joined the new Tibetan Youth League and became an early activist, encouraging others to attend meetings and dances and to keep an open mind to reforming Tibet. I had gone along to some of the youth affairs with him and found them fun. At that time there were no such things as social dances and the like, so these activities were all new and exciting. Söpela soon thereafter went to study in Beijing and excelled in Chinese in addition to his Tibetan.

A few days after we arrived and settled in, I decided to visit Söpela. When I neared his house, I saw him outside on the street. Spontaneously, I ran over and threw my arms around him. But nothing happened. He didn't reciprocate. He sort of just stood there limply, his eyes cast down and a frightened look on his face. Even though I was hugging him he seemed to be pretending I wasn't there. For a minute I couldn't figure out what was going on and didn't know what to do. Then I looked around and realized we weren't alone. When I had first spied him, he was all I saw. Now I saw that he had a member of the Lhasa Red Guards with him, and this meant that he had become a "revolutionary object of struggle" and was under the "supervision of the masses." He said virtually nothing and seemed terribly ill at ease, and since I feared that just by my presence I was making things worse for him, I quickly concluded our meeting, saying something brief and noncommittal—"good to see you," "I have to go now"—and moved on.

As I walked away, keeping my own eyes on the ground directly in front of me, I was genuinely confused. How could someone who had been such an activist and advocate of change have become the object of the current revolution? I thought there had to be a mistake. I learned, however, that what had happened to Söpela had happened to some of my other friends who had also been activists during those early years. This news puzzled and bothered me deeply. But when I gradually calmed down and thought about it, I realized (or perhaps rationalized) that they had become mid-level officials and thus fit the model of targets for the Cultural Revolution in the sense that they were people in authority who grew up in the old society and were likely to be hidden capitalist roaders. But I never believed that Söpela was an enemy of the revolution; he was a true modern Tibetan, and it was sad to see him broken like that. (I should add, happily, that Söpela survived the Cultural Revolution and became an important official after the reform policies of Deng Xiaoping were implemented in 1978.)

I also met a woman who used to be a friend in the old days. Her name was Sangyela, and she would in fact later become my wife. She was also upset and unhappy with life in Lhasa. By all rights, Sangyela was in no danger of being struggled against because she was definitely from the proletarian class, but she was also extremely religious and hated the government for closing the monasteries and prohibiting all religion, even in your own home. If a neighbor or cadre found out you were still practicing religion and reported you, you would be brought before the masses and struggled against, for the goal of the Cultural Revolution was to eradicate all remnants of old values, customs, and beliefs. But we Tibetans are a stubborn people, and many Tibetans from all classes and backgrounds risked punishment and struggle sessions by secretly saying prayers in their homes or by circumambulating holy temples as if they were just on a stroll, all the while whispering silent prayers. Sangyela was one of these. In her case, she went so far as to continue to burn butter lamps as offerings to the gods. She would save small amounts of butter from her scanty monthly ration and use it to light a small butter lamp which she placed inside the cabinet that used to be her altar (behind its closed doors) rather than on top, as was normally done. When she told me this, all I could think about was the danger of setting the whole house on fire by leaving a burning lamp inside the old, dry wooden cabinet. She laughed when I implored her to stop and paid no attention to my warnings about safety. Her religion was everything to her. I was surprised to be so vividly reminded of how religious—and, to be honest, I really thought superstitious—my countrymen could be. But I said nothing further about it.

The more opportunities I had to talk to old friends in Lhasa, the more dissatisfaction I encountered. The general feeling was that the relatively liberal Chinese policies of the 1950s had been a sort of honeymoon that had ended abruptly with the 1959 Lhasa Uprising. One person sarcastically explained what happened with an analogy. The party's policies, he said, were like a wet leather hat: at first when wet, the hat feels comfortable, but as it dries, it contracts and becomes painful.

It was also deflating to have friends ask me incredulously why I had left America and come home. At this point most of them wanted to get out, and they kept asking me, "Why did you come?" "What is the matter with you?" These were hard questions coming as they did so unexpectedly and from such a surprising source, and I didn't feel I could tell them I came back to help Tibet in a way that would make sense to them, so I usually didn't answer such questions. I was genuinely taken aback by what I was seeing and hearing, and conflicting feelings pulled me in several directions at once. I hadn't expected to see and hear anything like I was encountering. The fear and depression and the general poverty of conditions couldn't be denied. And in the current climate of opinion, there was no one among my comrades at the school to whom I could talk to about my doubts and concerns. The way things were now, if I dared to show any sympathy for my old friends or seemed to take their complaints to heart, I was in danger of being branded as an enemy of the revolution. I had to keep everything bottled up inside.

Unlike most of the students I knew, I didn't see things simply. To most of them—who were young, full of revolutionary zeal, and without much knowledge of life beyond their towns or villages—things were either black or white. Issues were clear-cut, the basis for their decisions unambiguous and seldom if ever examined. I was older, more educated, and had my own concept of change before I even decided to come back. When I said to myself that change had to occur, I didn't mean that everything that made up Tibetan culture had to be destroyed. I thought that improvements in hygiene, health care, and other services could and should be made as soon as possible. Tibet was a very backward country compared to more developed nations. I thought that the sooner we could improve the quality of life in these areas, the better. I felt strongly, too, that as a country Tibet should value education more—especially education for ordinary people. I didn't like the idea that all children would have to struggle as I had just to learn to read and write in their native language. I didn't see how we could move ahead into the modern world without a basically literate population. I also felt strongly that it was critical for the state to be separate from the church—at least in the political sense. In the old society about 15 percent of the total population were monks who were not engaged in producing anything. They relied on society to support them. I hoped there would come a time when monks would be self-sufficient and productive, and I totally favored a system in which there would be far fewer monks, but the quality and ability of each one would be higher.

But I also thought that there was such a thing as going too far. For instance, the example of Sangyela's strong and simple faith had touched me. I am not religious, and, as I have said, I supported fairly sweeping reforms of religion in Tibet. But I didn't think religion should be totally destroyed or forbidden. Abuse of the power of the monks is one thing, but the comfort and support people derive from their faith is another. I didn't see why it had to be either or. Similarly, I disapproved of the destruction of the ancient statues and religious texts. I didn't see what the revolution gained by destroying these things. They were already in existence, so why not just let them alone?

Perhaps more important, while I supported the idea that older people in power should be struggled against to cleanse the system of the old ways of thinking, I felt that the process was becoming much too indiscriminate. I couldn't get the example of my old friend Söpela out of my mind. I couldn't help thinking that the only reason he was singled out was that he was vulnerable—and perhaps because to keep its momentum the revolution had constantly to find new victims. Yes, Söpela had worked for the government in the old society. But they obviously didn't know him at all. He wasn't antirevolutionary. He was just in the wrong place at the wrong time.

Despite all these doubts and disagreements, however, I still identified with the students and was on the side of the new activism. I have discussed these events and my ambivalent reactions many times since with various foreign friends, and they always ask the same question: "Tashi, you are obviously a good nationalistic Tibetan who loves your culture and people. How could you be a Red Guard?" I have thought about that question many times and the answer is always the same. Like so many others, I felt that Mao's fundamental ideas would be good for Tibet. I believed that in order to create a truly modern society based on socialist, egalitarian principles we first had to root out those in authority who were secretly against the revolution. In retrospect, I think this line of thinking allowed me and many other Tibetan and Chinese students to rationalize the excesses and wrongs we saw as unfortunate side effects of a vitally important political movement. Although I was never fully accepted as a Red Guard, in my own mind I felt I had a pure revolutionary spirit and enthusiasm, and I worked to further the Red Guards' goals. Seeing the changes in Lhasa and the lives of her people had shocked me and sown deep doubts, and I spent endless hours in the quiet of the night thinking about these issues and trying to evaluate their significance. But in the end, I continued to be full of zeal for the revolution. And I was not alone. Tibet was full of Tibetan Red Guards and revolutionary activists, and, to be perfectly honest, I was proud to be a part of that movement. We were creating a new and more equitable proletarian culture in China and Tibet for the well-being of all Tibetans and Chinese. Or so we thought. How ironic considering what was about to happen.

9

The date was October 13, 1967. There was no warning.

The morning went normally enough, and after lunch I went to our regular afternoon meeting where political ideas and issues were discussed. I had just sat down, when the class activist sitting next to me suddenly stood up. In a loud, clear voice he said, "I suggest the anti-revolutionary Tashi Tsering be isolated from the people and placed under supervision." I couldn't believe my ears.

Obviously the whole thing had been planned well in advance. Even before the student who denounced me had finished speaking two others stood up and began to move toward me. A third ran out of the room and returned almost immediately with a slate blackboard with the words "Down with the counterrevolutionary Tashi Tsering" written in bold letters. While I stared at the blackboard, the two students who had been moving toward me took me forcefully by the elbows and marched me to an empty space near the front of the room. They forced me to my knees and pushed my head down so they could hang the blackboard around my neck. When the blackboard was in place my nightmare began.

In moments of trauma and crisis our minds race at amazing speed. As they were pressing my head down to receive the slogan-filled blackboard, my imagination began to play out the events of the past year, trying to see how I had been so blind to the possibility of what was now happening. People were yelling epithets all around me, but all

113

I could think of was my belief that I had done everything I was supposed to do and was not a counterrevolutionary. How could they be
accusing me? I couldn't get past that question.

The weight of the blackboard and the shouting forcibly returned me
to the present moment. The whole class left the classroom, pushing me
ahead of them. As they marched me around the campus, students from
other classes began to pour outside to see the new enemy of the revolution, and quickly a substantial crowd gathered for what was to be my
first struggle session. In the span of a moment, I had been transformed
from an agent to an object of revolution.

All eyes were on me when one of the class leaders raised his fist and
began to chant: "Down with the counterrevolutionary Tashi Tsering!
Down with the traitor to the Motherland." The crowd, numbering in
the hundreds, roared back, "Down with Tashi Tsering, remnant of the
big three exploiters."

The struggle session lasted several hours, but it was all a blur as one
student after another came up and accused me of this and that, dredg-
ing up things I had said even casually or as a joke. For example, one
female student from southwest Tibet screamed at me inches from my
face that I had slandered the People's Republic of China by saying
during a class a year earlier that there were so many people in China
that it was like an ant's nest. The Chinese people, she yelled, were not
ants, and this statement was proof of my counterrevolutionary views. I
tried to answer truthfully, to explain what I meant, but my effort only
seemed to make matters worse as students got more angry and accused
me of being stubborn and obstinate. Some took glee in physically
forcing me to bow at the waist every time the pain got too bad and I
tried to ease up a bit. They made sure that I was kept standing bent
over at the waist—that was the required style. I honestly don't know
how long I stood that way, but after what seemed like a full day it was
finally over and I was marched back toward the classroom. The real
struggle was to follow.

I was placed in what had been a storeroom, just adjacent to the
dorms. It was about three yards square and had nothing in it but two
crude wooden beds. While I was being taken there, other activists
searched my room thoroughly and took everything I owned, all my
clothes and possessions plus my suitcases that were in storage, and
even my watch and wallet. I had brought diaries and letters from my
years in America, and all these I later learned were carefully translated

into Chinese. Other students stayed with me and searched me thoroughly; in fact, the school doctor even looked into my anus. I was in a daze, unable to understand why they were doing all this to me. I had returned from a comfortable life in America to serve my people and here they were looking into my anus for God knows what. I don't think I ever felt so vulnerable and insignificant.

From then on, my every move was monitored by students every hour of the day. Someone watched me when I slept, when I went to the cafeteria, and even when I went to the bathroom. Normally, they didn't talk to me, just watched. And for the first full week I was humiliated before the students by being made to stand at the front of the cafeteria at meal times wearing a blackboard around my neck that proclaimed my crimes against the state. I ate only when the other students had finished.

That first night I could not sleep because I was so frightened and angry. I kept thinking about what I had done wrong to bring this on, and how I could have avoided it. The thought of being sent to prison—which I had heard meant terrible suffering—was more than I could contemplate. How should I act to avoid imprisonment? Thoughts popped into consciousness as if my mind had started to operate independent of me. And several times as I started to doze off, I had a terrible nightmare of a horse jumping on top of me, crushing me to death. It was horrible. I was so frightened that I began to think that the only answer for me was to make a run for the adjacent railway station and lie down on the track as a train arrived.

The next morning, after breakfast, my real interrogation began. Six or seven student activists came accompanied by an older Chinese textile worker named Mr. Chen and our political ideology teacher, Ma Ximei. They were the team that would handle me. Mr. Chen turned out to be a skilled interrogator, and my main adversary. I had been separated from the people but my "crimes" were not yet decided, so the goal of the interrogation was to get me to confess to the crimes they believed I had committed. The process was like squeezing toothpaste. That's how we sometimes described it. The substance was all there in the tube, but would not come out until somebody gave it a good squeeze. That morning the squeezing began. It lasted continuously for about forty-five days.

I was seated on a stool in the center of the interrogators, and they began by asking me if I knew why I was picked out. When I said no,

Mr. Chen said, "Oh, I don't think that's true. I think you know very well." I was nervous and unsure how to respond since I knew that there was a fine line between being totally obstinate—that is, admitting nothing—and being too cooperative and confessing to "crimes" the interrogators didn't even know about. One could survive this process, I knew. President Wang, the head of our institute, for example, had been released back to society because the students finally concluded that his attitude was positive and revolutionary. On the other hand, one of the vice-principals was ruthlessly struggled against for a long time because he was labeled "stubborn" and hostile toward the Cultural Revolution: he had insisted day after day that he had committed no crimes, that he had served the party loyally since he was a youth.

At first, I decided to tell the truth, and not to make up lies just to please them. I also would not admit that there was anything wrong with what I had done, so I answered Chen, "Yes, I do not know why I am here." Ma Ximei and the others had worked on my case carefully, and Chen was immediately ready with key questions from my earlier years. "Who sent you from Lhasa to India?" he asked, starting a whole line of questioning on this part of my life. What had I done there, who helped me there? Again and again he hammered away at me, first moving one way, then another, and then back to the first in a slightly different context. I didn't want to say I went mainly to study English, so I said I went to do business and see religious sites. But no matter what I answered they didn't believe me, and there seemed to be no end of difficult new questions. For example, they made a big deal about the fact that other young Tibetans who were supportive of socialism went to study in China and joined youth groups, and even the reactionary aristocrats brought their children back from school in India to Lhasa, but I had done exactly the opposite by going to imperialist India for years. Now wasn't that peculiar? Why was that? Did you not like to live in China? Were you opposed to our society? That day the interrogation jumped around a lot—or so it seemed—but came back to three main questions: Who sent me to India? Who sent me to America? And who sent me back to China? They saw my movements as too incredible to be just a coincidence. There had to be a deeper, more sinister explanation, and they were adamant about ferreting it out of me.

I said truthfully that nobody had sent me anywhere, that I went on my own. I started explaining how I raised the money I needed through trading, but Mr. Chen quietly interrupted to lecture me on the party's line regarding such interrogations: "Tashi, we examined your behavior and we have suspected you for some time. That's why we picked you up. You are now under the dictatorship of the proletariat. Chairman Mao gives you an opportunity to become a proletarian intellectual and serve the people's interests, but you must tell the truth and transform your old thoughts and ideas. If you resist cleansing your dirty mind, refuse to report your previous crimes, and do not expose your criminal partners in crime, we will show no mercy. The party's policy is that those who collaborate with us are treated with leniency; those who are stubborn and do not cooperate, we send to prison or a labor camp. So please tell us everything. We know what you have done very well, but it is up to you to confess and repent."

Day after day, they hammered away at me, asking endless questions: What kind of papers did I travel on? Who helped me find a British teacher? How did I pay for the expenses? What was my goal? What work did I do? As the days turned into weeks, I began to falter. They were very good at interrogation—at squeezing out toothpaste.

No matter what I answered, my interrogators wouldn't believe that I could have taken all the steps necessary to go to India and America on my own. While they had no proof the Dalai Lama sent me to India or that the United States was behind me, they pushed hard, trying to use logic to destroy my presentations. Sometimes these sessions were mild, and the interrogators simply tried to coax me to cooperate. But sometimes they would yell at me and threaten me with prison and so forth if I persisted in being obstinate. And all the time I thought over and over about what I should say. Should I tell them 100 percent, or should I leave out some things I felt they couldn't possibly know? Gradually, I began to admit "small" mistakes such as going to India rather than China or comparing China unfavorably with the United States—comparing the abundance of milk in the United States, for example, to the shortage of boiled water in China. Often I blamed capitalist influences that had invidiously affected my thinking, since I thought they would accept this explanation. But all the time I refused to accept blame for any serious crimes. Then toward the start of the third week of nonstop interrogation, as they led me once again through my years in India in great detail, I decided to tell them truthfully about how I had worked for Gyalo Thondrup, the Dalai Lama's older brother, and how he had sent me to Assam to interview newly arrived Tibetan refugees in 1959 just after the Lhasa Uprising. Since these accounts had ended up being the basis for the International Commission of Jurists' scathing report on Chinese aggression and atrocities in Tibet, I knew this admission was a risk, but I thought it was better to be frank and try to downplay my role as just that of a lowly worker (which was true). But it was a dreadful mistake. They rejoiced in this information and used it as proof that I was an advocate of Tibetan independence, a serious crime. I should never have told them about this work; they didn't know and probably would never have found out. But I wasn't sure and was too afraid to lie.

And so it went, day after endless day enduring tough interrogation sessions, each of which was followed by writing accounts of my life history in the evening—all the things I had done against the people, against the state, and against the revolution. During this period I was totally isolated and spoke to no one except the guards and interrogators. Usually these interrogation sessions were not violent, but sometimes a student would become abusive and pull my hair or kick or slap me around. I was miserable and sad and frightened all at once.

But no matter how many questions they asked, I refused to admit that I had been "sent" to America or that I was working for anyone when I returned. I insisted I came back of my own free will to serve the people. One day, about three weeks after the interrogations started, the interrogators were reading the notes I had written the previous evening when they came across a quotation I had used from Chairman Mao that said something to the effect that "the dark clouds will wither away and the bright twilight will soon break out." They immediately became livid with anger and started screaming at me: "How dare you use Chairman Mao's quotation like that. Do you think we are your enemy? Do you consider that we and the Communist Party and socialism are your enemies? Who is this darkness? Whom are you referring to when you talk about the darkness? And whom are you referring to when you mention the twilight? Tell me today what you are talking about, and why you wrote that? Do you consider us as your enemies, and are you threatening that some backers of yours are about to defeat us?" Nothing I said made the slightest difference to them, and they ended the session saying that my attitude toward the Cultural Revolution must be corrected.

The next day when the morning interrogation session began there were no questions. They at once put the blackboard around my neck and half-pushed, half-dragged me out to a hall packed tightly with about five hundred students and teachers waiting to struggle against me. This meeting, my second large struggle session, was organized by Chen and Ma Ximei for the purpose of teaching me a lesson for my use of Mao's words. They thought I was so arrogant and obstinate that I needed to be humbled. It was their strategy for breaking people. These large meetings were really not to find out information, but rather to intimidate and put you down.

The meeting started when the student leader yelled out, "Drag in Tashi Tsering the counterrevolutionary." As I was being pushed in others shouted, "Down with Tashi Tsering's arrogance," "Down with the enemy of the Motherland," and so forth. Then the highly theatrical public accusations began. The first accuser was a young girl from Nakchuka in northern Tibet. She started accusing me of being against Chairman Mao's thought and Marxism-Leninism. When I gave a good rebuttal, Chen himself jumped in and said that I was reactionary, stubborn, and arrogant—not with the arrogance of an ordinary man but with that of a counterrevolutionary. What he meant was that I was so counterrevolutionary that I had a very strong mind enabling me to dare to say clever things against the revolution and the interrogation. That's what counterrevolutionary arrogance meant. Chen then launched into questions about the quotation by Mao I had used: "You seem to consider that we are your enemy, is that right? If not, who is this darkness? To whom are you attaching the word 'darkness'? Whom are you referring to?" he asked me. "Who is the darkness and who is the twilight? Tell me why you said such things?"

I responded saying that the darkness was my situation. "I am here now and have become the enemy of the people. I'm sorry to have become such a man. When I said darkness I meant darkness for me, not for you and not for anybody else. It's darkness only for me." Naturally Chen wasn't satisfied by my answer and simply responded harshly with another question. "What is the twilight?" he asked, speaking to the crowd and looking smug and self-satisfied. I said that the twilight was also a description of me. "It's something I'm expecting to become; it is only something better than the darkness I am in now. That's what I consider to be my twilight. I really didn't mean to insult you or the proletarian class."

Chen, of course, was having none of it and retorted, "You are stubborn and persistent in your dirty ideas. Your attitude toward the Cultural Revolution is a disgrace. You know the Cultural Revolution of the proletarian class is so great. It is the initiative of great Chairman Mao, and it is guided by our great Chairman Mao." Then the whole meeting joined in, somebody shouting, "Down with the reactionary lackeys of imperialism," and "Down with the traitor Tashi." Finally, after several hours, the manager of the meeting said, "Tashi Tsering, the party policy is clear. You know it very well. There are two ways that you can choose. You can go along on the enlightened road or continue on the path of the black road, the hell road. This is totally your choice. If you are honest with us and show a good attitude toward the revolution, then you may get a light punishment. But if you maintain this stubborn opposition, we will find out everything and you will be severely punished."

The next day, after breakfast, the interrogations continued nonstop. After a few weeks more, I got so fed up with the same questions and insinuations every day that something inside me broke and I did something wild. I no longer cared what they did to me. All I knew was that I wasn't going to say what they wanted, and I wanted them to know that clearly. One of the guards was a rather nice boy, and that night he was on guard duty with me. I asked him to please write me a few sentences in Chinese since my writing skill in Chinese was not very good and I wanted everyone to be able to understand perfectly. He agreed, and I dictated a statement that had three simple points:

> 1. When I left Lhasa in 1957 and went to India for studies I left alone, on my own, and was sent by nobody.
> 2. When I went to America to study, the opportunity was obtained through a Williams College student named Robert Dunnam, whom I met in India, and I left against the wishes of Gyalo Thondrup.
> 3. When I left America, it was against the urging of my Tibetan friends. I made the decision on my own. Therefore, in all these three events nobody sent me. If you have any evidence that contradicts this, I will take the full responsibility.

At this point I wanted to let them know that this was my final word on these matters so I took a small needle and stuck myself in the finger to draw blood and then I signed the letter affixing my thumbprint in blood. Whatever the consequences, they now knew I would admit to nothing more. Afterward, the questions gradually stopped. My answers were not good enough to convince them I was telling the truth, but at least this phase of the questioning was now over.

My private prison ended soon after that, and I was sent to a large building near the center of campus that was a makeshift jail for people in my situation. It was so dirty and horrible that everyone called it the "cow shed." My fellow prisoners were mainly teachers, writers, intellectuals, and officials from the school. There were both Han Chinese and Tibetans there. The Cultural Revolution did not let ethnic background influence the targets. We numbered between 160 and 170 souls, each of whom was considered a class enemy in some way. By far the largest group were teachers and administrators. Ma Ximei's husband, Mr. Wu, who had been the head of the Education Department, was among them. Only those considered genuinely "proletarian" intellectuals had escaped persecution.

Our daily routine was rigorous. We were made to get up early in the morning, given some watery rice soup, and then sent to the fields to do intentionally demeaning manual labor. We worked in the pigpens or carried human excrement and urine from the institute to the fields, where it was used as fertilizer. We also, of course, were still subject to relentless and systematic indoctrination to correct our thinking. In the evening we were divided into study groups in which we read Mao's works, newspaper articles, and party documents. We were then made to write personal reports of our crimes and our thoughts about historical and recent events. We also had to include accounts of what they called "living thoughts"—our daily, hourly, and minute-by-minute mental activities. Periodically, individuals were called out for interrogations or to be the centerpieces at mass struggle meetings, like the ones I have described above. The interrogations were always one of two kinds—the rough ones that involved physical beatings and intimidation, or the more gentle ones that just involved yelling and insults. During those evenings in the cow shed, some of the worst experiences for me were when we were all made to stand for several hours before going to bed. While we stood at attention, members of the Red Guards would walk past and scream insults and slogans at us. We were made to bow our heads and not look at any of them above the chest as they shouted things like, "You are now under the proletarian dictatorship. If you clean the filth out of your dirty minds, if you honestly report your previous crimes, if you agree to report the criminal activities and thoughts of your colleagues and collaborate with us, the party will be lenient and reward you."

The private prison lasted into the next year, but in the spring of 1968 we got a kind of reprieve. The worst excesses of the Cultural Revolution were beginning to be seen for the disasters they were, and the Communist Party issued an order that private prisons like ours were to be abolished and the prisoners released. And so we were, but little in my own situation changed for the better. When I left the cow shed I discovered that the majority of my classmates had by then completed their work at the school and in many cases had already been sent back to Tibet for their first assignments. My heart ached with envy when I learned that they were being allowed to begin doing what I had risked so much to attempt, while I was still clearly under suspicion as a class enemy and forbidden to join them or return to my country. As it happened, though, I didn't have a lot of time to feel sorry for myself.

The threat of a war—it was feared a nuclear war—between Russia and China was brewing in the later months of 1968. (Actual hostilities broke out in 1969 and the whole school was evacuated.) Because of the general threat of possible nuclear attack, those of us who were left at the school were sent to Changwu County (a six-hour drive) to help dig fallout shelters. This was to be my period of what the Chinese called "mass probation." I was not in jail but not free and thus liable for all kinds of forced labor. This new status involved the same kind of indoctrination and intimidation and also some extremely hard manual labor.

We spent most of our days underground in tunnels not more than a yard high and two yards wide, where we hacked at the hard brown soil with pickaxes and shovels and carried out the loose soil by hand. We began early in the morning and stopped only for minimal meals that gave us just enough nourishment to allow us to continue the digging. And the evenings were the same as in the cow shed—the same routine of study, self-examination, and verbal or physical abuse. After the full evacuation of the school in January 1970, the atmosphere became even worse. Besides everything else, there were more people around whose duty it was to spy on one another and report possible criminal activities. There was a point at which I remember thinking that my situation couldn't possibly get any worse or seem any more hopeless than it had already become. I was wrong.

On March 23, 1970, there was to be another mass struggle meeting and this time I had a feeling something big was up. When the meeting was about to begin, two Red Guards escorted me to the meeting ground but kept me off to the side. I remember it was a crisp, beautiful day. The sky was a brilliant blue, and the air was clear. Suddenly I heard a voice saying, "Now the meeting is to begin, and Tashi Tsering, spy and advocate for Tibetan independence, should be brought forward." The two guards then marched me roughly to a spot before the platform and directly facing the crowd. I raised my head a little and saw that the meeting ground was packed; there must have been six or seven hundred students and teachers present. Before I even had time to think, one Red Guard forced my head and neck down and said in a voice that the whole assembly could hear, "You are now before the people's court, and you had better remember how to act." Then the chairman of the meeting read the order for my arrest, issued by the security office of Changwu County. When the arrest had been formally announced, two young soldiers tied my hands tightly behind my back. The blood seemed to have rushed out of my body, and I was trembling. After being released from the cow shed, my worst fear was being realized: I was being formally found guilty of being a spy and advocate of Tibetan independence. While I was still trying to understand my situation in full, a sharp pain brought me back to the reality of the moment. These first two students didn't seem to be able to pull the cords tight enough, so a Tibetan teacher stepped forward and pulled the ropes so tight that I knew he was intentionally trying to hurt me. The youth was extremely proud of himself. By this dramatic gesture, he had made himself a "people's hero," and he was later rewarded with a judgeship on the Chamdo high court.

When I was tightly bound, Ma Ximei walked slowly up the steps onto the platform and addressed the crowd. In a loud, clear voice she said she was there to expose what she called my "sky-full of crimes." The two principal charges against me, she said, were that I had received a letter from an American named Tolstoy directing me to wage war against the barbarian communists, and that in an article in an American newspaper (the school paper in Seattle) I had said that Tibet was independent. When the young, idealistic students and soldiers in the crowd heard these charges, they began to shout, and then hiss, as a sign of great surprise and disapproval. Both these events were partially true, but they had happened in America and Ma Ximei very cleverly had now made them seem as if they had occurred after I had been in China. Ma Ximei continued with a full report of my crimes, my work with Gyalola, and so forth. The meeting ran its course. And when it was over I was thrown tightly bound into an open truck, guarded by armed soldiers, and driven off to the Changwu County prison. My worst fear was now about to become reality.

10

The prison was only a ten-minute drive from the site of the mass struggle meeting, and the truck jolted to a stop before I had time to collect my thoughts. But when I realized that I was standing in front of the prison itself, my mind focused sharply. I remember small details even today.

The country around Changwu prison is stark and barren—no trees, no grass, no water, only the dry, brown hills. There were only a few brick houses in the area. Most of the peasants lived in what amounted to small, cavelike dwellings dug into the hillsides. At first I didn't realize I was standing in front of the prison, because all I could see was what looked like a doorway in a hillside that wasn't any different from many of the peasants' doorways. When I stepped inside, I knew different. It was like stepping into hell.

The doorway I entered was not flush with the hillside as it had first appeared. The minute the guards opened it and thrust me inside it seemed as if the earth had opened up beneath my feet. I found myself looking across and down at a large sunken courtyard, scooped out of the earth to a depth of nearly thirty feet. From the outside, you couldn't even tell it was there. The guards roughly pushed me forward and we descended to the floor by means of a steep staircase. When we reached the bottom I looked across the large open space. Directly opposite was a wall about ten feet high, which was patrolled by armed guards, who walked along the top, rifles at the ready.

My guards marched me directly toward that wall, and we passed beyond it through a small door. On the other side was a very small open space and beyond that a row of ten caves dug directly into the hillside. These were the cells. They were about 33 feet long, 10 feet wide, and 8 feet high. Ten prisoners had to try to live in each one of them. At least a third of the space inside was taken up by the earthen beds on which we had to sleep. When I was put into my cell, the other prisoners all looked up, suspicious but also curious about what was going on outside. Some were just peasants who had committed various crimes; some were hardened criminals—murderers and rapists; a few were political prisoners like me. What I remember best is their eyes. A few were fearful but had the eyes of people who still had hope. These, I later learned, were the newer prisoners. Most of the prisoners, however, had only expressionless stares, their eyes focused somewhere well beyond the prison and the horizon, without a flicker of hope. When the door closed behind me, the stench of human filth, sweat, and fear was so strong that I nearly vomited.

The first few weeks in this prison were one of the most miserable periods in my life. The filth was overpowering. We were allowed out to go to the bathroom only twice a day. The rest of the time we had to urinate and defecate in a large clay pot that was emptied every morning. We had no soap or towels and were forever surrounded by powerful nauseating odors. And we were under constant attack from an army of lice who called the cell and us home. You couldn't get away from either of them.

There was also the pain of hunger. At ten in the morning we were given two pieces of steamed bread, one boiled turnip, and one bowl of hot water. We got the same meal again at four in the afternoon, and that was it. Nobody actually died of starvation while I was there, but there wasn't nearly enough food, and I couldn't get used to the hunger and the weakness that this caused. Like the smells and the lice, the pain of hunger never went away, and I don't think I ever stopped thinking about food. Equally terrible was the inactivity and sense of total isolation. Except for the brief periods when we went to the bathroom and emptied the urine pots or when we ate, there was nothing to do. We were cramped together in our small, vermin-ridden cells day in and day out with nothing to occupy our minds. The guards discouraged movement or even talking. They patrolled the top of the wall that separated our cells from the main courtyard, and they could hear anything that was going on behind our doors. I remember sometimes a guard would call out sharply, "Hey there. In cell number three. What's going on?" You didn't want to answer—just stop talking.

The guards watched us all the time, and so we just had to sit there while our minds and bodies became numbed by the inactivity. I had experienced hard labor and physical abuse, but this was worse than anything, and I think the Chinese wanted it that way. They wanted to leave you alone with your thoughts, so that your mind was as much a prisoner as your body. I know that this period was as close as I have ever come to simply giving up. In fact, on the tenth day I actually decided to kill myself. I think I was a little bit crazy at that time, because I did the only thing I could think of to try to end my life. When it was my turn to empty my urine pot, I waited just a moment until the other prisoners went to the bathroom and then before anyone could stop me I actually drank the urine. I had convinced myself that if I did so it would kill me. I was sure of that and gulped down at least a quart. It didn't, however, kill me. Amazingly, it had no effect on me at all. I had gone over the edge and survived. I never got that close again. Somehow after that, in spite of the constant hunger and physical deterioration, my mental strength returned and carried me through. In fact, the Chinese didn't know it, but as I reflect on those days, they were the ones who helped me the most. They did it by making me angry.

The only breaks in the routine I have just described were occasional interrogations like those that I had to endure during my mass probation. My old tormentor Ma Ximei would return sometimes, and we would go through the same old routines. But one day it was different. Ma Ximei was there all right, but this time instead of bringing students from the Xianyang school she was accompanied by three policemen. When they called me from my crowded cell they did everything they could to make clear that this wasn't going to be just another routine interrogation. They brought me to a small room and handcuffed me to a low chair in the center. Then the whole group took their seats behind a table with a white cloth on it. The chair was so low to the ground that I had to look up to meet their eyes.

In front of me were Ma Ximei, the three policemen in uniform, and some Tibetans who were there because the Chinese always wanted to be able to say that the questioning had been fair, as my own countrymen had witnessed what had happened. They were all very formal and solemn, and the policemen were extremely arrogant. Though they

hammered away at the questions they always asked, they did everything they could to make the proceedings seem like a trial. As always,
they wanted to know more about my relationship with Gyalo Thondrup
in India. What had my responsibilities been? What was my mission—
then and now? They still wanted to know why I would have left the
security and abundance of America to come back to Tibet—unless I was
on a mission of some kind. That was what they were after. What was my
assignment? Who was I working for? I had better tell them or else.

I gave them the same old answers, which of course made them
angry. The policeman who was in charge of this supposed trial began
to bully me. What did I think I was doing? I had better cooperate,
because they were losing patience with me. In the relatively short time
I had been in the prison I had earned a reputation as a stubborn prisoner, a man with a bad attitude. Did I know what happened to people
like that? Of course I did.

In the time I'd been here we'd all known of a number of prisoners
who had been executed—just taken out and shot. The guards kept a
close watch on us, but news of such things raced through the cells like
a fire. There were no secrets. As I looked at the bullying officer in
front of me, I remembered a night not too long ago when we'd all had
to listen to the shouting and crying of a man we knew had been con-
demned to death. The shouting went on the whole night, and I remember listening to the guards taunting him in his misery, telling him he
deserved it, that he should have learned his lesson. I believed that's
what I was being threatened with now. They were hinting pretty
clearly that my life might depend on the answers I gave.

At that point something inside me just snapped. Instead of getting
frightened, I got angry, as angry as I have ever been in my life. I
remember looking at the table in front of me, the so-called judges'
bench. I could see that underneath the white cloth they had laid to
make the table seem imposing and ceremonial, the wood was dry and
cracked and the paint was peeling. My eyes glanced around the small
room and took in all the shabby details. The trial seemed to me like a
joke, a very bad joke. My interrogators were like children masquerad-
ing as adults, and I didn't fear them anymore. I was so tired of being
asked the same questions, so frustrated and furious that I lost all restraint and began to shout: "You want to kill me? Then go ahead, kill
me. You can do anything you want to me, but I'm not going to lie to
you. I'm not going to play these stupid games and say things that aren't

true just because you want me to. I believe in what I'm saying; I have told you the truth. If you won't accept it, then do whatever you want."

I meant what I said.

My inquisitors were angry, but they didn't do anything. I think the Tibetan witnesses were shocked. They just sat there, eyes lowered, staring straight ahead. None of them would meet my eye. And something seemed to happen in the room, though no one spoke about it. The so-called trial was over. No one said anything. My interrogators simply looked at one another, unlocked my handcuffs, and took me back to my cell. In the heat and adrenaline of the moment I felt I had won. I wasn't fooling myself. I knew that in fact they could kill me any time they wanted and that they still might. But I had won a victory in my own mind—whatever happened—and it felt good. My cellmates looked at me briefly when I returned, but nobody dared to ask any questions. I sat in silence, my mind racing, trying to understand what had just happened.

After the session in that broken-down little room, my life in the prison went on more or less as before. The routine was always the same. Each individual day became the same day that never varied and never ended. Summer dragged into fall. And then suddenly, one day in late November, with no warning or explanation, I was taken out of my cell and checked thoroughly by a doctor. And someone shaved my head. Nobody said why, and I didn't dare ask. All I could do was guess. I didn't think they were going to kill me. Why would they have given me a medical exam? I'd already seen how they treated the prisoners they were going to execute, and this didn't fit the pattern. But what was going on? Were they going to set me free? Were they getting ready to transfer me to another prison—and if so, where?

I didn't have to wait long to find out. A day or so later, on November 30, 1970 (a little more than 250 days since my arrest and imprisonment), I left the Changwu prison for good.

Gruffly and without explanation, two guards ordered me out of my cell. My hands were tied tightly behind me. I was loaded into a broken-down bus and driven over rough, snow-covered roads. I was accompanied by Ma Ximei and two policemen who never said what the final destination would be.

When we stopped, I was at the Xianyang prison, close to my school. I was foolish enough to hope that I had been brought here because I was going to be released soon and allowed to finish my course work and get on with my life. Of course I was wrong. After three days, I was ordered out of my cell and moved again. My hands were again bound tightly, and I was put on a train bound for Chengdu, the capital city of Sichuan Province.

In some ways I was glad. At least I was getting away from Xianyang prison, which, though I wouldn't have believed it possible, was even worse than the prison at Changwu. At Xianyang there had been only one prisoner besides myself, and I had almost no human contact. The food was even scarcer and more repellent than at Changwu. There were the same filth and vermin, and at Xianyang there was a constant dampness that never went away and that chilled you to the bone. At least Changwu had been drier.

When I got to Chengdu, things seemed better at first. There were six or seven other prisoners, so at least there were more people to talk to. The cells were cleaner, and the floor was dry wood planking, not the raw earth of Changwu or the near mud of Xianyang. By comparison, the food at Chengdu was wonderful. We actually got steamed rice and vegetables, and enough of both to fill your stomach. I think it was because I was so happy about the changed conditions that I made the mistake of letting my guard down, for which I was made to pay.

I let my guard down in the sense that I responded eagerly to the other prisoners' questions and friendship without thinking about what I was saying. The boredom of prison life is the same everywhere, and my cell mates were full of questions. Where had I come from? What crimes was I guilty of? Where was I arrested? They were curious about the fact that I wasn't Chinese. Was I Tibetan? What was a Tibetan doing in Chengdu prison?—a question to which I couldn't respond and to which I wished I had the answer myself. My response to their attention, however, was to answer what I could. And then I guess I just needed to talk, because I foolishly began to tell them what I thought about my experiences in Changwu prison.

As I've said, one of the horrors of Changwu was that talking among the prisoners had been forbidden. Until the privilege had been taken away from me, I hadn't realized how important it is to speak regularly and without fear to other human beings. Now that I had a chance again, I couldn't stop myself. I told them what a living hell I thought Changwu had been. I told them about the filth, the food, the cruelty. I didn't even think about what I was saying.

It was a big mistake. The very next day I was singled out by one of the prison officers who had heard about my description of Changwu. "You are a troublemaker," he said. "You are talkative and a liar, telling all kinds of stories about our very fine prison system. Your mind is still poisoned by your dreams about America. You'd do well to remember where you are—and who you are! You are a prisoner of the new proletarian dictatorship, and you'd better learn to behave properly, or else."

I knew immediately why I had received this reprimand. What had I been thinking about? Like the school during the early days of the Cultural Revolution, the prison was filled with spies. One or more of the prisoners I had spoken to had reported this evidence of my disloyalty—and perhaps had been rewarded for it. My punishment for being a troublemaker was that I was put into handcuffs that I had to wear day and night, even when I ate and went to the bathroom. It was terrible. Fortunately, I wasn't in Chengdu for long—only three days.

On my fourth day in Chengdu, I was roused from my cell once again. Ma Ximei and two armed policemen materialized as if on cue, and we were taken directly to the nearest airport, where we became the only passengers on a Russian-made plane that I was told would take me back to Tibet, my native land. I learned later that I got this kind of special treatment because I was being handled as if I were a dangerous international spy who was being taken to Lhasa for trial. I heard that was the argument Ma Ximei made to get the Chengdu security officials to pay for the plane. But I didn't know that at the time, and since I still did not know exactly what was going to happen to me when I arrived, I alternated between moments of excitement and moments of fear. On the surface, the news that I was returning home was wonderful. I could scarcely believe it. But I was returning as a prisoner, and perhaps I was getting my hopes up only to have them dashed even more cruelly than if I'd stayed in China.

I remember that the day we left was clear. We didn't talk much during the flight, and I spent a lot of time looking out a small window. As I watched the landscape change beneath us, my imagination began to stir, because when we got closer to Lhasa I realized that the snow-covered mountains below were the mountains of Tibet, the mountains that had been part of my consciousness since I was a boy.

When our plane landed it became clear immediately that I wasn't going home the way I wanted. It was December now and bitter cold. I was put into a car in handcuffs, though my cuffed hands were in front rather than in back (a much more comfortable arrangement). I was obviously not coming home to be released. The guards also put a white cloth scarf over my face with just a mouth hole to speak and breathe through. And they put a heavy fur hat on my head. I don't know whether this was to protect me from the cold or to prevent anyone seeing and recognizing me on our way to the Lhasa prison. I didn't know it at the time, but the "dragging through the prisons" was now at an end. Lhasa's Sangyib prison was to be my final destination.

Compared to the Changwu and Xianyang institutions, the Sangyib prison was immense. It lay three miles outside the city itself, near the Sera Monastery. The prison grounds covered an area large enough that there were separate complexes of buildings and distinct areas, almost like the grounds of a large university.

When our car arrived and passed through the gates, we stopped in front of a huge warehouse. There Ma Ximei took my possessions, which had been sent from the Xianyang school, and handed them to the Sangyib security officers. The two suitcases (one was Samsonite and one an Indian leather box) contained all I had in the world. I put them in storage myself, and when I was allowed a brief look inside the case I saw that most of my things were intact. But I noticed that a gold fountain pen—a Parker 61 from America—had been ruined. Ma Ximei or someone else had obviously intentionally broken it open, presumably to search for things concealed inside. The pen was one of my favorite possessions. As I looked at it there, broken and now impossible to write with, it seemed to be a symbol of what was happening to me. Like the pen, I thought, I could have been a productive instrument. I had wanted to use my education to help my fellow Tibetans. But I, too, had been broken into, and at the moment I was of no use to anyone.

I was to be a resident of Sangyib prison for the next two and a half years, until May 1973. By the time I had checked my personal items and put them away in storage, it was about two o'clock in the afternoon. I was then taken to a building that contained rows of small cells that held one prisoner each and placed in one of them. In spite of the extremely small cells, the physical conditions here were better than those in any of the prisons I had known in China.

The building that held the cells was a newly built concrete structure. There were dim electric bulbs in each cell, and the walls and floors were concrete and a good deal warmer and drier than anything I had seen before. We got more food and freedom, too. There were three meals a day here, and we got butter tea, tsamba, and sometimes even meat, although not in large quantities. We were allowed out every morning to empty and wash our urine pots, and we were given a basin of water a day to use for washing ourselves. Compared to what I'd been experiencing, these conditions amounted almost to luxury.

Not long after I'd arrived I saw groups of former Tibetan government officials working in the prison vegetable garden. They had been incarcerated because of their involvement in the Lhasa Uprising in 1959. I was told they had fixed prison terms, which meant that they knew when they were going to be released. They were assigned to work in the gardens during the day, and at night they were locked up in a large, communal cell. I actually envied them for their gifts of exercise and human contact, because though my material conditions were much better, I remained isolated from the other prisoners. I also envied their assurance of the length of their term. I had been classified as a political prisoner of a more dangerous kind, and so I was kept alone and denied what would have been the welcome relief of physical labor and society and a sense of when my trials would end.

For some reason, I wasn't as afraid here as I had been in China. Partly I think it was because even though a prisoner, I was at home in Tibet. Partly, too, it may have been because most of the prisoners, prison officials, and trustees were Tibetan and I was interacting mainly in my native language. Finally, I believe I had gained courage from my experience with Ma Ximei and the Chinese inquisitors after my sham trial at Changwu prison. Whatever the case, I became more assertive than I had ever been before as a prisoner. I was still haunted by the experience of hunger in the Changwu and Xianyang prisons. We got better food here in the Sangyib prison, but it was still not enough. So I began a sort of campaign to try to get more.

I approached the trustees and the Tibetan guards first. When they did not punish or mock my requests, my spirits rose, and I grew more insistent. At first a few of the guards took pity on me and occasionally brought me extra food. Then more decided to pitch in. At some point they all must have gotten together and talked about it among themselves, because eventually they regularly provided extra food not only for me but also for all of the prisoners in my block of cells. Eventually they made it a permanent arrangement, and everybody got the same extra rations. My fellow prisoners were grateful and treated me as if I had done something incredibly brave. Thus, isolated as I was, I got some much needed support and an image of myself that I am sure helped me continue to survive.

After six months I was moved to a different part of the prison where the cells were larger and the conditions better. For example, in my new cell there was actually a window that let the sunlight in and that I could open and close myself. That may not sound like much, but after months in the Changwu prison scarcely able to move around or talk without a guard checking up on me, even the smallest chance to control my environment became important. And there were other small freedoms allowed.

For the first time since I had been imprisoned I was given access to newspapers—both Tibetan and Chinese. I was so eager to have something to read that I asked and was granted permission to go to my things in storage and recover my Chinese-Tibetan dictionary. When I had it, I was able to read the Chinese newspapers with greater ease, and I added a lot of new words to my vocabulary.

The main problem, though, continued to be boredom—how to kill and fill the time. Because I had more relative freedom here, I was able to work out a series of activities and routines that allowed me to cope better. My method in general was to divide up the day. Mornings were my exercise times. I would do about two hours of physical exercises before breakfast each day. Sometimes I would jump or jog in place. Sometimes I would carefully stretch my limbs. And sometimes I would rehearse my old gadrugba dance routines. Though I hadn't danced in years, I had practiced so long and hard when I was young that my muscles seemed to remember every move. I especially liked the dancing, because I could do it almost without thinking and by giving myself over to the well-known ritual movements I could temporarily block out the reality of the prison.

Breakfast and washing would be over by about ten o'clock, and then I would use the hours between ten and noon to read newspapers. I would read the Tibetan papers first, and then tackle the Chinese papers with my dictionary in hand. I never let myself imagine that I was going to be in prison forever. I think if I'd thought that, I couldn't have gone on. So I treated the Chinese newspapers as an opportunity to continue to learn the language, which I was sure would be useful to me when I was released. I stopped reading the papers when it was time for lunch. As I said, in this larger cell I had a window to the outside world. It was barred, of course, but beyond the bars was a glass pane that admitted the sunlight, and so every afternoon that wasn't cloudy, I would strip to the waist and lie in the sun for as long as the light streamed through my window. It was one of my favorite things to do.

Another of the things I did to cope with the endless flow of time was to sing songs. They weren't traditional songs; they were songs I made up as I went along and that helped keep me in control. I would sing to myself about how, though I was locked alone in a room, I could breathe freely, and in my mind I could range all over the world. I would sing to myself about how I knew I was going to be free some-day. I would say that, yes, it was a dark day now but I could see good things on the horizon. And I would sometimes construct the arguments or accusations the Chinese were always using against me and then rehearse my answers and counterarguments. The fact of just saying such things over and over again made it easier to believe that the events I wanted would actually happen or that the arguments I made would eventually work.

I also spent a lot of time reminiscing, conjuring up images of people, places, and things I couldn't see otherwise. I pictured my village and my parents as they were when I had last seen them. I tried to see if I could tell whether they were well, how they might have changed. I tried to imagine how Lhasa looked when I had danced for the Dalai Lama as a child or worked for the government as a clerk. I tried to bring back some of the happier details of the city seen when I had made my visit with the Red Guards in 1966. I even brought back some fond images of my time in America. I remembered people who had been especially kind to me, and when I was hungry I would remember what American apple pie looked and tasted like. Sometimes, when I was feeling de-pressed, I would remember the details of my conversation with Gyalola in San Francisco. I would make myself remember his telling me that I didn't know myself and that I wouldn't be able to stand up to the Chinese. This always helped me strengthen my resolve. In short, I did literally everything I could think of to keep my spirits afloat.

But the months dragged on and turned into years, and I found that although my routines were extremely helpful, they weren't always enough. And so I would seize anything that would give me a sense of hope and protect me from the darker, more pessimistic side of my imagination. I remember, for example, that I was very excited when I heard on a Beijing National Radio broadcast in 1972 that Richard Nixon, the president of the United States, had come to China to visit

Mao Zedong and Zhou Enlai. I was excited because I thought that in general it would be good for China to end its closed-door policy and perhaps become a part of the international community. Indeed, I thought that if China became a part of the international community, then Tibet would, too, and that therefore the process of modernization could be speeded up. But part of my excitement was also selfish. I hoped that if Communist China became a part of the international community, then some of its most ruthless policies against its own citizens might have to change and that eventually conditions for prisoners like me would change for the better. It didn't happen, of course. The hoping helped, but only for a while.

One of my few fond memories from this period is of the way I was able to knit myself a pair of wool socks. I don't remember how or when exactly I got the idea, but I noticed that the saddle blankets on the mules I saw in the prison yard were leather on one side and woven wool on the other. One day I asked a guard I knew pretty well what happened to them when they got old and worn. When I learned that the blankets were either thrown away or stored somewhere, I asked if he could get me some. He found me several badly torn and worn out pieces fairly quickly and then I went into action. I separated the wool from the hide and then untangled the wool fibers and respun the yarn. At that point I searched the prison yard for some sticks I could use for needles. I found some about the size of chopsticks and sharpened them on the prison stones. With my needles I began to knit, always making sure the guards weren't around. I don't know that they would have prevented me from doing this, but I liked the sense that I was getting away with something.

Perhaps it was the memory of all those evenings at home in the room with the fire with my whole family, talking of course but each of us always doing something—knitting, sewing, or mending. Maybe some of the knitting skills just rubbed off by my watching my mother and sisters. Whatever it was, it kept me going. I worked a long time on the knitting, and when I was done I had myself a fine, warm pair of wool socks for the winter. I had more than that, too. Looked at objectively, a pair of socks is next to nothing. But I took enormous pleasure in having made them in these circumstances. As I think back on it, it was a way of asserting myself, a way of proving that even though I was in prison there were things about my life and my environment that I could still control. It was the little things like those socks that I think got me through the terrible experience of not knowing when or if I would ever be free again, because though my level of comfort was higher than it had been in any of the other prisons, the idea that my sentence was indeterminate preyed on my mind. My spirits often flagged, and it didn't help matters that I had some health problems.

I had developed chronic problems with digestion in the Changwu prison. My system wasn't working properly and I began to suffer regular bouts of severe diarrhea, stomach cramps, and gas. I talked to the guards, who allowed me to see a prison doctor. He gave me medicine, but it wasn't very effective, and over time I developed my own techniques for dealing with the pain. When the attacks hit, I would quickly lie down on the floor and begin to control my breathing by first holding my breath as long as I could and letting it out in a very controlled way. Then I would tense the muscles in my stomach and begin to move them in something close to peristaltic waves while I massaged my stomach with my hands. I can't tell you why it worked, but for some reason this combination of controlled breathing, muscle control, and massage got rid of the worst cramps and gas. And I still sometimes resort to it.

During my time at Sangyib prison there were also periodic interrogations and endless written reports I had to make. In the reports, I was supposed to give an account of my past crimes and detail my new thinking. They were a real challenge, because of course my thinking hadn't changed. But I knew that my eventual release would be at least loosely tied to the Chinese sense that I had in fact "reformed." So I used to make up anything I could think of that I thought would be what they wanted to hear, without, of course, admitting to the serious charges. I would confess that I now realized that I had made a mistake in criticizing socialism while I was in India—things like that. I felt very helpless and frustrated about having to play these kinds of games.

The formal interrogations occurred less frequently than in Changwu (and a bit less violently), but I was still occasionally questioned by Chinese officials who represented the Autonomous Region of Tibet. In some ways it was like a well-rehearsed theatrical performance. They always asked the same questions, and I always gave the same answers. My responses had become so automatic that I think by that point I could have gotten through the interrogations in my sleep. I remember only one of these sessions more distinctly than the others.

In the middle of 1972 I was interrogated by an officer from the Chinese Intelligence Bureau and a short, fat Tibetan as well.

What I remember is the behavior of the Tibetan interrogator. The Chinese officer was very demonstrative. He shouted at me all the time. But the one who hit me was the Tibetan. He seemed to love his work and would slap me for the smallest matter. The idea of my own countryman treating me that way is what stays in my mind.

My eventual release was as much of a surprise and a mystery to me as my imprisonment. One day, with no warning or preparation, I was sent to the office of the director of the prison. I had no idea what was happening or about to happen and so was extremely suspicious. The director's name was Mr. Qiao, and my suspicions increased when I stepped into his office. I remember it was wintertime and extremely cold. But Mr. Qiao's office was warm and friendly. There was a fire burning, and instead of shouting at me or firing hostile questions like my usual interrogators, Mr. Qiao was mild and even courteous. With a friendly gesture he pointed to a chair and asked me to sit down. There were a cup of green tea and a cigarette waiting for me. It was only after I had made myself comfortable that Mr. Qiao began to speak. He was a calm, elderly Chinese man, a veteran of the revolution. After a sort of preamble that was full of general praise for the Communist Party and its policies, he smiled, looked directly at me, and said, "When a man makes a mistake, it is sometimes allowed because he may not have understood what he has done; and if he recognizes his mistake, then it is our policy to let him have a brighter future. I want you to think about that—what it means to you—because I hope you will be one of the ones who can become a new man." I was used to bullying and accusations in situations like this. I wasn't prepared for kindness. What was going on? What did he mean? Was this another trap? Would I end up harming myself if I talked freely as I had in a weak moment at the Xianyang prison? My mind raced furiously as I was trying to think of what to say.

Mr. Qiao sat there smiling and expectant, and in the end I trusted my instincts and instead of responding with the numbed recitation of my usual bland answers, I decided to take a chance and be more forthcoming. I thanked him warmly for inviting me to his office and for his thoughtfulness. And then I tried to tell him what was honestly in my mind when I decided to return to Tibet. I told him that I now knew that I had repeatedly made mistakes, used bad judgment at times, and was extremely grateful for the leniency I had already received. I also tried to make clear that my main concern was for the Tibetan people; that I supported the Communist Party because I thought it would help the ordinary people of Tibet. I told him that from the earliest days of the Chinese presence in Lhasa I thought that the communist system was going to make it possible to modernize Tibet, to make my people competitive citizens of the modern world. Therefore I accepted the leadership of the Communist Party and the idea of the Autonomous Region of Tibet. My loyalty was to the Tibetans living in Tibet and especially to the working classes, and of course socialism and the Communist Party.

When I was finished speaking I realized that I was shaking. Mr. Qiao said nothing for a moment, and I knew that whatever the result, the interview was now at an end. We both rose and Mr. Qiao seemed pleased. He patted me on the shoulder and smiled. "Do you need anything?" he asked. "No, thank you," I said. And the next thing I knew I was back in my cell, without even remembering how I got there.

What occurred then was all very mysterious. At first nothing happened. My days went on as usual, and there was no reference to my meeting with Mr. Qiao. There were certainly no apparent consequences. For the first few days I was both nervous and excited. Was I going to be punished? Had it really been a trick after all? Or was I going to be released? That possibility was so exciting that I scarcely let myself hope. It was the spring of 1973—a little over three years since that day in March 1970 when I was denounced at my school and taken to Changwu prison. Three years and who knew how many more were to come?

Months passed and because nothing happened—either good or bad—I had pretty much decided that nothing was going to come of my talk with Mr. Qiao. It was just going to be another one of those experiences with the Chinese authorities where they don't tell you anything and there's no way of guessing what their intentions are. At just about the time I had resigned myself to the idea that the meeting had meant nothing I had a visitor, a Mr. Wang, who was a senior Chinese security officer originally from Shanghai. His message was simple: "Today we are releasing you," said Mr. Wang. "Your arrest was correct and so our decision now is to set you free. We now consider that you have been properly educated and have become a new person. You are a new man now, and our only hope is that you will serve the people well."

I was stunned. When you hope—even dream—for something as

much as I had hoped and dreamed of my release, you make it so magical and remote that it's hard to believe it when it actually happens. For a moment I couldn't find my voice. When I did, all I managed to say was that I was extremely grateful and that I would indeed work hard to serve the people. I was literally in a daze.

There were a few formalities to be gone through before I could be set free, which was a good thing because they gave me time to regain my composure and begin to experience the full impact of what had happened. There was some important paperwork to be done. When you are arrested in China there are specific steps that are supposed to be taken. A letter of arrest must be issued and signed by the appropriate authorities. None of the proper forms had been filed when I arrived at the Sangyib prison in Tibet. And so, ironically, on the day of my release I had to wait while officials filled out, signed, and backdated all the forms that were supposed to have been filed over two years before. Of course, I couldn't have cared less about the breach in procedure. Nothing mattered but the thought of freedom.

When Mr. Wang had finished all of the official business he told me what was going to happen next. "According to regulations," he said, "you will be sent back to Xianyang to the Tibetan Minority Institute where you were arrested. There they will arrange a permanent job for you." I thanked him and said again that I would do the best I could to serve the people as they wished. All I could think about was that finally I was free.

11

My new freedom began on May 17, 1973.

After the months and then years of waiting with scarcely any hope of escape, things suddenly seemed to move with remarkable speed. Mr. Wang had no sooner finished filing the proper papers than he sent for my belongings, which had been put in storage on my first day in the Sangyib prison. When I had inspected them, he helped me put them into a jeep, and before I knew it we were outside the prison walls on the road to Lhasa.

For a while it was almost overwhelming simply to be back in the normal world again. It was a warm, sunny day. What clouds there were hung near the tops of the familiar mountains. As we drove along the road we passed fields that were covered in the soft haze of green that you see when the crops are beginning to send up new shoots. There were houses and occasionally a shop, all the sorts of things that when you are free you don't even notice because you take them for granted. I saw them now with unusual clarity and watched the familiar scenery speed past with the avidity and enthusiasm of a child.

When we got to Lhasa, Mr. Wang drove me to a large house that at one time had belonged to the fourteenth Dalai Lama's parents and that now was being used as a guesthouse. He gave me some food coupons I could use to buy food and about 30 yuan (30 yuan was less than a month's wage for a low-paying job), which would be enough to tide me over until I got back to my school. I stayed in the guesthouse for several days, during which time I was able to visit old friends. I also had some visitors, among them Sangyela, the woman with whom I had become reacquainted when I went to Lhasa with the Red Guards. I had known Sangyela since the 1950s when I was still in Lhasa and was surprised and delighted that she had come to see me. I was struck by what a kind and good person she was.

I was also grateful just to see people and be able to move among them without restraint. But I also saw clear evidence of what would remain a problem for years.

The majority of the people who came to see me treated me well, but with caution. (Sangyela was a rare exception.) Most of them kept a distance, and I could feel the tension immediately. There was no mystery about why. To my friends, just as to people who didn't know me, I was an ex-convict, a political prisoner who was still suspect. Under the best of circumstances such a status would have been a problem. In the political climate of the moment, all the normal effects were magnified. Thus, as my elation over my release from prison began to subside, it was replaced by the knowledge that in some senses I was still going to be a prisoner—of my reputation and my past.

Another thing began to bother me that I could not have anticipated. Here I was in the city where I had lived for some very pleasant years. I knew the location of the several houses where I had stayed formerly, but Lhasa didn't feel like home any longer. I no longer felt that I belonged. So much had happened since I left, both to the city itself and to me, that we seemed like strangers or perhaps old friends meeting after years of separation who didn't recognize one another at first. I think this process had begun when I was shocked by so many things during my earlier visit. Now—at least for the time being—I didn't really feel at home.

I was afraid the same would be true of my village, too. My parents, who had been denounced by many of the people who used to be our neighbors, did not live in our old home any more. So where was home? Guchok? Lhasa? Somewhere else? Where did I belong? Suddenly free, I felt rootless and adrift. I hadn't expected this feeling, and it made me sad and a little frightened. In that sense it was fortunate that the Chinese had such definite plans for me.

In a few days a colleague of Mr. Wang came and put me on a plane for Chengdu. At Chengdu I was met by a security officer, and together we boarded a train for the Xianyang school. We arrived on May 30, 1973.

It became immediately clear that there were going to be real limits to my freedom. While I was waiting to learn what their decision would be I was told that I was to room with a man named Lobsang Thondrup, a former Tibetan monk official who had been accused of molesting boys. That I was put in the same room and therefore the same category as him told me everything I needed to know about the way the Chinese still viewed me. The two of us were free to roam about in prescribed ways. There were no cells or bars. But they watched us constantly and treated us more or less alike.

Waiting to learn what the school would decide to do with me was extremely frustrating, and so to take my mind off my worries I went with the current class of students to do a day's labor in the country. Nobody told me I had to go; I decided on my own. It felt good to work in the open, to be part of a larger community, and to be happy in what I was doing. I returned refreshed and then learned that I had been assigned to the school's printing workshop, where I would work as a bookbinder. My status would be that of a worker at a salary of 43 yuan per month, or about $15.

The job was less than I had hoped for. The prospect of binding books was, of course, far better than going back to prison, but I was disappointed that the plans to train me as a teacher had been changed because I thought of myself as an intellectual and wanted to use my mind and learning to help Tibet. For the moment, however, I could do nothing.

The printing workshop was under the direct supervision of the Education Department and had a total of about sixty workers. Wei Shibu, a peasant from the Shaanxi highlands, was the monitor and technical teacher for the unit I worked in. His superior was Liu Peiyuan, a veteran of the revolution and supervisor of the entire printing workshop. The workshop printed textbooks, exercises, stationery, envelopes—all the necessities for the day-to-day operation of the school.

We worked eight hours a day. Everything was all new, and the work was hard at first, because I had to learn it quickly on the job. I learned how to bind books, fold pages, and use a bamboo knife to control and crease the pages properly. There was only one actual machine in the modern sense, a primitive mechanical paper cutter that we used to cut paper to various sizes or to trim the edges of the finished textbooks. Sometimes when Wei Shibu was absent I had to use this paper cutter on my own; and in my haste to finish my tasks and appear to be contributing, I made mistakes or handled the machine clumsily. My co-workers (some of whom were illiterate peasants) were amused when I struggled and used to call me *men kan gui,* or "monster master." What they meant was that I tried to do too much too fast, without first mastering the requisite techniques. But my biggest problem at first was not mastering the techniques of printing; it was the very practical one of how to live on my salary.

At the current prices, my salary of 43 yuan per month meant that I would be living close to the subsistence level. I worried about money continually, until finally I made a strict plan for myself. Of the money I had, I decided that I ought to spend the highest percent on food. My health was not good, and I knew that I had acquired some chronic digestive problems in prison. Moreover, my experience there had also taught me that physical deterioration makes it harder and harder to keep up mental and emotional strength. So for the time being I decided to spend 36 of my 43 yuan a month on the eggs, milk, rice, grain, vegetables, and oil that I needed to rebuild my strength and maintain my health. I used to get up early and have a big breakfast each day. A milkwoman came by at about five every morning, and I got up then to buy my milk fresh. Each day I would make myself two eggs, milk, and steamed bread and have it all cooked and eaten by the time the rest of the workers were beginning to rise. I also followed this routine because I still remembered what it had been like at my school during the Cultural Revolution, and I didn't want anyone to see the size of my breakfasts and start spreading rumors that I was leading a "bourgeois" or an American-style life. For lunch every day I would try to have vegetable soup and more steamed bread or rice, which I found was soothing to my digestion. For dinner I used to have a huge bowl of noodles with no meat but steeped in vinegar, soy sauce, and onions. I waited for dinner every day, and sometimes that steaming bowl of noodles tasted better to me than a steak dinner in America!

Because I spent almost all my money on food, I had to be creative when it came to taking care of my other necessities. The cost of my room and the electricity was paid for by the school, but all the other household goods plus my clothing had to come from the 7 yuan each month that was left, and I did everything I could to cut corners. Coal was expensive, so I had to limit cooking at home. I ate at the public dining hall when I could, and when I cooked at home I used rolled-up balls of wastepaper from the bindery instead of coal. The burning paper created a lot of smoke, and since my prison experiences had taught me to avoid calling attention to myself whenever possible, I used it to cook mainly outside and early in the morning. But I saved myself a lot of money in a year that way, too. And I think because the physical plant at the school created a lot of smoke and soot, nobody ever noticed my little contributions when I fried my eggs in the morning.

My other economies had to be even tighter. I used to watch the garbage dumps carefully for any household items I might use. I regularly found things like still-usable brooms and washbasins there. I think my greatest triumph, though, was my clothes. Fortunately when I left the prison I had all of my former clothing, which had been kept safe in storage. I even had a few things left that I had bought in America, and I had all of the quilted denims that I had been given when I first arrived at the school. This initial stock of clothing served me quite well, but of course eventually it began to wear out. When it did I became a master of patching and mending. It started with a square here, a square there. I got the cloth for the patches anywhere I could find it, and soon my appearance began to be affected. The squares began to grow into clusters and the clusters began to move toward one another. I patched some of my clothing so often that after a while you could scarcely see the original garment anymore. In short, I became a sort of master scrounger. I pulled used shoes out of the garbage cans, washed them carefully, and made them wearable if they were anywhere close to my size. One day, I remember, I got a real prize. I saw that Mr. Lhawangla, a Tibetan teacher, was about to throw away what had once been a fine fur coat. I told him that if he threw it away I would pick it up and wear it, so he just gave it to me instead. It was in fact in pretty bad shape, but I worked on it for days in my spare time and finally got it into usable condition. And I became known far and wide for my ability to darn socks. I was famous for my trick of using material from completely worn out socks to mend others and do so in such a way that you sometimes couldn't tell where the original ended and my own knitting began.

Although this time of my life was hard for me, I think back about the steps I took to make my clothing last as long as I could with both irony and amusement. By today's standards I must have looked like a clown or a vagrant most of the time. But at that particular moment in history and in that particular place, my increasingly "proletarian" look was almost a badge of honor. Because of my denunciation and imprisonment, I never forgot that period in my early days at the Xianyang school when my much more fashionable American clothing had been a matter of comment and eventually suspicion. My fellow students had told me that I looked too American and that I needed to heed Chairman Mao's advice and "reform" my clothing, so grudgingly I did. For example, I had a pair of wonderful shoes with sharp pointed toes that the Dalai Lama's third brother had given me in New York. The students used to call them "rocket shoes" (I suppose because the pointed ends looked like the nose cone of a rocket), and after some additional negative comments, I duly took my rocket shoes to a cobbler who cut off the offending points and made the shoes more politically acceptable. I also had American-cut suits retailored and made to conform to Chinese style, and I even had a few fairly broad and colorful ties recut and made into belts. All to no avail, of course. It was ironic, I thought, that now, after all I had gone through, necessity—rather then politics or ideology—was making me a model of proletarian perfection.

This routine of working hard (six days a week, with breaks on Wednesday afternoons for political study) and cutting every corner I could became my life for the better part of a year. In some ways that was a blessing. The days were so filled either with tasks at the bindery or all the little things I had to do to find fuel to burn and clothes to wear that I had little time to think of anything beyond practical matters. I spent most of my time alone, and my best companion was a Chinese-made Red Flag radio on which I listened to the Voice of America and the BBC whenever I could. Unfortunately, after a month or so I found out that some of the students learned of my practice and reported me for "listening to the enemy's radio." I felt I had to give up the practice and so was forced to go without one of my best companions in those very lonely days.

Made to feel I had to give up the radio, forced to room with a man accused of molesting children, and treated as guilty by association by co-workers who acted as if I were a sort of second class citizen, I began to feel increasingly pessimistic about my prospects. There was nowhere I really belonged. The main problem, I felt, was my dubious political status. Although I had been released from prison, I was still labeled as the worst possible kind of criminal, a political enemy. Therefore, even though I was technically free, people had to keep their distance from me. I wasn't openly shunned, but for the most part people were reluctant to allow themselves to get too close to me or to admit me fully into the circles of their friendship and communities. Their hesitation was very hard to deal with psychologically and all the more so because the whole reason that I decided to risk hardship and danger by returning was that I wanted to do something meaningful to help my fellow Tibetans. And now here I was—in China, not Tibet— working at a menial job of little direct use to my people and treated as if I carried some kind of communicable political disease. The more I thought about it, the more I felt I had to take active steps to achieve— or perhaps I should say to salvage—some portion of my former hopes and dreams. And so in the autumn of 1974 I asked and was granted permission to take a leave from my job and return to Lhasa and visit my parents. I had a plan.

I had thought about my situation a good deal since I had been back at the school. I decided that it was natural to feel as I had during the first few days after my release from prison. I had been away from my homeland for an extremely long time, and of course I couldn't establish the old closeness right away. But now as I faced the prospect of working in China indefinitely, I was even surer that Tibet was where I wanted to be. Given the Chinese attitude about me, I knew that getting permission to return would not be easy. But I now knew that I would have to keep trying. You had to do one thing at a time, I reasoned. When I had been sent to the school, I had to adjust to hardships. When I had been denounced and sent to prison, I had to concentrate on simply surviving—both physically and psychologically. Now that I was free-but-not-free, and living in China but not Tibet, I had to change my status and try and get back home. Even a journey of a thousand miles begins with a single step.

One of the first steps I decided to take was to get married. I knew it was a possibility, because when my old friend Sangyela visited me in the first days after my release from prison, she had made me an offer of sorts. Not in so many words, of course—she is a shy and tactful person and would never have done anything so direct. But when we talked she made it clear that she was living alone now and that she was lonely. We had known one another for some time, and it wasn't hard to read between the lines. I wasn't ready to commit at that time, though. I had been out of prison for about two days, and the idea of marriage was simply too much too soon. But the more I thought about it and my present situation, the more I was attracted to the idea and the more convinced I became that Sangyela would be an ideal partner.

I knew that she was a good woman who, like myself, had had a hard life. While she and her sister were still young girls, both the parents died and the two young women were forced to fend for themselves. With what little money they had, they tried to set themselves up in business selling chang in a shop in Lhasa. But running a business of that sort is tricky at best and is no life for inexperienced young girls. Few of the customers in their chang shop were decent people. They were rough, hard-drinking men who would often refuse to pay their bills and always made unwanted sexual advances. What law enforcement officers there were in those days were not much help. They didn't exhibit much sympathy for two women trying to run a chang shop, and the officers themselves sometimes got drunk and became a problem as well. The business slowly began to fail, and living as they did the two girls had little opportunity to meet decent men who might have married them or at least helped salvage the business.

When the chang shop failed, Sangyela was desperate. At her wits' end she turned for a short time to prostitution to try to make enough money to live. But she was so shy and unassertive that men often took advantage of her and then refused to pay, and so even this desperate expedient was a failure. In these circumstances, she tried to save herself by marrying a carpenter. But he turned out to be what in America they would call a playboy. He was not a faithful husband, and he often neglected his work. He was gone much of the time, and in his absence, Sangyela's new father-in-law made sexual advances to her. When her husband was at home, he frequently beat her, and at some point she tried running away to India. She almost lost her life on her flight to Kalimpong, and her plan didn't work. Her husband followed her and forcibly brought her back to Lhasa. Eventually, she ran away again, this time successfully, and settled in Yadong, near the border with Sikkim and Bhutan.

There Sangyela met a well-off businessman whom she married and with whom she was very happy until he died in the early 1960s. At that time, she took all the wealth she had (mainly a beautiful solid gold necklace and gold charm box that her second husband had given her) and moved back to Lhasa to be closer to her sister. Like me, in a few short years she became caught up in the Cultural Revolution and along with many other Tibetans was made to sell her jewelry, including her gold necklace and charm box, to the Chinese for an absurdly low price. The Chinese exploited many powerless people in this way.

With her valuables gone, Sangyela had to live carefully during the next few years. That was her situation when I met her in Lhasa when I came with the Red Guards in 1966.

I decided to ask Sangyela to marry me for a number of reasons, many of them practical. For one thing, I thought that marrying her would give me a home base in the city where I had lived for so many years. For another, the fact of having a wife and home in Lhasa would, I thought, make it easier for me eventually to apply for a transfer out of my present job and find a position in Tibet, where I wanted to be. Also, a wife would help solve the problem of always feeling isolated, of people keeping their distance, keeping me always on the outside. Finally, Sangyela was the right age and the right kind of person. We were both in early middle age now. I still had plans for myself, even some hopes and dreams. If I had tried to marry a young girl, there would probably have been children. I couldn't afford a family on my salary, and children would have needed looking after and raising. I wouldn't have had any time to pursue those dreams. And there was another reason why I was drawn to Sangyela. I knew her and she knew me. We had none of the foolish expectations of the young. We'd both survived difficult times. We had both had to make hard decisions and painful compromises. We knew what it meant to live with the consequences of our actions. I respected her, and she respected me. We both knew how to appreciate the simple things in life and could keep our troubles in perspective.

Looking back, I think my decision to marry Sangyela was one of the best decisions I've ever made. She has always been a kind, capable, independent woman. We have always lived in a state of peaceful co-existence, because we understand one another. When we agreed to become husband and wife, we made a verbal agreement. Sangyela is a very religious person, and I am far more interested in modern science and technology. We agreed from the beginning that we would never challenge or belittle one another's beliefs and values. We never have, and we have had a good life together ever since.

There was one problem, though. Technically, I was already married to Tsenjenla in Seattle, in America, in what seemed like a completely different life that had no relation to my existence now. I never expected to see Tsenjenla again. After my experiences in China, my denunciation, and my imprisonment, my American life was no longer a part of my present reality or of any of the possible futures I could imagine for myself. I had been gone from America for many years, now. For part of that time I believed I might die at any moment, and now that I had survived, I saw no possibility of ever returning to the United States. Therefore, I felt that the fact of my previous marriage should not prevent me from marrying Sangyela. I did not feel that I was doing anything wrong.

I was able to stay in Lhasa and live with Sangyela for about two months. At that time she was employed as a construction worker and earned only 1.2 yuan per day, barely subsistence level. Her apartment was tiny, not much more than 10 by 15 feet. Like everyone else at the construction site, she wore patched and ragged clothes, and whenever she could she would gather sticks and any other burnable materials she could find on the way home to cook with. In fact, her narrow existence reminded me very much of my own back at my school.

The Lhasa that I now lived in was the same Lhasa that had shocked me when I saw it as a Tibetan Red Guard. Staples were in short supply, and economies were strict. Necessities were rationed to city dwellers: so many *jin* (pounds) of butter, grain, and only occasionally meat for festival days. And these rations were provided only to people who could prove permanent residence. Families who did not have the proper credentials were not given grain or allowed to send their children to school in the city. (The Chinese enforced these regulations here and in China during these lean years to prevent mass migrations to the major cities.) The markets had only turnips and potatoes for sale. Even people with money to spend could not buy meat or butter nearly as easily as in the old days.

Nevertheless, for a short while after my marriage, I lived in a kind of happy dream. Sangyela made only enough money to take care of herself, and now that our expenses were increased because I was living with her we had to watch every penny. She continued to work at the construction site; and I took every odd job I could find. I went to the houses of people we knew and mended the children's clothes. Sometimes I would go to the nearby marshes to pick the reeds that people dried out and sometimes used for fuel. It may sound like a very hard life, but I remember it fondly. Somehow or other we didn't mind the poverty. Partly I think that was because I felt I had a home again and someone I cared about who cared for me. Sangyela was a lovely Tibetan lady capable of strong emotions and with a kind and compassionate heart. As we got to know one another in the ways people do only by living together, I was surprised to discover that she had been thinking about me for a long time. I was touched to learn that when I had been in prison she had kept a photograph of me beneath her pillow at night. The ties between us grew strong, even in so short a time. As strained as our circumstances were, it was a wonderful time for us and one that I was very sad to see come to even a temporary end. But I knew that eventually I had to go back to Xianyang. I had no choice. My school was expecting me, and I knew I would suffer if I did not return. And so, after a brief visit to see my parents and my old village, I left Lhasa on a cold, drizzling morning that looked exactly like I felt.

I found nothing on the trip to lift my spirits. The bus route was through what had once been the dense, unbroken forests of Kongpo and Kham. For seven days we wound our way through the mountains to Chamdo, and then it took another six days to get from Chamdo to Chengdu, where I caught a train that got me overnight to the Xi'an railway station. The trip had been long enough to give me plenty of time to think. As I considered what I had seen, the happiness of my new life with Sangyela was tempered not only by the changes I had seen in my country but also by the brief and painful trip I made to see my parents.

Nothing prepared me for what I found when I visited my old village. My mother and father were still alive, but the suffering they had endured was written on their faces. They seemed half-dead from a chronic lack of nourishing food, proper clothing, and adequate medical care. They told me that their property, including sheep and other animals, had been confiscated twice since the time my brother was caught with a gun. They had lived for years at or below subsistence level. Their physical situation—their drawn faces and thin bodies—nearly broke my heart. I didn't stay more than a week because they didn't have enough food to feed me and themselves adequately; in fact, my being there was cutting their available supplies nearly in half. Also I felt awkward, because I had not come home to stay. I was still under a cloud of suspicion and could do nothing to relieve their sufferings or change their status (although I was able to help them considerably a few years later).

Though the visit to the village itself was not as shocking as the sight of my parents, it was equally disturbing. From the minute I returned to Guchok, it was easy to see that the old village was poorer than it had been in my youth. I learned that it had been turned into a commune in the early 1960s, and it was easy to see the unhappy results. When I was a boy, though the village had not been a center of wealth or prosperity, it had functioned quite well under the old system. There were some well-to-do families, a few very poor, to be sure. But the majority made a decent living and were relatively happy. Each extended family acted as an independent economic unit. Each had its own land, animals, and equipment. There was healthy competition and a chance for significant rewards for those who worked hard and successfully.

Under the commune system all of the land, equipment, and livestock were taken away from the individual families to be owned jointly by the village. The net result was that individuals produced less than they had before. The population grew, but the wealth of the village didn't keep pace. By this time, there were more people and they had less. And there was no encouragement or desire to break out of the system. So I had a lot to think about as I jolted over the mountain roads, going steadily away from my new wife and toward a country that wasn't mine and a job that was not fulfilling.

When I arrived at the Xi'an railway station and made my way back to my school I soon encountered difficulties about my marriage. I immediately went to ask the appropriate officials for formal permission to legalize the marriage and was furious when they told me that they could not sanction it. They knew that I was already married to a woman in Seattle, and since bigamy is not legal in China, the head of the school refused to provide the necessary papers. I was determined to pursue the matter, so I went to see Mr. Meng, the head of the Education Department, and argued that since my marriage to Tsenjenla in Seattle had taken place under American law, it was not a valid marriage under Chinese law. Therefore, technically, I was not married to anyone. I was so determined, and pressed my case so forcefully, that at last Mr. Meng gave up his argument and issued the necessary introductory letter that made my marriage here official. But that was by no means the end of my problems.

Though my marriage was now officially recognized by the school, there was no indication that I was any nearer to my hope of being allowed to return to Tibet in the foreseeable future. And so the months began to drag by, and eventually the months became years. And nothing changed. Sangyela lived in Lhasa, always hopeful that eventually I would be able to come home. I continued to work at the book bindery but couldn't find the way to push my situation to any kind of permanent resolution.

Then in 1976 something dramatic occurred. In the autumn of that year I was working at the Xianyang railway station unloading boxes of paper for the printshop. Around midday we heard a shocking announcement over the loudspeaker: Mao Zedong had died.

The moment was electric, and I remember it vividly. I acted shocked and saddened like everyone else, but I really wasn't. Although I believed Mao was one of the greatest revolutionary leaders in the history of the world, I had become disillusioned with his idea of endless class struggle and his policy of dividing the population into agents and objects of struggle. How had ruining so many people's lives helped China? At the same time my mind was working a mile a minute. Maybe this was the event that would change China. Perhaps Mao's death would mean the end of the domination of his ideology and the Cultural Revolution. And if the political atmosphere began to become less suspicious and a bit more democratic, perhaps the policies and assumptions that had been controlling my life and determining my fate since I returned would relax as well.

I knew I had to be careful, because the nation itself was in deep mourning, although I suspected that many only feigned sadness, as I did. But I am also sure that many were genuinely devastated, especially among the peasants. I heard that people fainted when they heard the news of Mao's death, that many wept openly in the streets. I did not see such things personally, but reports were common. It was a very tense time in some ways, too. I heard a story about a woman who apparently had not heard the news. She dressed up to go out, putting on a lot of makeup and finery, and was attacked by the people in the street who felt she was being intentionally disrespectful. My course was clear enough. I continued to play the part I knew I was expected to play, and like the rest of the nation, I waited.

Not surprisingly, nothing changed at all for a while. Although we knew that fierce struggles must be going on in Beijing, at first scarcely a ripple made it as far as Xianyang. But unlike before Mao's death, there was reason to hope. There was an air of expectancy. And eventually things began to happen. Before too long, the architects of the worst aspects of the Cultural Revolution, the famous Gang of Four, had been denounced and put in jail. Then at the Eleventh Party Congress that began in 1977, it became clear to everyone that the moderates in the party had gotten the upper hand. Two major policy changes came directly out of that congress. The first was that the Cultural

Revolution was completely discredited. The second was that the party's official emphasis on class struggle was replaced by a push toward economic reconstruction. All the energy and resources that had fueled the class struggle would be shifted to help support policies for economic recovery and greater modernization. I couldn't have been happier. I thought that these changes would not only take the pressure off me but would also help all Chinese and Tibetans. I not only hoped that I would soon be allowed to return to Tibet but also that this new official wish to modernize would make it easier for Tibet to do the same. I was full of new hope, but as usual things took a turn rather different from what I expected.

Encouraged by the tone and tenor of the Eleventh Party Congress, I went to my superiors at the school and asked them to transfer me to a work unit in Lhasa. I knew that there was a party document that said that husbands and wives should be brought together in the same work unit whenever possible, and I thought now was the time when this policy was most likely to be honored. But it wasn't that easy.

Under Chinese law you couldn't just go to another city and find a job. You were assigned to a work unit and could move only if another unit agreed to take you. It was a clever system that gave the Chinese a great deal of control over individuals. If you tried to move about without permission, you couldn't find work. Because there was no way to make a living, there was no place for you and you eventually had to come back into the system or foolishly try to live outside it. For most people, the latter choice was not an option.

At first my superiors simply refused my request for a transfer. They told me that they could not find a work unit in Lhasa to take me. When I pressed them, they finally agreed to let me go to Lhasa for three months on my own. They said that if I could find a position in a work unit that would take me, then I could get the necessary transfer. That was a lot easier said than done, and I'm sure they knew it would be.

I did go to Lhasa and though it was wonderful to be reunited with Sangyela again, the experience of trying to find a job was extremely discouraging because the deck was stacked against me. For most of that first three months I followed lead after lead but with no success. The story was the same every time; I would hear about a possible position for which I was qualified. I would go and talk to the people; they would ask questions, and I would have to tell them about being in prison, about being a political prisoner. The minute they knew my history, you could see in their eyes that the interview was over. I went from one work unit to the next, and the same thing happened each time: so sorry. Nothing at the moment. Thank you for applying. The doors just kept slamming, and it made me more and more frustrated, discouraged, and angry. It was such a waste. I was in my late thirties. I had a good education. I could speak and write three languages. But I was officially classified as a menial worker, and I was wrongfully saddled with a political and criminal record that virtually guaranteed that no one would be willing to take a chance on me. It was like still being in prison. The bars were invisible, but they were there just the same.

By the end of three months I had found nothing, and I petitioned my school to give me some extra time to find a job. The school wouldn't hear of it. My leave was over, and I was to return immediately. A second petition produced the same results and an even harsher warning. If I did not return, they would cut off my salary. At that point I decided that I wasn't going to go back to the school, no matter what. I simply had to find a job in Lhasa. And so I lied. I sent them word that I was ill, that I had to be taken to a hospital. Then I told them that my wife had health problems that required that I stay with her. I told them anything I could think of to buy time. And I stayed an additional three months, knowing that my salary would be stopped, trying to find a position that would allow me to transfer to Lhasa.

I don't know what would had happened if I had not succeeded. But finally, after about a month, when I had all but lost hope, I found a courageous and extremely kind woman who worked in the Tibet Autonomous Region's Health Bureau and was willing to give me a chance. She offered me a job teaching English at a disease prevention station. She wasn't afraid. I was grateful beyond what I can express, and I foolishly thought that my struggle might be over, because I now had someone willing to take me and was able to get the proper papers.

When I had the documents I needed in hand, I went directly to the Autonomous Region's Labor Department in Lhasa. I hoped they could handle my transfer from there and that I wouldn't even have to go back to my school at all. My luck seemed to continue. I was given a temporary teaching assignment. My students were some of the staff at the Health Bureau, and the money I received helped me to get back on my feet financially. But of course it wasn't that easy. The work unit in Xianyang would not allow the transfer to be made while I was in Lhasa. My orders were to return to China immediately.

So again I boarded a bus and set off for Xianyang. When we stopped in Chamdo, I stayed overnight with one of my former schoolmates from the Xianyang school, who greeted me very cordially and treated me extremely well. Since I had become used to coldness, suspicion, and fear from most of my classmates, these kind attentions were extremely welcome. Grasping at straws, I hoped they might be another sign that my fortunes were about to change for the better. But by the time I got back to my school once again, I learned differently. On the day after I returned to Xianyang, I went eagerly to see the official in charge of my work unit, told him about my offer of a job, showed him my papers, and asked for assurances of the transfer to Lhasa that they had promised. "No," he said. He was sorry. I would simply have to try to understand. Despite my letter of approval from the Labor Department in Lhasa, the Xianyang school authority had decided not to keep its promise.

There is no way to describe my anger. I now thought I saw my situation clearly for the first time. The school's sending me to Lhasa to look for work had been a sham, a cruel expedient. I had had no chance from the beginning. The officials at my school were never going to let me go. They simply weren't going to take the chance. They didn't trust me, and it was easiest for them, far less risky, just to keep me here indefinitely. I had never really allowed myself to think about the possibility of being at Xianyang forever. Now it was all I could imagine. For a time I was almost frantic. I was so close to the kind of freedom I wanted. I had a wife in Lhasa and at least one person who was willing to take a chance and give me work. I couldn't stand the thought of staying at this school and in my menial job in the bindery for the rest of my life. If I didn't get my status changed, I would never feel that I was a man like other men. As it was now, I could not look people in the eye. I felt instead that I ought to apologize for myself.

I believed that my criminal record and official classification as a menial laborer were the keys. I simply had to do something to change them, and after thinking about it for a while I decided that if I couldn't get satisfaction at my school, I would try to go to Beijing, without the school's permission, and plead my case before the State Council. It was an act of pure desperation.

Technically, I felt I had the right to take my case to Beijing. After Mao's death and the downfall of the Gang of Four, intellectuals—and everyone— who felt they had been wronged during the Cultural Revolution were being officially encouraged to come to Beijing, describe what had been done to them unjustly in their respective work units, and seek redress. The State Council was supposedly willing to listen to all such pleas. But I knew that I would never get permission from my school to make such a journey—to accuse them (among others) of bad treatment! In fact, if the school officials realized what I was thinking of doing and if I were caught, I wasn't sure what the consequences might be. I might even be sent back to prison again. But how much worse would that be than the kind of life I was living now? I honestly felt I had the truth on my side, and, whatever the risk, I would try. So I began to make my plans.

The first school Tashi built in 1990 in his home village of Guchok. The school had three classrooms, two apartments for the teachers, and forty-six students.

A group of village students with their teacher at Guchok school.

First year village students learning to write in school on a traditional Tibetan wooden writing board.

Students and their teachers in front of their new school.

A new school completed in 1994 that contains three classrooms, two teacher's apartments, and over ninety students.

Students and their teachers in front of their new school.

Students dancing in traditional style at the Khartse school in front of other students and villagers.

A Tibetan boy practicing writing the Tibetan alphabet on a traditional Tibetan writing board.

12

On September 25, 1978, at about five in the afternoon, I put a small bundle of clothing under my arm and slipped out of my room, which was in a one-story brick house not more than a few hundred yards from the railway station. I was sure everyone was watching me. There were plenty of teachers and students around, most of them washing the vegetables they would soon be cooking for dinner. At first, nobody seemed to notice, but then I locked eyes with my roommate, Lobsang the child molester. He was just about to enter our apartment but had turned and was looking in my direction. It was clear that he had seen me, and when he noticed that I was heading toward the station I saw him turn and begin to walk quickly toward the school office. I didn't want to break into a run and call more attention to myself, but I quickened my pace, and when I reached the railroad yards I darted in among the lines of empty cars on the siding.

I had no doubt about what Lobsang was up to. I'm sure he saw my escape as an opportunity to gain favor with the higher-ups. I was also sure that they would be searching for me soon. My heart was pounding, and I had to stop, calm myself, and try to think what to do. I didn't know how much time I had before the search for me would begin, but it wouldn't be long.

I looked around frantically. It was only a little after five, and the train for the provincial capital of Xi'an (about forty miles away from the school at Xianyang), where I could get a ticket to Beijing, wouldn't be leaving until much later. I needed somewhere to hide. There were trains of heavily loaded coal cars on the siding and among them a boxcar or two. I saw that the door of one of the boxcars was open, and I slipped inside and closed it behind me. Alone in the darkness, I could literally hear my own heart pounding.

Within minutes the first of the searchers reached the station. Through the cracks in the sliding door I watched as the people from the school ran around angrily, asking questions, and looking in the station and among the railroad cars. Soon they began to fan out and search more systematically. A few got close enough that I could hear what they were saying, and I tried as hard as I could not to move and to control my breathing. At one point, a Chinese official climbed up on top of one of the coal cars just across from the boxcar where I was hiding. He was only yards away, and for a few moments I was so frightened I couldn't breathe. He looked directly at the car I was in, and I felt as if our eyes locked. But I didn't move a muscle, and although he was looking right at me, he didn't see me. The search continued, and for a while I thought I was safe. But every time I thought they were gone I would suddenly hear voices terrifyingly close: "He's there, right there." "Look under the cars." "Watch for anything that moves." They were all around me at one point. I don't know how they missed me. But as dusk turned into darkness the search became increasingly less active and finally stopped altogether.

I was extremely lucky. I had made no secret about my anger at being refused permission to return to Lhasa, and therefore the school officials decided that I must be going to try to go west, toward Tibet. So they watched the westbound trains going to the railway station at Liuyuan on the Qinghai-Tibetan border. It never occurred to them that I would try to go east, to Beijing. And so at about nine o'clock I was able to sneak onto a slow-moving train that took me to the central Xi'an City station. When I got there, I walked right in and bought a ticket to Beijing with most of the remaining money I had in the world. Nobody tried to stop me. They were all looking on the wrong track!

As the train rolled through the dark night toward Beijing, I had plenty of time to think. Most of the other passengers were asleep, but I was so keyed up I could scarcely stay in my seat. I had decided to take this step in a moment of rashness and desperation, but from the minute

I left my school without permission, the die was cast. I couldn't go back without dire consequences. I could only keep going forward and hope for the best. I had so little money that I didn't buy any food that night. My stomach churned with hunger and anxiety, but there were no second thoughts. Whatever was going to happen would happen.

The train didn't reach Beijing until the next evening. During the day I spent the pittance I had left to buy a meager breakfast of steamed bread and a vegetable dish. I got through most of the rest of the day by drinking hot water, but hunger was the least of my worries. When we arrived at the station, I could see that something was up, and I was terrified. There were policemen everywhere. They were looking people up and down and stopping some to search their luggage. My heart sank. Was this the way it was going to end? Had they gotten word of my whereabouts already? I was completely numb with fear and almost in a dream state.

Mechanically, I went through the motions of gathering my belongings and following the other passengers off the train. I was sure it was the end for me. Even if by some chance I wasn't the one they were looking for at the moment, if they stopped me for any reason it was all over. I had no travel documents, no introductory letter from my work unit. If I were detained for any reason, they would check with the school. And that would be it.

I walked slowly down the platform trying to avoid people's eyes but also trying to avoid acting strange or calling attention to myself. I was sure that at each step I would suddenly feel a rough hand on my shoulder or hear a sharp voice call out to me, asking to see my papers. But it didn't happen. I don't know what or who the police were looking for, but for the moment at least it wasn't me. Grateful even to have made it this far, I had no idea how much longer my good luck would last. So without waiting a moment longer, I searched until I found a well-lighted part of the waiting room in the station itself, and there I drafted what would later become my formal petition to the State Council. Since I had nowhere to stay until morning, I spent the rest of the night in the station writing. I wrote in Chinese, which was hard for me and took longer than I thought. But I knew exactly what I wanted to say, and the ideas themselves came readily. Part of the time I was concentrating so hard on my petition that I almost forgot where I was. But the other part of the time I was afraid. Nobody seemed to mind my spending the night there, but the policemen would come by periodically on their normal rounds. I tried desperately not to look suspicious and not to let the terror I felt show. I comforted myself with the thought that if they caught me now, they would find the document I was writing. They would know why I was here, and perhaps my case would still get a hearing, whatever happened to me.

As the next day broke I was still without a definite plan. I didn't know exactly how to go about presenting my petition or to whom. And I was going to need a more permanent and less public place to stay. Moreover, I knew that my school wasn't going to forget about me and that if the school officials had no accurate information, they could accuse me of almost anything—of trying to run away to Tibet, of trying to flee to India, whatever they wanted to say. To protect myself, I walked nearly six miles through the city to find the nearest telegraph office, and I sent a telegram to my school in which I told them where I was, why I had come, and exactly what I was going to do. I'm certain that the school officials were furious when they received it, but what could they do at that point? If they had caught me during my escape, I would have had little chance. But the Communist Party had publicly invited people with grievances to come forward. I was already in Beijing, and it was unlikely that anything the officials of my school back in Xianyang could do would keep me from at least having my day in court. There might be hell to pay if and when I had to go back, but I was certain they would now be forced to let the events play themselves out. I wasn't out of the woods entirely, but suddenly I began to feel much better.

After I had sent my telegram, I continued to walk the streets of the city, trying to decide what to do next. On a hunch, I walked to the Beijing radio station, where I knew I would find an old classmate of mine from Xianyang school, Mr. Wangchuk, who worked there as a radio announcer. At first, when he met me and heard the facts of my story, he was nervous, and I could see he was a little bit frightened. But he decided to befriend me and went directly to his superiors. When he had told them why I was here, they gave him permission to allow me to stay at his apartment where he lived with his wife and daughter, which I did for one night.

It was an act of courage and friendship for Wangchuk to agree to take me in. I will never forget his friendship, and we are still close today. He not only gave me a place to stay for a night, but he helped me in every way he could. When he learned that I had no money, he gave me 25 yuan to live on. I offered some of my clothing as security for the loan, but he would have none of it. He didn't ask questions or make demands. He just gave me the money I needed. I had become so used to people avoiding me, staying away from me, not wanting to take a chance, that I was almost overcome with his kindness to me in my time of great trial.

I stayed with Mr. Wangchuk for only one night, because on the next day (my third day in Beijing) I learned that the State Council had a guesthouse that provided low-cost rooms for those coming to seek redress for grievances committed during the Cultural Revolution. The house was easy to find, and when I arrived it was crowded almost to overflowing with people from all the provinces of China, all there to complain about wrongs committed against them. There were even people from as far away as Inner Mongolia. As I saw the sheer number of citizens, every one of them in situations much like my own, I began to feel less lonely. And when I entered the house itself and took steps to find out what the process was by which I could make my own complaint, seek my own justice, I began to believe that there might be some hope for me after all.

I talked first with one of the officials whose job it was to interview and process the new arrivals. He asked me some very direct questions: Where was I coming from? Did I have the proper travel documents? I told him the truth: that I had no documents and that I had left my school without permission. And I also told him a little bit about my history. He seemed to understand my situation immediately. Many of the others who had come were in similar circumstances and had taken similar or even greater risks to get here. Without hesitation the officials decided to let me stay.

I took a deep breath, asked for directions, and went next to the office of investigators. The number of people who had come with complaints was so great that there were rows of investigators' offices. As instructed, I went to a large general office first. There I identified myself and gave a brief history of my persecution to an officer, who was very attentive and took notes continuously. When I had finished my initial statement, he took me to the office of Mr. Wang, the man who would be the principal investigator in my case. As I was about to enter, the young man from the general office took me aside for a moment. "Remember," he said in a kind voice, "you can say anything to Mr. Wang. You don't have to be afraid." After all the years during the Cultural Revolution in which even your best friend might become the one who denounced you, the idea that I could speak completely freely was a bit hard to believe. On the other hand, every indication so far was that the party was completely serious about redressing the wrongs that had been done in the past. And what did I have to lose at this point?

Mr. Wang was a calm, elderly gentleman who took my case seriously from the start and encouraged me to speak freely. He wanted me to begin at the beginning and give him a full account of my situation and my particular grievances. I did and then presented him with the petition I had written in the railway station on my first night in Beijing. I told him what it was and made a formal request that he present it to the State Council for me. Mr. Wang didn't seem surprised or act as if my request was anything out of the ordinary. He took the document from me and began to read through it quickly. As he read he made notes and asked me questions about particular events and episodes.

In my petition I had made three points. The first was that I was an innocent victim of the Cultural Revolution because I had been unjustly denounced and imprisoned as a Tibetan nationalist and an American spy. I was neither of those things and never had been. The second point was that I had been imprisoned and persecuted without a formal trial, to which I had a right, and that I was released without any formal resolution of my status or my case.

The third point was that I now had a wife who lived in Lhasa while my work unit was in Xianyang, and that although it was party policy to allow husbands and wives to live together, my work unit was refusing to permit me to transfer to Lhasa.

My petition was an emotional document. In it, I expressed feelings that had been building for years. I talked about the cruelties I had seen at my school, the physical and mental suffering I had undergone. I wrote about what it was like to be released from prison but not be free, to be treated as a criminal even though I had never been formally tried or convicted, to be an educated and potentially valuable contributor to my country and then to be classified as a menial laborer and kept far away from home. As I remembered the details of what I had written, I became bit nervous, because I knew how much of my anger I had poured into that document, written as the railroad police walked back and forth past me in the station. But I quickly saw that I didn't have to worry. Mr. Wang didn't seem at all surprised and was neither judgmental nor critical. When he had finished reading, taking notes, and asking questions, he told me to go back to the guesthouse, get some rest, and come back to see him in two days. He said that during that time he would consider the facts of my case and my petition and discuss them with his superiors. He was very kind. As I was leaving he told me to be careful, because he knew I was one of many who had no travel documents. I left the office emotionally drained but more hopeful than I had been in years. It was true that I still had to wait while others determined my fate. But the seriousness and kindness with which everyone was treating me were extremely encouraging.

As I waited back at the guesthouse, I had time to reflect on my experiences. The system here seemed to be a series of hurdles that each petitioner had to cross. At each stage my story—like everyone else's—was being evaluated and then either dismissed or sent to another group for further review. The process was, I assume, designed to weed out improper or groundless petitions. If your case kept leaping over the hurdles it was eventually considered by the men at the highest levels of the State Council. There were dangers, however.

Though Mr. Wang never told me about it (I only learned about it later), it seems that during this two-day waiting period my school made an attempt to intervene in the process. Mr. Zhou, who worked at the Xianyang school, happened to be in Beijing on a business trip during the time that I was there. After the school got my telegram, school officials contacted Mr. Zhou and ordered him to go to the State Council and "keep an eye on Tashi Tsering." I learned that Mr. Zhou had not only gone to the State Council but had spent some time talking with Mr. Wang. I don't know for certain that the school gave him any specific instructions, but I do know that Mr. Zhou did nothing to harm my case. In fact, he may actually have helped me. Though Mr. Zhou was now "liberated," he himself had been persecuted during the Cultural Revolution, and, having seen many good friends persecuted as well, he had many bitter experiences. Again, though I don't know the particulars, the result seems to have been that he was sympathetic and confirmed many of the details in my report. If the Xianyang school officials had hoped to harm my case, they picked the wrong person to send to check on me, because when I returned for my next interview with Mr. Wang, he made it clear that my petition was still alive. After questioning me closely about details, he told me that my case would be discussed next by the larger group of which he was a part. I was to return tomorrow to learn its decision.

When I returned, Mr. Wang went straight to the point. He told me that his group had judged that I had done exactly what I was supposed to in making my petition and that it would be sent to the highest council for final judgment. I was overjoyed when I heard the news, but with the next sentence I was brought swiftly back to earth. There was another part to the decision. While my petition would reach the highest level, it was also their conclusion that my case could be resolved for good only at the place where my troubles had arisen—at my old work unit and the Xianyang school.

I was stunned. All of my previous bad experiences came flooding back to me, and I thought for a minute that this whole process of petitioning was just another bad joke. It was just to make the people imagine that something was being done to help them. The result would be the same as it had always been. Mechanically I thanked Mr. Wang for his and the party's kindness and consideration. And then my emotions took over. "I am not going back to that school," I burst out. "I am going back to Tibet, where I belong. I hate the Xianyang school, and you can't make me go there." By then I was shouting. I couldn't stop myself, and Mr. Wang looked both surprised and shocked. He didn't try to argue with me, though. He waited a moment and then looked me right in the eye. "Tashi Tsering," he said, "if you do what you've just threatened to do you will be making a big mistake." That was all he said, but there was something about the way he said it that calmed me down immediately. Instinctively I trusted Mr. Wang. He had been honest with me and a supporter throughout the whole process. I felt bad that I had shouted at him, and after a few moments I was able to swallow my disappointment and suspicions and agree to go back to my school once again. I tried to convince myself that I wouldn't really be going back alone. The State Council would send its report and recommendations to my work unit. I would just have to hope and trust that justice would be done. I had only one final request. I pointed out to Mr. Wang that I didn't have any money. How could I even afford to go back? He smiled and told me his office would provide money for the trip home, which they did without further question.

I had plenty to think about on the train on the way back to Xianyang, and I kept going back and forth in my mind. One minute I would be cynical and pessimistic and imagine that when I returned I would be criticized and then punished, that nothing would come of my petition after all. The next minute I would be filled with hope. I would be certain that the school officials would finally have to take my case seriously, because the State Council did and because it was the wish of the national Communist Party that wrongs committed during the Cultural Revolution be redressed. I had no regrets, but I wanted things settled quickly, one way or the other. I had my hopes raised, and I didn't want to wait longer.

Early on the morning after I arrived back at my school, I went directly to talk with the president at his home. He was a revolutionary intellectual who had been persecuted at this school during the Cultural Revolution, but he had been cleared and "liberated" long since and had become extremely hard-line in his policies, as if to show his former persecutors that he was above suspicion and could be trusted completely. I was sure he already knew about my unauthorized trip to Beijing, and as I knocked on his door I worried which president I would find—the one who understood what it meant to be persecuted unjustly or the one who still felt that the eyes of the community were upon him and assumed people would be judging him on the basis of how he dealt with me. I didn't have long to find out. The president's wife answered the door and quickly took me to Mr. Wang, who was still seated at the breakfast table. The first thing he said when he saw me was, "Tashi Tsering, you have made a very bad impression on the students and staff of this school. No one has ever done what you have just done! I don't say that you had no right to go to Beijing and present your case, but you went without permission. You violated school discipline. This is an extremely serious offense."

My emotions had begun to rise from the minute he began to speak, and I could feel tears of anger in my eyes as I replied hotly. "I didn't ask anybody's permission to go to Beijing, because I was sure the school would not have granted it. This school has always been my biggest enemy. I came here in good faith, but it was here that I was denounced unjustly. I was put on mass probation here and then arrested and imprisoned at the request of the people at the school. There was no formal trial, and when you released me you crippled me by giving me the status of a criminal and the classification of a menial worker, far below my training and abilities. I don't say that you have done all these things yourself, but everything bad that has happened to me has happened since I came to this school. How can you imagine that I would feel that I could go to it for help?"

I paused for a moment, but the president said nothing and so I continued but in a more conciliatory vein. The tears were running freely as I tried to remind him of what it had been like to be denounced at a mass struggle meeting, what it had been like to feel powerless to defend yourself and to be unable to appeal to the facts or the truth. I said I was sure he could sympathize with someone like me who was also accused unjustly, who had hopes of helping his people and his country, and whose hopes had been dashed unfairly and repeatedly. "Please forgive me for my bluntness," I kept saying, "but also please try to understand." Because he did nothing to stop me, I let all my anger and frustration go. I pointed out that even though I had been released from prison I was obviously not trusted. I was not allowed to join my wife in Lhasa even though party policy specifically states that husbands and wives should be allowed to work together. "Don't you see," I said finally. "I didn't ask anyone here to help me, because I didn't believe anyone would. I went to Beijing on my own, because I felt it was the only thing left for me to do!"

I was finished. The president said nothing at first, and the room became so quiet that I could hear the clock ticking. Finally he spoke. "Your actions have reflected badly on the school and its staff. You must write a letter of self-criticism in which you apologize to your co-workers for breaking the school's code of discipline. When you have finished your letter, you will give it to your supervisor." And that was all. The interview was over.

The president's reaction and his decision were both more and less than I had expected. It was less in the sense that I suppose I had foolishly hoped that the school might have acknowledged its mistakes on the spot and that something truly decisive might have happened at once. It was more in the sense that—as I thought about things realistically—there was no talk of prison or direct punishment. There was no outburst of anger; there were no threats. I even had the feeling that this command to write a self-criticism letter might be an easy way to let the school save face. I didn't know. But there was little else I could do, so I went back to my room and began to write.

The first version of my self-criticism letter was emotional, full of anger and justifications for my actions. In it I detailed all the wrongs I felt had been done to me, much the same things I had said to the people at the State Council. When I gave this version to my supervisor for approval, he returned it to me almost immediately. It was unacceptable, he said. It was too full of excuses and self-justification. I wrote a second draft that I thought was much more moderate and reasonable, but he returned that, too. So now I understood the game, even though I still wasn't sure what was at stake. So I wrote an even briefer, highly apologetic letter in which I said that I was extremely sorry for breaking the school's discipline and embarrassing the students and staff.

This draft was acceptable, as I knew it would be, and so my supervisor called for a self-criticism meeting. It was a big meeting. There were at least sixty people there, all workers or staff from the school— no students. The idea was that I was to apologize to my peers, presumably the group my actions had directly embarrassed. I still remember how nervous I was and, of course, why. I had extremely vivid memories of the mass struggle meetings during the days of the Cultural Revolution, especially the one at which I was denounced. Was history about to repeat itself?

When the meeting began I was made to stand up and read my self-criticism letter aloud, which took about five minutes. When I had finished, I was permitted to comment on what I'd said, and so I began to try to explain why I did what I did, why I felt I had no choice. I was interrupted a number of times by workers who criticized me. Why didn't I trust the school? If I had just talked to my superiors, they would surely have supported my request. They said they thought I was just interested in justifying myself, even now.

I can't say I was surprised by such reactions. That sort of thing is exactly what went on at such meetings. They weren't just occasions to punish and publicly humiliate the offender. They were also opportunities for public displays of loyalty and correct thinking. If anything was unusual about this meeting, it was that someone actually supported me—publicly. Among all the self-righteous and critical voices there was one woman—Mrs. Suan—who actually reacted sympathetically to my story. "Let us listen to him," she said. "He has so many things to say. He is full of reasons, and we should listen to him." I was nearly overcome. Nothing like this kind of sympathy or support had ever happened to me in the past; it scarcely could have. Mrs. Suan was courageous, there was no question about it. But the fact that she spoke at all was clearly a sign that the worst excesses of the Cultural Revolution were over, even here at the Xianyang school. Slowly but surely, things were changing.

The meeting lasted about two hours. By the time it was over I had conceded that I had broken the school's discipline. I apologized to my fellow workers and then went back to my room to await the school's official response. I didn't expect an early decision. I knew the Chinese now. They would tell me what they wanted when they wanted. There was nothing I could do to speed up the process. Day followed day, and I soon got back into my old routines at the book bindery. I had returned from Beijing at the end of September 1978. The self-criticism meeting had taken place about two weeks later. Soon the days turned to weeks and the weeks to months, and still no word.

I heard nothing until December 19, 1978. When I finally learned the school's decision I was shocked. I could scarcely believe it. The school's officials issued a formal document in which they said that I had been wrongfully arrested and imprisoned; that they would refund all of my lost salary, including that due during the time spent on mass probation; and that I would immediately be reclassified from worker to intellectual. It was everything I had asked for. In my wildest dreams I never imagined I would succeed to this extent. I went back to my room in a daze, trying to make myself realize that after all those years of struggle and despair, I had finally won.

13

My liberation this time was completely different from my more or less conditional release from the Sangyib prison years ago. Good things began to happen to me right away, reassuring things. My work status was changed immediately, and within days I was reassigned to the National Language Research Center, which was in a different part of the school from the bindery. Since I was classified as an intellectual now, not a laborer, my future work would obviously be consistent with my new status. I also ceased to have to room with Lobsang. He was moved elsewhere, and I had the room all to myself. I was no longer to be stigmatized by being linked with a reputed sex offender, and therefore those prison bars that were invisible but had so seriously affected the way people looked at me (and the way I viewed myself) were disappearing.

I was almost giddy in my new freedom, because along with it came at least temporary prosperity. I was immediately given the money that I would have earned during the years I was in prison. Though my monthly salary had been extremely low, the money had been accumulating for a long time, and because I got it all at once it was a considerable sum for me. In those first exciting days, I used some of it to buy myself a big Japanese radio–tape recorder. With it I could begin listening again to the BBC and the Voice of America, old friends whose company I had missed for a long time. The political atmosphere was now such that you could be much more open about such things, and for a while I listened almost greedily.

At the National Language Research Center I learned that my training as an English teacher, which had been interrupted when I was imprisoned, was to be resumed, and this news, too, made me extremely happy. I felt that education was an area in which I could genuinely play a role not only because of my training but because of my life experiences. My own pursuit of a modern education had given me the knowledge and perspectives that made me to want return to Tibet. I thought my example might be one that other Tibetans like me might want to follow, and I was immensely pleased at the thought that I could help them do so.

Because I had been out of practice with English, the school decided to send me to the Xi'an Foreign Language Institute to take a six-month refresher course. So in January 1979 I boarded a train for Xi'an, this time with the school's permission. I was excited and glad for the opportunity to study English once again because I knew already that I needed some help. When I had first begun listening to the Voice of America on my new radio I was shocked at how much my skills had deteriorated. By the time I left the University of Washington, so many years ago, I had gotten used to hearing English, and I read and wrote it regularly and with some facility. But I had been nearly completely cut off during the years in prison, and for a short time I was worried that I had lost everything I had previously learned. Happily, just listening to the radio began to bring the old abilities back, and I was eager for the chance to sharpen my skills at the Foreign Language Institute. After a detour of nearly twelve years, I was back on track once again.

There were more students than I had expected. They were from most of China's many provinces and in such numbers that we were broken into separate groups for study. I was put in a group commensurate with my level of previous experience. Among my classmates were teachers, of course, but also businessmen and professionals in various fields. Many were there to brush up their English because they were going to be sent abroad, either to study further or to represent China in some capacity. It seemed clear that the central government was in a mood to look outward now, to think more in terms of participation in the world than at any time since my return. It was a good sign—good for China and, I thought, good for me, especially good for my chances of getting back to Tibet sooner rather than later.

I was impressed by the classes. The textbooks were written by Westerners, and even some of the teachers were from abroad, like my friend Mr. Norman, who was from Australia. The presence of these teachers from "outside" was, I thought, another sign that the Chinese were beginning to look outward. There would never have been foreigners teaching in the schools during the Cultural Revolution. The books were in English, of course. We spoke English in class as well, and I got up to speed quickly. I found that most of the students in my group could write English better than I could. But I seemed to have retained much of the ability to speak that I had gotten from my years in America, because my conversational skills were better than those of most of my classmates. The whole day was used for learning. At night we were not only allowed to listen to the BBC and the Voice of America, we were encouraged to do so, and the listening helped immensely.

It was a very happy time for me. I was shaking the rust off. I not only felt my skills returning, I felt I was reconnecting with the world. For the first time since returning to China I actually sent a letter out of the country. I wrote to Professor Terry Wylie at the University of Washington, because his was the only address I still remembered. Somehow or other, through all the years, the Cultural Revolution, the deprivation, and imprisonment, his mailing address stayed in my mind. In my letter I asked about Tsejen Sakya and some of the other professors and students I had known and told him I would love to hear from him. Professor Wylie never answered my letter. I learned later that he was angry with me because he felt I had betrayed the Dalai Lama by my independent actions and refusal to work with the government-in-exile. His anger was just one of many reminders I would get of how politically complicated the relations between Tibet and China had already become, how many different sides there were, and how strong the feelings could run. Happily, though I did not hear from Professor Wylie, I did get a letter from my friend Mel Goldstein, who told me about many common acquaintances and let me know that he was coming to Beijing soon for a conference. I was very happy to reestablish ties with at least one of my friends in America, although I was unable to meet him in Beijing. What pleased me the most was the still new sense that I was going to be able to have much more to say about the direction my life took than I had had for years.

When I returned from the six-month course at the Foreign Language

Institute, I was eager to go home to Tibet and immediately applied for a transfer to Lhasa. I learned, however, that the school wanted me to stay for a while at least, because school officials were planning to establish an English Department and they wanted me to help. Their attitude was completely different from that in earlier times, however, when they had simply denied my requests. They genuinely seemed to want me to stay, and so I didn't become angry. Instead, I asked that if I couldn't go to Lhasa right away I be allowed to bring my wife here to the school to stay with me. The officials agreed and even paid for my plane fare and Sangyela's, and in a short time I was on my way to Lhasa—not to the Sangyib prison as before but to my home, to bring my wife back to live with me!

I stayed in Lhasa for about two weeks, but though Sangyela was delighted to see me I had a harder time than I thought getting her to follow me back to China. For one thing, she didn't want to leave her sister. The hardships the two had suffered had made them very close. And that wasn't her only objection to leaving. As I have said, Sangyela was religious, and she didn't like the idea of going to what she felt was "Godless" Communist China. I respected her feelings and was patient and tried to reason with her. I reminded her that she could pray in our house in Xianyang just as well as she could in Lhasa; and that we wouldn't be there forever. It would be all right.

In the end, Sangyela agreed to go, and once she had decided to make the journey, the excitement took over. She had never flown before, and so everything about the plane ride was new. She was fascinated by the fact that when the plane gained its cruising altitude we were above the clouds and she could look down on the snow-covered mountaintops.

When we deplaned at Chengdu, Sangyela was frightened by the crowds at first. She didn't speak a word of Chinese, and she was so afraid of getting separated from me in the crowds that she clung to me with an iron grip and wouldn't let go till we were safely on the train for Xi'an. Since it was also the first time she had ridden on a train, she was interested in everything about the train itself and fascinated by the images of the foreign countryside that rolled rhythmically past the windows. I think she was a bit shocked when we arrived at the school and she got her first look at my apartment. Since Lobsang had cleared out I had it all to myself. It was a single room but a big one with a high ceiling, and after some of the tiny prison cells I had seen in the past few years, I was very proud of it because it seemed so large and spacious. To me it looked very neat and tidy. There were my bed and quilt, a desk and chair, and a box or two on the floor with all my things. Everything in apple-pie order. But the rest was just empty space. Sangyela said nothing at the time, but she told me later that she thought the bulk of my possessions must have been in storage somewhere else. It was hard to believe I had so little.

Sangyela was not dismayed for long, however. She had known real hardship, and once she had agreed to come with me, she was not daunted by removal from her home, by the new surroundings, by the fact that she didn't speak Chinese—or in fact by anything. The school found her a job, and she threw herself into it. She began with janitorial work at the school's hospital, where she quickly became known to her Chinese co-workers as "the woman who never sits." Always on the move and impatient with the slower workers around her, she talked her way into another job that amounted to her doing the work of two—and for twice her original salary. As soon as she began this new position, she would get up early in the morning and have the hospital's courtyard cleaned by dawn, and then have cleaned the patients' rooms by about three in the afternoon. She worked so hard that some of my Tibetan friends began to tease me about my wife who was now earning more than I was!

Once we were settled, I threw myself into my job as well. As the plans for developing the new English Department began to go forward I had what I thought was an excellent idea. As I thought about my own experiences learning English and remembered sitting across from Mr. Cumming with a dictionary between us, I realized that one of the things we would need most was a good dictionary—preferably one that had the definitions in both Tibetan and Chinese as well as English. As far as I knew there were no trilingual dictionaries available. So my idea was that I be allowed to compile one. I first discussed my ideas with Liu Dejun, who was in our group and who had come from the Xi'an Foreign Language Institute to help facilitate the Tibetan education project. When I described my project to him he said, "That's a wonderful idea! That's exactly what we need." I was very encouraged by his immediate enthusiasm and ready offer of support, and so together we made a formal proposal to the school that I be given time and support to put together an English-Tibetan-Chinese dictionary for the specific purpose of helping students at the school learn English more quickly and efficiently. My superiors liked the idea and encouraged me to go ahead with it, which I did—immediately.

My operation was very small at first. The school didn't have a lot of extra money to spend. But school officials did give me a room of my own to work in; they provided all the reference books they could, even though there was no budget for reference books; and they relieved me of all other duties. Basically they paid me my salary for working on the dictionary. They also gave me an assistant. I had been thinking about whom I would like to have work with me, and the obvious choice was Liu Dejun, especially because he had seemed so enthusiastic about the idea. When I approached him, he smiled and agreed on the spot.

We began work on November 13, 1979. In the beginning we were only thinking of compiling a small dictionary to be used by the students at the school. Since we were starting from scratch we had to begin by deciding how we would choose the words to be included and how we would classify and present them. We began by including the simplest, everyday kinds of words that everyone needs to carry on a practical conversation. Our first principle of inclusion was frequency of use. Then slowly we began to branch out and add more specialized and sophisticated words as well. At first we used Liu Tengyan's *English Daily Use Vocabulary* as a source of words. Eventually, however, our most valuable resource and guide was a copy of A.S. Hornby's *Advanced Learner's Dictionary*, which I had first seen at the Foreign Language Institute. Mr. Norman, the teacher from Australia, had given me a copy. We adopted Hornby's system of presenting the words, because we found it extremely useful. Hornby's was only a bilingual dictionary, however. So as we began to build our own dictionary we had to adapt his system to a trilingual format.

Although I didn't realize it at the time, the dictionary project was going to become my principal occupation for many years to come. The work was extremely tedious and time consuming. What I remember more than anything is that small room we worked in and the boxes and boxes of note cards. By modern technological standards, our methods were primitive indeed. As we acquired the words, we wrote them down, one to a card. On each card we began with the word in English, then the international phonetic pronunciation, the part of speech, and the definition, first in Tibetan, then Chinese. I remember that at first Liu Dejun and I argued about the order of the definitions. He wanted

Chinese first; I wanted Tibetan. I am still proud of the fact that I won the argument and Tibetan came first!

We worked tirelessly that first year even though the job was terribly boring and repetitive. The cards piled up, because we had to hand copy each of the definitions and then check and cross-check our work. Since I knew the three languages, I collected words in all of them. But Liu Dejun worked as hard. I knew I had made a good choice when I asked him to help me; we worked effectively together. He was so diligent that he learned to copy Tibetan script just by looking at it. Though he couldn't read Tibetan, he could copy anything accurately and was eventually able to do almost as many tasks as I could. By the time we were finished with this phase of the project, we had collected approximately ten thousand lexical items, including about six thousand headwords. We did it all by hand, mainly just the two of us and without any assistance from modern machines or techniques. And besides the lack of secretarial help, we had some other problems.

In January 1980 both Sangyela and I got very ill. Sangyela became so ill that she had to be hospitalized. I was quite worried and visited her every day until I suddenly fell ill with what was diagnosed as hemorrhagic fever. I was put immediately into intensive care and was terribly sick for a week. My doctor, Mr. Li—who was very kind to me—told me later that I came very close to death. The fever broke at the end of a week's time, and then I became aware of other problems.

It happened that I had been put in a room which was just down the hall from Sangyela's. But the disease had stricken me so suddenly that I hadn't been able to tell her what happened to me and nobody else did, either. I learned later that she was worried when I stopped coming to see her. She feared either that something terrible had happened to me, or that I was deserting her. For a short time she was frantic, until finally some of the hospital staff realized her concerns and set her straight. By then I was recovering and soon able to get around and so we solved the problem between us. But we were both sick or at least fragile for most of the rest of the winter. Until we could get back on our feet we were helped enormously by Jigme Surkhang, who at the time was a football coach at the Xianyang school, and also his wife, Dechöla. We had known one another from the tea shops in Lhasa as far back as the 1950s. He had been a good friend through the bad times of the Cultural Revolution, when we had both been denounced as spies. He and his family did Sangyela and me a thousand kind offices while we were in the hospital and as we were recovering, and we will always be grateful to them.

The winter of 1980 was extraordinarily cold, and our health came back slowly. But our strength returned with the warmer days of spring, and eventually I was back at work on my dictionary, putting in the long hard days that I suspect were indirectly the cause of my illness. And if the work was tedious, it had rewards of other kinds, because I could sense that people's attitudes about me were changing for the better and as a result I was being treated differently. Where I had formerly seen only suspicion and fear I now saw friendship and respect. Word had obviously gotten around about my unauthorized trip to Beijing and the outcome, and it was clear that many admired what I had done and felt freer about showing their feelings than at any time in the past. My co-workers were treating me as an equal now. The school community knew that I was working on a dictionary and that was also perceived to be a good thing, something to be admired. It was nearly a complete turnaround. Where before I had been seen as a politically suspicious type who had been to America and become "Americanized" in all the bad senses typical of the Cultural Revolution, I was now seen more as someone who had studied in a foreign country and learned a number of valuable skills, especially language skills, that could be of great use. Where before my actions had been called stubborn and indicative of a bad attitude, I was now talked about as being courageous, full of persistence and determination. In short, I could look people in the eye now and take pride in my work. Because other people's attitudes always affect us to one degree or another, I drew strength from the newly positive reflections of myself that I saw in my colleagues' eyes and behavior. I was happy with myself and my life to a degree that I wouldn't have thought possible a year or two before, and because I knew what it was like to be distrusted and shunned, this new feeling was particularly sweet. My plans changed slightly, as they always seemed to do, but this new conviction of respectability and value never went away again.

My plans changed slightly because it appeared that there were going to be problems with the school's proposal to establish an English Department. We had gone ahead full tilt with the preliminary plans. We were a staff of about twenty teachers and had even gotten to the point of setting up classrooms, moving furniture, and stockpiling supplies. And of course Liu Dejun and I were hard at work on our dictionary.

But eventually it became clear that we weren't going to have enough Tibetan students to justify a department of the size proposed. Our problem was, I think, a comment on the level of general education in Tibet at the time. The school had sent people to Lhasa and elsewhere to canvas for qualified students, but they couldn't find enough to fill a single class, much less support a department of twenty faculty. When it was clear that the idea for a department was going to have to be scrapped, I knew immediately what I wanted to do.

The collapse of the proposed English Department at my school was, in one sense, an opportunity for me. I had not been unhappy working on the dictionary and living with Sangyela under the same roof at long last. But although Sangyela had thrown herself into her work here, she missed her sister badly and never fully reconciled herself to living in the country she called "the place of the ghosts." And so since the teachers who had been scheduled to be faculty in the English Department at the school now had to be reassigned, I asked that I be allowed to return to Lhasa to teach. The school did not resist or put obstacles in my way this time. All I had to do was find a job in Lhasa, which I did—as an English teacher at the Tibet Autonomous Teachers' College (which would become Tibet University in 1985). And before I left, school officials did some very nice things for me. They promoted me two degrees in salary, claiming that they were now willing to count my years in American schools as preparation for which I could be rewarded. And they gave me the title of "lecturer" (though at the time I had never taught a class), which ensured that I would be eligible for a better class of housing when I got to Lhasa. And so in the autumn of 1981 Sangyela and I left "the place of the ghosts" and returned to our native land.

I didn't realize how much I disliked Xianyang and the school until I knew that I was getting away from it for good. Even though things had recently taken a turn for the better, the school had been the scene of so many painful experiences for me that I could never get them entirely out of my mind. And it was in the middle of nowhere, an island far away from the place I wanted to be. So I was more excited and more emotional than I had anticipated when Sangyela and I touched down in Lhasa again. As it turned out, it was fortunate that my spirits were so high, because for a while life was very hard for me.

Before I left Xianyang I had discussed the dictionary project with the school officials. We all agreed that it was important and should be continued. And now since there was not going to be a small English Department at Xianyang, the idea was to expand the scope of the dictionary considerably to make it a more useful resource. The officials at the Autonomous Teachers' College in Lhasa agreed to support my work. But the job was even bigger now and although they generously gave me time and some office space, I got very little financial support and not even one assistant. There was no money even for typists and copyists, and so I had to do everything myself. Soon I did literally nothing else. When the job began in earnest it was common for me to work seven days a week and at least ten hours a day. In the beginning I was able to sustain this kind of pace, because I strongly believed in the value of the project. And I was pleased that my new school appreciated my effort. I not only felt that I was finally doing something that I wanted to do, but I also believed that my work on the dictionary would be a way of leaving something permanent behind me. It would be a contribution whose value would continue and perhaps even increase long after I was gone. This was all well and good, but after a while the work and the impossible schedule threatened once again to take its toll on my sanity and my personal life.

I also had trouble at home. Though she had wanted badly to come back to Tibet, Sangyela surprisingly began to be very unhappy after we arrived. She had worked hard in Xianyang, earned good money, and had been supported by the routines and community her job provided. At first after our return to Lhasa she had no way to earn money and little to do all day but worry about it. Without her income, we were suddenly much poorer than we had been in Xianyang, and our poverty was no longer romantic; it simply added to the strain of living day to day. Sangyela blamed me for the fact that she wasn't working. I had taken her away to a strange place and prevented her from developing her chang-selling business in Lhasa. Now she had no work and wasn't able to set up her shop again.

We quarreled often in those days. My time was so taken up with the project that I did literally nothing at home; thus the entire burden of running our household, every practical aspect and day-to-day activity, fell on Sangyela's shoulders, and this burden sometimes added fuel to our quarrels. I was aware of the sacrifices she was making, but I could see nothing I could do at the time. When my dictionary was finally finished, I made a special point of thanking Sangyela in the preface, which was highly unusual. Tibetan culture is patriarchal, and my colleagues often questioned me about why I would thank my wife. I told them it was because I was so grateful to her for her help in those years. I may have been making the money, but in order to live the money has to be turned into food for the table, fuel for the cooking fire, and the dozens of other practical necessities that hold a family together. For a while she did everything.

Although Sangyela and I spoke many harsh words during that time, we loved one another and slowly but surely we worked out our problems together. Sangyela decided that in spite of the difficulties she knew she would encounter she would try to open up a shop that sold chang, our home-brew beer. The problem was getting a license. There was a heavy demand for licenses, and for a time we simply couldn't get one. We tried every trick we knew, used every friend whom we thought could help us. Sangyela, however, was determined, and began to sell chang illegally. It was very risky, but eventually we got the proper papers and that part of our life began to stabilize. At the same time, though, my work on the dictionary had become impossible for me to handle alone. Even if I continued to work the long hours I was working, I couldn't get anywhere because I had to do even the smallest and most mechanical jobs myself. I sometimes had to go literally from place to place on foot to get references or to talk to people who could help me. A cousin of Jampa, my son by Thondrup Dromala all those many years ago, was kind enough to give me a brand new bicycle to help me get around, and I appreciated it much, but that was the level of support I was operating at. The school had no tradition of providing funds to underwrite a project like mine, and so I couldn't expect money from it in the present circumstances. And as I considered how much work was still to be done, I got fairly desperate. Then I found a way to help myself.

In April 1982 there was a large public meeting sponsored by the Tibet Autonomous Region's government. Its purpose was to listen to representatives of the intellectual classes—teachers, writers, engineers, technicians, and so on—who had ideas about how the government could help them contribute to the new society. It was an open meeting, but not everyone could attend. The various schools, companies, and institutions in Lhasa were to send one or two people—intellectuals— who had already made some kind of contribution. I was one of two teachers sent by my new school. School officials felt that my work on the dictionary was the kind of project that made me eligible, and I was extremely pleased. Besides the fact that it was a recognition of my work and the long hours I was putting in, it was also the first time I had ever been allowed to participate in a high-level meeting like this. It was, I couldn't help noting, exactly the opposite of my previous experiences with the old-line aristocrats in the Tibetan government-in-exile. I was optimistic about my chances for finding support for my project. I was still grateful to the Chinese government for taking me seriously when I went to Beijing and doing something to redress my grievances. I felt that perhaps this might be another situation in which speaking up might get me what I wanted.

The gathering was held at the meeting hall of the Tibet Autonomous Region government. The room was long and rectangular, and in the center there was a large oval table. We were encouraged to sit where we wanted, and I decided to sit exactly opposite the man who was going to preside, Yin Fatang. I sat between the two other representatives of my school, Nyima Öse and Tsewang Gyume, both senior officials. As we took our seats, we could feel the excitement and anticipation in the air.

When all were seated, Yin Fatang rose to speak. He told us we had each been specially invited and that the purpose of the meeting was to seek our opinions, especially about what were the best ways for the government to implement policies to help the intellectuals. He didn't say it in so many words, but what he meant of course was that the government now wanted to try and help the intellectuals who had been so neglected and persecuted during the Cultural Revolution. Most of Mao's policies had been based on class struggle, one class pitted against another—workers against intellectuals, and so on. According to the new policy, intellectuals were now to be considered as part of the laboring people, their intellectual labor to be seen as potentially valuable as physical labor. Yin welcomed us warmly. He made a special point of emphasizing that he truly wanted to hear our ideas, that we might speak freely and without fear of reprisal. In the old days I wouldn't have paid any attention to such statements. But in the new political atmosphere I believed him, and both the format and the outcome of the meeting confirmed my instinct.

It was a genuinely open discussion. Most meetings I had been familiar with had clearly been carefully scripted. The agenda had been planned in advance, and there was no dialogue, only a sort of public performance. This was a real meeting, and I didn't hesitate to participate. I spoke early, but before doing so I had decided on a strategy.

From the moment I began, I made it clear that I wasn't there to complain about anything that had been done in the past. I was grateful to have an opportunity to speak at a meeting like this. Since party policies had changed in the last few years my life had gotten much better, and I appreciated the fact that I didn't have to play the old games. I said that I didn't even know how many times before I had mindlessly praised the party, afraid to say what I really thought. I felt that the chance now offered was the chance of a lifetime, and I wasn't going to waste it in false praise or selfish complaints. I simply wanted to tell about the project I was working on, describe the difficulties I was laboring under, and explain how the government could help me. Nobody told me to stop, and so I continued.

I started with a brief history of the dictionary project and emphasized its potential value. Then without whining or accusing anyone, I spoke of the purely practical hardships I was encountering. I explained how little money I had to support my research and all the things I had to do, that I had only one assistant at Xianyang, and that now my school could not afford to give me even one such helper. I explained that the scope of the project was much bigger now and that to complete it I needed a typist who knew the three languages in question. I needed assistants to work with me—preferably more than one—who knew the languages and could help with the copying and endless cross-checking. I said that I was grateful to the Autonomous Region's Teachers College for paying me my salary to work on the dictionary and giving me the space to work in. But without further support I simply didn't see how I could complete the work. I was at the end of my rope. I had no more money. Either I had to stop now, or sell my expensive radio–tape recorder to allow me to continue for a few more months. By that time I guess I had gotten fairly emotional.

While I was talking I wasn't aware of how much time I was taking, but I spoke for quite a while. I remember that at one point the other teacher from my school, who was sitting next to me, began to tug at my sleeve, trying to get my attention to tell me to finish up! I remember him doing it, but while I had the floor I decided that I was going to say everything that I wanted to say. And Yin didn't seem to mind. In fact he seemed genuinely interested. He listened carefully and periodically asked me very sharp, specific questions—exactly where was I in the process now, how did I do such and such.

When I finally sat down, I was emotionally drained and had no idea what would happen next. To my delight and astonishment, Yin Fatang publicly approved my request. Right there in front of everybody he told the officials who had accompanied me that the college should give me the financial support I needed. He said that all humankind can benefit if the people in power know how to use correctly people like those assembled today. I was extremely pleased, though at the time I was uncertain about exactly what that would mean, how Yin's statement of support would help me directly. After I had finished, others took the floor. Most of them tried to be more careful and political than I had been. They spent large amounts of time praising the party and in general trying to butter up the officials. I just sat there quietly, surer than ever that the strategy I had used was the best one—at least for me. And so it proved to be.

At Yin Fatang's direction, my new school suddenly gave me 2,000 yuan to spend on my project, and it made all the difference in the world. I immediately hired three new people. The first was a very talented woman typist who was fluent in the three languages. She proved to be a tireless worker and was, I believe, the best copyist I ever had. I also hired Mr. Wangdor, who knew all the languages and became an invaluable proofreader. With what suddenly amounted to a "staff" to help me, the work began to move swiftly ahead, and my life in general improved substantially. In the meantime, Sangyela had finally gotten her license to sell chang and had developed a thriving business. Within three years I was able to send a manuscript of the enlarged and revised dictionary to the Nationalities Publishing House in Beijing, where it was accepted and eventually published in 1988. I was, I think, justifiably proud of my achievement. I said in my preface that the dictionary's main purpose was "to meet the growing needs of young, mid-level educated Tibetan and Chinese speakers using English." It was, I said, "meant to promote cultural exchange between nations and among nationalities." In fact, I saw the dictionary as the first concrete step I had taken to help my people catch up with the twentieth century and learn to function and compete in the modern world. I still believe that this book is a major contribution. But during the years I was working on it I began to see that there might be another project whose effects would be even more lasting.

14

My first few years back in Lhasa were spent almost exclusively working on my dictionary and watching Lhasa change and grow under Deng Xiaoping's new "Open Door" policy. Tourists and businesspeople began to arrive from all over the world, and a growing need for English-speaking tour guides emerged. Tibetans, however, were not well positioned to capitalize on these new opportunities because our schools did not teach English. Moreover, since Tibetan students were already studying Tibetan and Chinese, adding English to the curriculum would mean either dropping one of the current languages—a political impossibility—or adding English as a third one, a logistic and pedagogic impossibility, at least in the short run. Chinese students, however, did not have to take Tibetan, so they generally studied English as their second language. Something clearly needed to be done to provide an equivalent opportunity for young Tibetans.

My colleagues and I at Tibet University often talked about this problem, and in the course of one such discussion I recalled that when I was living in Seattle I had seen night schools that taught English to immigrants after work. That seemed like just what was needed in Lhasa, at least as a stopgap measure, so in the fall of 1985 I decided I would try to set up such a school. By that time my work on the dictionary was under control, and the number of details that had to be attended to had lessened considerably. So I asked the university for permission to go ahead, and when it was granted, I went to work quickly.

There was no such thing as a private school in Tibet in those days, and I had to start from scratch. First, I persuaded a small "tourist" hotel called the Banak Shol to rent me several rooms to use as classrooms. The hotel gave me a special price because my night school would help Tibetans. Then I had furniture made for the classrooms and I hired some teachers, making a point to get as many foreigners as I could, because I knew they would give the school instant credibility and status. Next I advertised. I put flyers everywhere encouraging young professionals and middle-school graduates to sign up. I even put advertisements in the Lhasa newspapers with photographs of our classrooms and some of the foreign teachers. I didn't ask anyone for official permission to do these things, because I felt certain I would have been turned down or that the project would have been buried in red tape. I just did them, and it worked! There was a new flexibility in Tibet that hadn't been seen since the Uprising of 1959.

My first class met in September 1985. The teacher was Camille Moore, the daughter of Professor Robert Moore, a colleague at Tibet University who was helping the university launch an English Department. In a short time I had two full classes, had hired several more teachers, and was offering instruction in both writing and conversation. I copied textbooks on a rented Canon copier, and I ran a tight ship financially. The tuition was high because I wanted people to understand that the school was serious. Though I didn't teach myself, I was there every night to see that all the details were attended to. I was tough on the students. I made them sign a paper saying that they realized that if they attended even half the classes, their tuition would not be refunded if they dropped out after that. They saw me there every evening, and they knew I meant business.

The general public immediately took to the idea of an English night school, and the project was an enormous success. The students felt that they got their money's worth. And I did as well. I was able to pay all of the operating expenses out of the tuition and had enough left over to give my teachers a small pay raise in the second year. And the government didn't object. I know this because one of my students happened to work in the office of municipal public security. He told me that his superior had talked with him about the school and said that at one point the city was thinking about stepping in. But officials decided not to, and I like to think it was because the project was working so well. Whatever the case, the idea itself was clearly a good one, and today Lhasa has a much larger night school with more than a thousand students! My success in getting this going was gratifying but it created something of a problem for me—and an opportunity.

The problem was a very pleasant one. At the end of the first year, I discovered I had realized a profit of 10,000 yuan! Given the fact that the average salary for a professor in Tibet was 2,300 yuan, this profit represented a small fortune and a serious temptation. A part of me simply wanted to use the money to buy things that I had been unable to afford for years—to buy presents for Sangyela, to do crazy things. When I think back on it, I am embarrassed to remember how close I came to wasting it all. What saved me was the fact that at about the same time I made an eye-opening visit to my home village of Guchok to see my mother and brother. While it was wonderful to see my family again, it was also so depressing to see that my young nieces and nephews were just as illiterate as I had been when I was a boy. Forty years after I had left Guchok to become a member of the Dalai Lama's dance troupe, little had changed in the village in terms of education. There was still no primary school, and virtually all the inhabitants of Guchok were illiterate in their own language. Coming face to face with this reality had a profound effect on me and set me along a path that has since consumed my energies. Sitting in the village with my relatives I found myself thinking over and over again, "How can Tibet become a modern society on such a foundation of illiteracy? What was the problem with education in Tibet?"

The Cultural Revolution had, of course, been a disaster for education in Tibet. Not only were schools closed or turned into centers of political activism, but also minority nationalities such as Tibetans were pushed to assimilate into the larger Han Chinese linguistic world. The Tibetan language was not used in offices, and such schools that existed taught primarily Chinese. The 1978 reforms changed this, articulating a policy that overtly expressed respect for Tibetan language, religion, and culture. Hu Yaobang, the first secretary of the Communist Party, in fact visited Lhasa in 1980 and publicly said that there were too many Chinese officials in Tibet and that in the future Chinese officials who stayed in Tibet to work had to learn the Tibetan language. For Tibetans, the announcement of this policy was a great victory.

In the years following Hu's visit, the Tibetan educational system was reformed, and great emphasis was placed on expanding the use of the Tibetan language. The Chinese government built new schools, and a 1984 government document officially decreed that in Tibetan institutions of higher learning the majority of students ought to be Tibetan and that Tibetan should be the main language. One of the slogans that captured the spirit of the time was "Learn Tibetan, Use Tibetan, Develop Tibetan." I have always believed in the importance of literacy and education in a general way and continue to feel very strongly that the Tibetan language should be the main vehicle for the modernization of Tibet—that is, that it should become a fully modern language capable of discussing science as well as esoteric Buddhist philosophy. These changes were welcome and sounded very promising—in theory. But as I looked at what had transpired in the first half of the 1980s, I was disappointed to see that in many ways the policies had not always worked out well in practice. For example, the higher the grade level in the educational process, the fewer Tibetan students were enrolled—and the more Chinese. It galled me that the number of native Tibetans was highest in the primary schools, began dropping in the lower middle schools, dipped substantially in the senior middle school, and was lowest at the university level, where roughly half of all students were Chinese.

There were a lot of explanations. A few highly nationalistic intellectuals saw this structure as a calculated Chinese strategy to benefit the Chinese, but far more thought that the problem was the flawed implementation of an essentially good policy. As the reforms were operationalized down the line—from Beijing to the autonomous region government, to the districts, and so forth—the intent and spirit of the policies grew weaker. Ordinary Tibetans joked about this, comparing the process to the dilution of the alcohol content of chang. The best chang (the strongest) comes from the first addition of water to the fermented barley. However, water is added several more times to the barley, and with each subsequent batch, the beer becomes weaker. The idea, of course, is that the fundamentally good policies conceived in Beijing became diluted down the line in an analogous way.

Another line of reasoning emphasized the low value placed on educational achievement in traditional Tibetan society, where education was seldom available to peasants and ordinary people. My own experience was, I believe, both unusual and yet typical. It was unusual in the sense that I actually succeeded in getting a modern education. It was typical in the sense that I had an extremely hard time finding ways to learn even the basics, and the initiative always had to come from me. A cultural value on secular education either as an end in itself or as a means to an end was simply absent. Even though my parents had wanted the best for me, they made no connection between my possible success in life and my education. From their point of view, the one didn't necessarily have anything to do with the other. An assumption of a need for education for someone of my class was simply not part of the old society's way of thinking, and this assumption was even true to an extent at the higher social levels. For more than simple reading and writing, there were no modern schools in Tibet at all in the old society, and the children of aristocrats who wanted a modern education had to go to India to study at missionary-run schools. Indeed, in 1944 the Tibetan government tried to establish a school that combined elements of both traditional Tibetan and modern Western education in Lhasa, but dobdo monks known for their wild behavior threatened to steal the students for homosexual purposes unless the school was terminated. The powerful forces of conservatism in Tibetan society, especially the religious establishment, clearly saw modern education as a direct threat to the dominance of Buddhism and the old theocratic power structure. Therefore, except for one or two isolated experiments, the old government had no commitment to broad-based education. In some important ways, this attitude has carried over to contemporary Tibet, where, it is sad to say, many rural and working-class Tibetan parents do not see a good education as especially important.

There were important grains of truth in all these views, but as I looked into the situation at several of the middle schools in Lhasa, I found that the lack of Tibetan students wasn't owing to a simple process of dilution or to flaws in Tibetan culture. There seemed to be several important structural factors at work.

First, despite the minuscule proportion of Chinese in the entire Tibet Autonomous Region, there was a substantial population of Chinese government officials and civil servants living there with their families. These were educated officials who valued learning and wanted their children to succeed educationally. Consequently, the government felt it had to accommodate this need and created a separate Chinese language track in Lhasa's schools for these youths, of whom there were many. One middle school in Lhasa, for example, contained about 55 percent ethnic Tibetan students, the rest being Chinese and children of mixed marriages.

These Chinese students worked very hard and scored well on the comprehensive exams, so they moved up to the higher levels—to senior middle school and college—in numbers disproportionate to their percentage in the overall population. Tibetans, although far outnumbering the Chinese in primary schools, did just the opposite. They scored poorly on the exams and moved up to higher levels in far smaller proportions than their numbers warranted. Language played a large role in this differential. Basic subjects such as chemistry and physics were taught only in Chinese, and the national examinations were also in Chinese. Thus Tibetan students had to master the difficult subject matter of science through a foreign language and then take exams in that language in competition with native speakers. For many Tibetans whose Chinese was poor or mediocre, this hurdle could not be overcome and it is not surprising that Tibetan students rarely did as well as their Chinese counterparts. The consequence was that as one went up the educational ladder, proportionately fewer and fewer Tibetans scored well enough to reach the next rungs. For example, according to my figures, in 1979 the whole of Tibet sent 600 students to institutions of higher learning in inland China, but of that 600, only 60 (10 percent) were ethnic Tibetans. In 1984, there was a total of 1,984 students in the Tibet Autonomous Region's three colleges. Of that number, only 666 (34 percent) were ethnic Tibetan. Consequently, although Han Chinese represented only a few percent of the total official population of the Tibet Autonomous Region, they utilized a disproportionate percentage of its educational resources and finances.

I was extremely bothered by this situation. It seemed obvious to me that in the *Tibet* Autonomous Region the resources should overwhelmingly be used to improve life for Tibetans. The Chinese had plenty of opportunities available to them in the rest of the country, and I thought it was just not fair to allow them to utilize such a high proportion of our area's scarce resources. Although I had no particular position of power or influence, I remembered that, early in the 1980s, Deng Xiaoping had said that in the new China we should be guided not by ideology but should "seek truth through facts." I had some important "facts," and since I recently had had so much luck speaking my mind, I decided to do it again for Tibetan education.

In August 1985, a meeting was held in Lhasa to celebrate the twentieth anniversary of the founding of the Tibet Autonomous Region. I knew that there would be high party officials in attendance, and so I drew up a petition in which I stated my views about what was happening to Tibetan education and what should be done to change things for the better. I talked of what I had seen and heard in the schools I knew about. I tried to provide relevant objective statistics—"facts"—that showed how few Tibetans made it to the university. In conclusion, I made three suggestions: first, that the government do more to ensure equal opportunity for Tibetan students; second, that the money spent on education be more fairly allocated, by which I meant that more of it be used to help Tibetan students and that the Chinese language track classes not always get the best teachers, textbooks, and equipment; and third, that more money be spent on the primary and lower middle schools where most Tibetan students attended, even if this emphasis would mean that less would go to the colleges and universities.

When the word got out that my petition contained what could be considered criticisms of Chinese policies, it caused quite a stir in Lhasa. There was even a story about it in the newspapers. My suggestions would not have been especially noteworthy in a modern Western country—maybe a small piece on a back page. But public "suggestions" like mine simply weren't made in Tibet in those days. Having learned the lessons of the Cultural Revolution well, people were shocked and even frightened by my audacity. Some of my close friends actually feared that I might be sent back to prison.

I did not share their fears. I had found the Chinese in the post-Mao era to be willing to listen to complaints and opposing points of view— even those of ordinary citizens like me. I had been impressed by the way I had been treated in Beijing when I ran away from the Xianyang school. The officials in Beijing told me I could speak openly and without fear about the injustices I had experienced and they had been as good as their word. So, though I wasn't foolish enough to assume that my petition would cause major changes, I did not believe I was in any danger for having made it. And my instincts turned out to be correct. I received encouraging reactions and replies to my ideas from several high-ranking Tibetan officials.

One official wrote to tell me that he felt my picture of what was happening was accurate and that he would send my documents on to the People's Congress of the Autonomous Region. Another, a party vice–secretary, thanked me for my honesty and sincerity. He went on to say that he felt my suggestions corresponded with the spirit of the central government's policy on Tibetan education and that he had given them to the appropriate people in the Education Department. It felt good to get those feelings off my chest.

However, after the stir my petition made had died down and I had received all the congratulatory letters from officials that I was going to get, the world went on much as before. Nothing dramatic happened. Education has steadily improved, to be sure, and just last year a trial program was successfully completed in which physics, math, and chemistry were taught in several middle schools in the Tibetan language. But Chinese students still outperform Tibetans and constitute a far greater proportion of the students at the higher levels than their numbers in the population warrant.

It was at this point, soon after the twentieth-anniversary meeting, that I had visited my home in Guchok and saw firsthand the abysmal educational situation there. As a result of that experience, I realized that operating a night school in Lhasa was not addressing the real problem. The key to change in Tibet was to make high-quality education available to all Tibetan children at the village level, even in places like Guchok. There would never be more qualified Tibetans in high school and college if a high-quality educational foundation did not exist at the grass-roots level. I knew I couldn't change all of Tibet, but I became obsessed with the desire to at least do something so that the children in my home village would not have to continue to live in ignorance. Consequently, I decided to use my newfound wealth to build a primary school in Guchok.

Knowing what I wanted to do was one thing; getting it done was quite another. In Tibet individuals simply don't go out and build schools on their own; governments and departments of education do that. And 10,000 yuan was a hefty sum but not enough to pay for everything. I knew I would need help and that I would have to work with the government if I wanted to succeed. So I did a lot of thinking in a very short time, and in 1986 I came up with my first proposal, which I presented to the head of the Department of Education in my home county of Namling.

I told the officials quite simply that I had some money I was willing to contribute, that I wanted to use it to help build a school in my home village, and that I hoped they would help me. I told them that as far as I knew there had never been a school in Guchok. Of course, there were some children who became monks and learned to read in the monastery, but there was nowhere for the children of ordinary people to go. I made the old argument—which is still a good one—that people are human capital. I argued rather strongly therefore that neglecting the children in the rural areas meant wasting a potentially valuable resource.

For some months after I sent in my proposal I heard nothing. I had no idea what would happen. Then suddenly one day some representatives of the Namling County Department of Education actually came to my home in Lhasa to talk with me. I again tried to make it clear that I wasn't threatening to do anything rash on my own. I wasn't trying to work independently of the government or the residents of Guchok. How could I? I had a handsome sum of money to contribute. But more would be needed. I couldn't build a school if the village wasn't willing to accept it. I told them that I was willing to pay for all the raw materials and supplies necessary to construct a simple school building and get it ready to receive pupils, but the county and its government would have to support me by agreeing to maintain and operate the school, hire the teachers, and so on. After we had talked for some time, the officials told me that they thought my idea would work and that they would support it. They said a lot of fine-sounding things—that it was very patriotic of me to wish to contribute in this way, that it was important to help the children, that they were the hope of the future, and so on. It actually seemed that my dream was about to come true. But it took another four years before that first school opened its doors.

There were a host of reasons for the delay. Partly I suppose it was my fault. While detailed negotiations with the county officials dragged on, I was informed that I had to go to Beijing to do the final editing of the page proofs of my dictionary, which was finally published in 1988. In addition the political situation heated up as a series of violent riots occurred in Lhasa in 1987 and 1988. But there were other problems as well—with my family and the people of Guchok themselves!

My own brother, Lhapka Damdul, was dead set against the school project and in fact was very bitter. As I have said, my family had been treated badly during the Cultural Revolution. They had suffered terribly. When my brother learned about the money I had and what I wanted to do with it, he was furious and felt betrayed. Why, he wanted to know, why if I had all that money didn't I think of my own family first? Why on earth did I want to build a school? People in my family were obviously in need. Why didn't I help them? His response was completely unexpected and was very painful for me, and for a while it got even more so. My brother was adamant. He kept hammering away, and after a while the rest of my relatives pitched in. At times even Sangyela joined them: Why won't you help your own family? What's the matter with you? What made them all especially bitter was the idea they had that if I actually built a school in Guchok I would be helping the very families who had done such terrible things to them. In their eyes I wasn't just neglecting them and my familial responsibilities; I was actually helping their enemies.

The other members of the village didn't help either. None of them had ever been to school, and they were suspicious and wary of the value of education. They objected to having to contribute free labor to build the school—some of them may even have still been resentful about the tax burden that fell on them years ago, because I had become a gadrugba dancer—and some also thought I must be making such a proposal in the hopes of becoming famous thereby. "He is just seeking fame," they said. "He just wants to be a big shot." There were even rumors that I was simply playing a game, that I intended to take the money supposed to be for the school and build myself a mansion in Guchok that I could eventually retire to and lord it over all of them.

Because I knew how my family had suffered in the past, their opposition was one of the most painful experiences of my life. But I knew what I believed, and I had faith in my ideas. I told them emphatically that I was not trying to build a school to help the people who had treated them so badly. The people who had made them miserable were not the children who were being disadvantaged today, and it was wrong to punish the children for what their parents or grandparents might have done. Indeed, I told them I believed that education was the way perhaps to prevent others from being treated as badly. As painful as their criticism was for me, I kept talking to them, and eventually my family and the village quieted down. And so the project went forward.

The final agreement I arrived at with the county was simple and practical. We agreed that I would donate my 10,000 yuan but that the school when built would be owned by the citizens of Guchok. We also agreed (in writing) that the two teachers would be paid for by the county's Education Department. And we agreed that the school would be operated and maintained by the county with direct involvement from the citizens of the village. The students would be children ages six through twelve who would attend the school for two years, studying Tibetan and simple math. If at the end of that time they could pass the standardized examinations administered to all students at that grade level, then they would have the right to attend an official county primary school and go on up the ladder as far as their abilities and determination would take them.

At that point we were ready to begin. Materials were bought, the schoolhouse built, books paid for, and teachers hired. The school opened with forty-six children. It had taken a long time to work out the arrangements for the Guchok school, but when I saw the village children sitting there learning to read and write, I was thrilled and moved. The kind of school I had yearned for as a child was now operating in my home village, and I had played a role in bringing it about. My dream of helping create a modern Tibet now had a concrete manifestation.

When I started the Guchok project I didn't really have any grandiose plans, but once the school opened it was obvious that it would be relatively easy to repeat the process in other villages in Namling County that were without primary schools. All it would take was money and effort on my part and the continued cooperation from the county. But where to get such money? I had closed my Lhasa night school when I went to Beijing to oversee the publication of my dictionary, so I no longer had profits flowing in from it. I would have to figure out a new way to raise substantial amounts of money. But though raising the funds seemed formidable, it also seemed possible. I had by this time retired from the university so had plenty of free time. Sangyela, moreover, was doing well in her chang-selling business, so with her income and my nice pension from the university, our finances were comfortable. I didn't have to worry about our family's livelihood. Thus I decided to dedicate all my efforts to raising money to build schools. It seemed so clear to me that this was the challenge I had been seeking my entire life, and I could not turn away from it just because it was hard. I had to find a way to raise money.

After much thought, I turned to what Americans call a nonprofit business venture. Over the years, foreigners doing research or business in Tibet had considered me someone who would give them sound advice or even help them in their work, so it was common for foreigners to stop by my house in Lhasa to chat and have a cup of Tibetan butter tea or chang. I enjoyed these visits because my guests generally loved Tibet and were trying to do something good for its people. But now as I thought of alternatives, I realized that these frequent visitors gave me regular access to a group of foreigners who might also be interested in helping my school project. Rather than just ask for donations, I decided to try to do business with them. Foreigners, I knew, loved to buy mementos of their trip and often asked me where to buy Tibetan handmade rugs or other local handicrafts, so I decided to keep a number of rugs in my house for direct sale. Initially I got ten beautiful rugs on consignment from one of the best Lhasa rug factories and started showing these to the foreigners who stopped by, explaining that the profits from these went entirely to my school project. Since I had no overhead, I could sell the rugs at less than market prices. I even learned how to make things easy for the visitors by shipping such items directly to their homes. This arrangement led to my taking orders for custom-made rugs. And, to my joy, many of these kind people believed in the importance of my project and not only bought a rug or two but also made a donation of money for the school project. At the same time I was able to make contacts with a few shop owners in Europe and Japan and started buying and shipping Tibetan books for them on a regular basis. It was fantastic, like a dream. Soon profits grew and in a short time I was able to fund a second school, which opened in the autumn 1991 in Khartse, another poor village in Namling County.

We learned a lot as we launched each new school. We learned, for example, that getting good teachers was even more crucial than we had imagined, and also harder. There wasn't an oversupply of teachers, and the counties were always looking to save a little money. We would ask for the best, but sometimes we had to settle for less. Often we had to take students who had gotten into the middle school but had not passed the examinations that would have enabled them to go further. They weren't always ideal, but they could usually teach our students well enough. We had to make a lot of compromises such as these, but my enthusiasm never flagged. The building continued apace, and it wasn't very long before we began to get indications of success, which were very encouraging.

In 1994 I learned from the county's Education Department that on the examinations given to all students in the Namling County schools, the students from my schools had one of the best records in the county. In my first school at Guchok, sixteen out of forty-six students passed the examination and earned the right to go on. Among them was my nephew, who thus became the first member of my family who ever went to school in the modern way! The percentage of those succeeding (35 percent) may seem small by Western standards, but this sort of success was unprecedented in villages like mine. I think it is fair to say that these events changed my life. Because of my role in the building of those first few schools I realized that I had finally found what I had been looking for when I left the safety of America so many years ago. I had found the way I could help the people at home, especially the ones growing up in the rural areas where I had come from.

Since then my life has revolved around my schools, but I was also able to make a trip to America in 1992. My old college classmate, Professor Mel Goldstein, invited me to come to his research institute at Case Western Reserve University to help in some of his research, and a Tibetan businessman I had been helping in Lhasa to develop a joint-venture carpet business offered to buy me the airplane ticket. I jumped at the chance.

The pleasure was, of course, getting a chance to see the United States again and visit old friends. But I had another mission as well. I brought with me samples of Tibetan carpets and handicrafts, which I showed at both private and public exhibitions. The exhibitions allowed me to let a wider public know of the existence of such Tibetan products, and I sold a good many things as well. In fact, I made quite a good profit, which went directly back to Tibet to help build more schools. Indeed, by 1996, six years after the first school at Guchok opened, our project had built a total of thirty schools in Namling County, and the average number of students in each school has increased to ninety—double the number who first attended the school in Guchok.

I don't know how many more schools I will be able to build before I die, but I hope I will live long enough to see every Tibetan get the opportunity to go to school and advance as far as he or she is capable.

Epilogue

I received a phone call early in January 1994. The voice on the other end of the line informed me that if I could get myself to Beijing I would find a ticket waiting for me at the United Airlines office and a visa at the U.S. Embassy. I was going back to America once again.

This second trip abroad in such a short time was a delightful surprise, and I was pleased when the Chinese quickly approved. Fortunately my good friend, Mr. Wangchuk, agreed to take charge of my school-building projects, because at the time I was in the process of negotiating for some high-quality building materials for the next schools. I knew Mr. Wangchuk could handle the transaction and that an independent woman like Sangyela could manage our home and her own business with ease, so I had few worries as I boarded the plane.

The arrangement was that I would again be based at Case Western Reserve University in Cleveland, Ohio, where I would continue to help Professor Goldstein on a new edition of his Tibetan-English dictionary. But it also turned out that I had plenty of time to travel and visit old friends, and I made the most of the opportunity to further my plans for more schools. I worked hard in Cleveland and visited friends in Virginia, Michigan, and at Williams College. It was a wonderful opportunity to try to raise more money, and everywhere I went I told people about the school project. Sometimes I spoke to people in private houses. Sometimes I addressed small groups. I showed a videotape of my schools, and everywhere I went I found individuals willing to contribute.

As I was preparing to return to Lhasa in January 1995, I had some time to think about my visit. It was a satisfying trip in every possible way, and I couldn't help comparing this visit to America with my earlier experience in the 1960s. So much had happened in the interim; so much had changed. When I was in America in the 1960s I was struggling with the English language at Williams College and eventually with my conscience at the University of Washington. My thoughts and ideas were still forming then. I was experiencing the political awakening that would radically change my life, but I wasn't really able to process all the information I was receiving or control all the ideas and emotions I was experiencing. The things that happened to me when I returned to China in 1964 had put me severely to the test, but they had focused my thinking and matured and hardened me. I knew what I wanted now and what I could and couldn't do. When I left America for China in 1964 I was making a blind leap—almost a leap of faith. When I returned home to Lhasa in 1995 after this visit I would as a matter of course continue the school building work that meant so much to me. On the brink of my departure, I also thought about a very special and unexpected meeting I had with His Holiness, the Dalai Lama, in Ann Arbor, Michigan.

When I left Tibet in 1994, I had not known of His Holiness's plans to come to America. But when I learned that he was to speak at the University of Michigan, it was so close to Cleveland that I couldn't miss the opportunity to see him once again, and when I made the trip I was lucky enough to get to see him twice. The first time was in the morning in a receiving line in which all the Tibetans present were allowed a public audience, called *jeyga*. I was surprised and pleased that His Holiness seemed to remember me from my earlier audience more than thirty years before. "It has been a long time. You have changed a lot," he said. I moved on down the line, and after everyone had met him, the Dalai Lama spoke to all those assembled there. He talked only about general things, safe nonpolitical subjects like "how best to be a human being." It was more or less just a ceremonial appearance. I was lucky enough, however, to get another, more private interview.

My friend Gelek Rinpoche, the spiritual leader of a Tibetan Buddhist group in Ann Arbor and Cleveland, had arranged for me to talk to

His Holiness alone, later that afternoon. As I walked into his room I offered him the traditional white khatak and touched his hand with my forehead. When he invited me to sit down, I sat opposite him in a comfortable chair and we had a surprisingly good talk. The reason this visit is so vivid for me is that from the moment it began I was struck by how different it was from my earlier audience when I was about to leave India and go to America—how different I was. That was more than thirty years ago and in Dharamsala. His Holiness had been very kind, and I had felt a bit ill at ease. Even then I was pulling away from more direct involvement with the government-in-exile. Because the moment had been an anxious one, I remembered it clearly, and as His Holiness and I talked of this and that in Ann Arbor in 1994, images from that earlier conversation began to superimpose themselves on our present one. What did I intend to do by going to America? he had asked me then. "I am going to do something to help Tibet and Tibetans. But at this time I cannot tell you exactly how," was all I had been able to say. "Be a good Tibetan," he had said. "Study hard. And use your education to serve your people and your country." Would he think that I had done so? What did I think myself? So many years had passed since then; so much water had flowed under the bridge.

When my attention returned fully to the moment at hand, I realized that our present conversation, though pleasant, was still about rather neutral and safe subjects. But I wasn't the young man of thirty years ago anymore, and I decided to speak about serious matters. I told him how much I respected his commitment to nonviolence, but I also suggested that we—meaning Tibetans—needed to know how to oppose the Chinese when their policies seemed unreasonable and also to learn how to live with them. I had confidence in my opinions. I felt great reverence, but I no longer saw myself as a supplicant. Instead I felt I was someone who had something to say. I told the Dalai Lama that he had an extraordinary opportunity. He was in a unique position to strike a deal with the Chinese that could be beneficial to both themselves and the Tibetans. "Both the Chinese and the Tibetans would listen to you," I said emphatically. I wanted him to unite our people once again, to end the government-in-exile and return to Tibet.

The Dalai Lama listened and looked at me thoughtfully. "Tashi Tsering," he said. "You know the Chinese better now, from experience. And I will tell you that I have thought myself of many of the ideas you have just expressed. I value them and your advice, but all I can tell you is that I do not believe that the moment is right." I wasn't surprised, and I wasn't discouraged. I had said what was on my mind, and he had listened with attention.

I don't pretend to have answers to the big questions anymore. I am in my sixties now, and as I look at the faces of the children at one or another of my schools, I worry about things that I didn't even think about when I was younger and had more energy and less experience. Who? or What? I sometimes ask myself now is the Tibet I am trying to help? Who represents Tibet? The Dalai Lama? The old elite now living in exile who made people like me wait outside the door when it came time to discuss important issues? The more progressive intellectuals in Tibet, or those in exile in India, America, and Europe? Is Tibet the Tibetan librarian I met in Austin, Texas, who would scarcely even talk to me because he thought I was a communist? Is Tibet the soldier who interrogated me at the Changwu prison and wanted to be even more Chinese than the Chinese, or the villagers in Guchok who were so quick to suspect my motives when I wanted to build them a school, or the brave woman who trusted me when I was classified as a political criminal and who gave me a job when I desperately needed one? The older I get, the harder it is to find simple answers.

I can see more clearly now why my Tibetan and American friends thought I was crazy when I wanted to return in the 1960s. And many of the things they said would happen did happen. Just as they predicted, I was distrusted from the start. My motives were always suspect—not only by the Chinese but also by the people in my own village. I was foolish to think I could stay above or outside of politics. Back then when I was so full of enthusiasm and resolve, I saw myself first and foremost as a Tibetan nationalist who represented the interests of the common people, the serfs. I have always considered myself a Tibetan nationalist and patriot, but I now understand that these terms mean different things to different people. And my own views have mellowed under the relentless pressure of history. I adamantly do not wish a return to anything remotely like the old Tibetan theocratic feudal society, but I also do not think that the price of change and modernity should be the loss of one's language and culture. The Cultural Revolution taught me how very precious those are. So, while I genuinely welcome Tibet's march to modernization, I also believe we Tibetans must struggle to ensure that we do not lose our linguistic and cultural heritage. Education seems the key to these goals.

While I was waiting in Havana for permission to return to China, I wrote a letter to my friend and classmate Larry Epstein at the University of Washington, Seattle, who kept it and later gave it to me. In it I proudly said, "I am glad because I am going home. A month [from now] I will be in Beijing, where I plan to study for a few years before beginning to work to build socialism, democracy, and happiness in Tibet." How naive I was then, how foolishly optimistic. And yet, I think if it had not been for my naiveté and foolish optimism, I would never have survived and accomplished what I have.

Index

Advanced Learner's Dictionary
(Hornby), 174
Arithmetic system, 10

Baldwin scholarship, 64
Banak Shol hotel, 184
Beijing, 104-107, 158-164
Buddhism, 8-9, 111-112, 187

Calcutta, 49-51, 58
Calligraphy, 10, 28, 32-33
Case Western Reserve University,
viii-x, 195, 197
Celibacy, 27
Central Intelligence Agency, 59
Changwu prison, xi, 123-128, 129, 133
Chen (interrogator), 115-116, 117,
119-120
Chengdu prison, 129-130
Chiang Kai-shek, 60, 103
China
annexation of Tibet, 35-36
Cultural Revolution in, 100-123
Eleventh Party Congress in, 152-153
invasion of Tibet, 35
at Mao's death, 152
Nixon's visit to, 134-135
"Open Door" policy of, 183
prisons in, 124-129

China *(continued)*
State Council of, 155-156, 159,
161-164
See also Tibetan Minority Institute
Chinese in Tibet
arrival in Lhasa, 36, 40
atrocities of, 57
commune system of, 150-151
in Cultural Revolution, 107-112,
147-148
and Dalai Lama, 55, 57
education policy of, 41-43, 185-
186
in education system, 187-188
prison of, 131-139
rationing of necessities, 149
rebellion against, 55-56
social change through, 40-43, 77, 79,
85, 90, 111, 112, 138
See also Tibet Autonomous Region
Chushul, 20
Class system, 31, 38, 42, 60-61, 62, 63
Commune system, 150-151
Cultural Revolution
in China, 100-107, 113-123
end of, 152-153
redress of grievances, 155-156, 159,
161-168, 180

Cultural Revolution *(continued)*
  in Tibet, 107-112, 147-148, 185
Cumming, Mr., 52-53, 173

Dalai Lama, 51, 60, 62, 70, 80, 171
  audience with, 64-65, 198-200
  dance troupe of. *See* Gadrugba dance
    troupe
  flees to India, 56
  government-in-exile, 58, 83-84
  and Lhasa Uprising, 55-56
  and return to Tibet, 199-200
  treasure of, 57-58
Damdul, Lhapka, 191-192
Darjeeling, 36, 51
Deng Xiaoping, 109, 183, 188
Dharamsala, 64-65
Dictionary project, 173-175, 177-178,
  179-182, 191
Domala, Thondrup, 37-40, 47, 179
Drepung Monastery, 19-20, 70-71
Dunnam, Robert, 63-63, 72, 88, 120

Education in Tibet, 177
  calligraphy, 28, 32-33
  during Cultural Revolution, 185
  Chinese policy and, 41-43, 185-186
  of Chinese population, 187-188
  class system and, 31
  in English language, 183-185
  lack of opportunities for, 9-11, 111,
    185, 186-187
  of low value in traditional society,
    186-187
  modern attitude about, 36-37
  Tibetan language usage in, 185-186
  village school-building project,
    190-195
Eleventh Party Congress, 152-153
English Daily Use Vocabulary (Liu
    Tengyan), 174
Epstein, Larry, 201

Foreign Language Institute, Xian,
  170-171

Gadrugba dance troupe, Tsering in
  abuse by host family, 18-19

Gadrugba dance troupe, Tsering in
    (continued)
  end of term in, 32-34
  escape from, 19-23
  lashing by director, 3-5, 32
  return to, 23, 25
  selection for, 11-15
  tax exemption for service in, 23, 44
  training period in, 17-18
Gambala Pass, 20-21
Gangtok, 58
Gelek, Rinpoche, 198–199
Geshi Wangyela, 70
Goldstein, Mel, vii-ix, x, 171, 195,
  197
Guchok, 6-7, 44, 150-151, 185
  school project in, 190-195
Gyaltsen, Lobsang, 51, 58-59, 62
Gyangling, 3
Gyantse, 22, 49
Gyentsenla (monk), 43
Gyume, Tsewang, 180

Homosexuality, of monks, 26-30, 38
Hornby, A. S., 174
Hu Yaobang, 185
India
  Dalai Lama in, 56, 57-58
  government-in exile in, 83-84, 180
  Tibetan activists in, 59-65
  Tibetan community in, 20, 49-55,
    86-87
  Tibetan refugees in, 56-57, 81-82,
    117-118
International Commission of Jurists,
  57, 118

Jampa (son), 179

Kalimpong, 20, 21, 49-50, 51, 52, 60
Kennedy, John F., 74, 79, 80
Khartse school project, 194

Lenin, V.I., 73, 76
Lhasa, 140-141
  Chinese arrival in, 36
  Chinese modernization of, 40, 41-42

Lhasa *(continued)*
  Cultural Revolution in, 107-112,
    147-148
  English language school in, 183-185
  Gadrugba dance troupe in, 11, 13-14,
    16-19, 20, 24-34
  living conditions in, 108, 149
  Sangyib prison in, 131-139
  Tibet University in, 177, 181, 182,
    183
  Uprising of 1959, 55-56, 60, 110,
    132
Lhawang, 53
Literacy, 9-10, 24-25, 185
Liu Dejun, 173, 174-175
Liu Ten-yan, 174

McPeek, Miss, 69, 70, 74-75
Mao Zedong, 35, 76, 82, 95, 118, 180
  audience with, 104-107
  Cultural Revolution and, 100-101
  death of, 152
Marriage, traditional, 7-8
Marx, Karl, 73, 76
Ma Ximei, 95, 97, 103, 115, 116, 119,
    121, 123, 126, 130, 131
Meng (Education Dept. official), 151
Milarepa (hermit), 76
Monks
  deviant *(dobdo)*, 29, 187
  at Drepung Monastery, 19-20, 70-71
  homosexual partners for, 27-30, 34,
    38
  nonproductivity of, 111
  officials, 14, 26, 27, 32, 34, 38, 43,
    51, 62-63
  opposition to Chinese, 43
Moore, Camille, 184
Moore, Robert, 184
Mussamari refugee camp, 56-57
My View of the American Way of Life
  (Tsering), 78

National Academy of Sciences
  Committee for Scholarly
  Communication with the People's
  Republic of China, viii

Nationalities Publishing House, 182
National Language Research Center,
  169-170
National Minorities Institute, 104, 105
Nehru, Jawaharlal, 50
New York, 66-72, 88
New Yorker, 69-70
Nixon, Richard, 74, 134-135

Öse, Nyima, 180

Panchen Lama, 21
People's Liberation Army, 35
Polyandry, 7-8
Potala Palace, 3, 13-14, 71, 107
Potala Treasury, 32-34, 36, 40-41, 48,
  62-63
Profiles in Courage (Kennedy), 79
Prostitution, 50-51, 147

Qiao (prison director), 137-138

Ramoche Temple, 107
Raymond, Mr., 67-68

St. Joseph's College, Darjeeling, 36,
  43, 53-54
Sakya Pandita, 24
Sakya, Tsejen Wangmo (wife), 78, 80,
  148, 171
Samden, Lobsang, 70
Sangyela (wife), 141, 151, 153
  background of, 147-148
  chang shop of, 179, 182
  in China, 172-173, 175-176, 177
  relationship with Tashi Tsering,
    146-147, 148-150, 178-179, 192
  religion of, 109-110, 111

Sangyib prison, 131-139
Seattle, 76-80
Sera Monastery, 29
Seventeen Point Agreement for the
  Liberation of Tibet, 36
Shigatse, 21, 22, 50
Sienbenschuh, Bill, ix-xi
Sikkim, 49, 57-58

Snowland Hotel, viii
Sonam (student), 53
Söpela, 108-109, 112
Stanford, Father, 53
Stanley, Father, 76
Surkhang, Dechöla, 175
Surkhang, Jigme, 175-176

Tashihunpo Monastery, 21
Taxation, 11, 23, 44
Thondrup, Gyalo, 64, 79, 88, 117, 127, 134
    and CIA, 59
    class attitudes of, 60, 61
    friendship with Tashi Tsering, 51-52,
        56, 58, 60, 62
    opposition to Chinese, 80-87
    refugee camp visit by, 56-57
Thondrup, Lobsang, 142, 157
Tibetan House, India, 83
Tibetan Minority Institute, Tsering in,
    91–93, 139
    in Beijing visit, 104-107
    denunciation during Cultural
        Revolution, 113-120
    dictionary project of, 173-175
    English Department plan and, 172,
        173, 176-177
    escape from, 157-160
    illness of, 175-176
    labor transformation in, 97-98
    in Lhasa visit, 107
    in National Language Research
        Center, 169-170
    physical conditions of, 94-95
    political lessons in, 95-96
    in printing workshop, 142-146, 152
    Red Guards in, 100-104
    redress of grievances from, 161-168
    refusal of transfer to Lhasa, 153-155
    social interaction in, 96-97, 176
    student body of, 93-94
Tibetan refugees, 56-57, 81-82,
    117-118
Tibetan Youth League, 108
Tibet Autonomous Region
    educational reforms of, 185-186

Tibet Autonomous Region (continued)
    foreigners in, 183, 193-194
    public government meeting in,
        179-182
    twentieth anniversary of, 189
    See also Chinese in Tibet
Tibet Autonomous Teacher's College.
    See Tibet University
Tibet House, New York City, 84
Tibet University, 177, 181, 182, 183,
    184
Tolstoy, Mr., 64, 68, 88
Tolstoy Foundation, 64
Trade, 43-44, 48
    with India, 49, 50
Trappist monastery, 75-76
Tsbei (wife), 30–32
Tseden, Dorje, 44-47, 98-99
Tsering, Sonam, 78, 80
Tsering, Tashi
    America, impressions of, 66-67,
        74-78, 80, 87-88
    business venture of, 193-194, 195
    at Case Western Reserve University,
        viii-ix, 195, 197
    childhood of, 6, 8-9
    in China. See Tibetan Minority
        Institute
    on Chinese modernizing role, 40-43,
        77, 79, 85, 90, 111, 112, 138,
        200
    and class system, 31, 38, 60-61, 62,
        63
    collaboration on autobiography, ix-xi
    and Dalai Lama, audience with,
        64-65, 198-200
    in dance troupe. See Gadrugba dance
        troupe
    decision to go to America, 63-65, 78,
        120
    decision to go to India, 43, 47, 78, 120
    decision to return to Tibet, vii-viii, 5,
        78-91, 120, 137-138, 200-201
    departure from Tibet, 48-49
    dictionary project of, 173-175,
        177-178, 179-182, 191

Tsering, Tashi *(continued)*
  educational opportunities denied to,
    9-11
  educational reform proposals of,
    189-190
  education of, in India, 51-54
  education of, in Tibet, 24-25, 28, 31, 32
  English night school of, 184-185,
    193
  English studies of, 36, 52-54,
    170-171, 173
  family of, 7-8, 44-47, 98-99, 150,
    185, 191-192
  finances of, 38, 43-44, 48, 51, 58-59,
    64, 67-68, 169, 178, 185
  friendship with Gyalo Thondrup,
    51-52, 56, 58, 60, 62
  historical studies of, 73, 76
  imprisonment by Chinese, xi, 59,
    121-138
  in India, 49-65
  intellectual and social life in Lhasa,
    36-37, 41-42
  and Mao Zedong, audience with,
    104-107
  marriage to Sangyela, 146-150, 151,
    172-173, 178-179
  marriage to Tsebei, 30-32
  marriage to Tsejen Wangmo Sakya,
    78, 148-149, 151
  Marxist influence on, 73, 76
  as "modern" Tibetan, 76-77
  monk patrons of, 26-30, 32, 43
  in New York, 66-72
  Potala Treasury job of, 32-34, 36,
    40-41, 48, 62-63
  as Red Guard, 100-107, 112
  refugee camp visit by, 56-57,
    117-118
  relationship with Thondrup Domala,
    37-40, 47
  release from prison, 138-141
  return to America, 195, 197-200
  return to Tibet, 107-112, 130-131,
    153-155, 177

Tsering, Tashi *(continued)*
  school-building project of, 190-195
  son of, 39, 179
  with Tibetan activists, 58-65
  on Tibetan independence, 90
  on Tibet University faculty, 177, 183
  at University of Washington, vii, 74,
    76-77, 198
  village of, 6-7, 150-151, 190-195
  at Williams College, 72-74, 198

University of Michigan, Dalai Lama
  at, 198
University of Washington, vii, 74,
  76-77, 171, 198

Villages
  commune system in, 150-151
  Cultural Revolution in, 98-99
  school-building project in, 190-195
  traditional life in, 6-7

Wang (investigator), 161-164
Wang (security officer), 138-139, 140
Wang, Jingzhi, 102, 116, 165-166
Wangchuk, 160-161, 197
Wangdor (proofreader), 182
Wangdu (monk), 26-30, 32, 33, 48
Wei Shibu, 142
Williams College, 63, 64, 67, 72-74,
  198
Wylie, Terry, 76, 80, 171
Xi'an, 93, 158, 170-171
Xianyang prison, 128-129
Xianyang school. *See* Tibetan
  Minority Institute

Yadong, 49
Yarlung River, 20
Yin Fatang, 180, 182

Zhang Guohua, 107
Zhao (interpreter), 91-92
Zhou, 163

Melvyn C. Goldstein is the John Reynolds Harkness Professor and Chair of the Department of Anthropology at Case Western Reserve University as well as the Director of the University's Center for Research on Tibet. He has conducted extensive historical, anthropological, and linguistic field research in Tibet and is the author of *A History of Modern Tibet: The Demise of the Lamaist State, Nomads of Western Tibet: The Survival of a Way of Life,* and a number of other books and articles including an *English-Tibetan Dictionary of Modern Tibetan* and a *Tibetan-English Dictionary of Modern Tibetan.*

William R. Siebenschuh is Professor of English at Case Western Reserve University. He received his B.A. from Grinnell College in 1964 and M.A. and Ph.D. from the University of California in 1966 and 1970 respectively. Professor Siebenschuh is the author of books and biographical and autobiographical texts and regularly teaches courses in eighteenth and nineteenth century British fiction, biography, and autobiography.